HOLY FATHER,
SACRED HEART

HOLY FATHER, SACRED HEART

*The Wisdom of John Paul II
on the Greatest Catholic Devotion*

Carl Moell, S.J.

A Herder & Herder Book
The Crossroad Publishing Company
New York

The Crossroad Publishing Company
16 Penn Plaza, 481 Eighth Avenue
New York, NY 10001

Published with the permission of Superiors
Reverend Richard J. Baumann, S.J.
Provincial, Chicago Province of the Society of Jesus
April 12, 2003

Nihil Obstat: William B. Smith, S.T.D., Censor Librorum
Imprimatur: +Robert A. Brucato, Vicar General, Archdiocese of New York
Date: June 18, 2004, Feast of the Sacred Heart

Documents originally published in the English edition of *L'Osservatore Romano* are reprinted here with permission. Documents not published in English have been translated with permission of *L'Osservatore Romano*.

Credit for the artwork on p. 2: "Abide in Me," by Sr. Mary Grace, O.P.

Printed in the United States of America

Library of Congress Cataloging-in-Publication Data

John Paul II, Pope, 1920-
    [Selections. English. 2004]
    Holy Father, Sacred Heart : the wisdom of John Paul II on the greatest of Catholic devotions / [compiled by] Carl J. Moell.
       p.   cm.
    Includes bibliographical references (p.   ).
    ISBN 0-8245-2147-1 (alk. paper)
    1. Sacred Heart, Devotion to.   I. Moell, Carl J.   II. Title.
BX2157.J54 2004
232 – dc22

                                                                        2004013048

1   2   3   4   5   6   7   8   9   10   10   09   08   07   06   05   04

To
Reverend Walter O. Kern,
ardent devotee and tireless apostle
of devotion to the Sacred Heart of Jesus

Contents

Part Three
VARIOUS MESSAGES

Part Four
SAINTS AND BLESSEDS OF THE SACRED HEART

Part Five
PRAYERS TO THE SACRED HEART

Foreword

Pope John Paul II was not long into his term in the papacy before he became the pope who had written and spoken more on the Heart of Jesus than any other pope in history. He continued to do so consistently. Thus, for anyone to attempt to collate and to comment on all that the pope said on this topic is a formidable accomplishment.

Father Moell formulated this objective early in the pope's reign. Thus, he was alert to whatever Pope John Paul II said or wrote about the Heart of Jesus. In those early years of this publishing project, he was stationed in Rome at the Jesuit General Headquarters, almost next door to the Vatican. He could follow closely the various talks and writings of the pope as they appeared in *L'Osservatore Romano*, the Vatican newspaper.

The author's ability at collating and commenting on what the pope said and meant was shown in the publishing of all the pope's meditations on the thirty-three invocations of the Litany of the Sacred Heart. The pope began these Angelus Meditations in June 1985. He completed them after numerous interruptions in November 1989. They were published with commentary in *Prayer and Service,* no. 4 (October–December 1990). This is the publication of the General Office of the Apostleship of Prayer in Rome. The eighty-five pages provided a unique service to all interested in the spirituality of the Heart of Jesus. It was a harbinger of the high quality of commentary contained in this latest published achievement by Father Moell. Chapter 6 in this volume contains a summary of the author's commentary on the pope's meditations on the invocations of the Litany of the Sacred Heart. The litany itself is published in chapter 29.

It is obvious that Pope John Paul II is so convinced of the importance of this spirituality of the Heart of Jesus that he has sought every possible opportunity to pass on his own deep appreciation of its relevancy for the Church today. Perhaps his most successful effort to do so has been achieved through the inauguration in 2000 of Mercy Sunday to be observed each year on the Sunday following Easter. Chapter 24 treats of this initiative of Pope John Paul II. The "mercy" aspect of the Heart of Jesus seems to have caught the imaginations and hearts of today's faithful with exceptional vigor. May I point out that it has the advantage of being celebrated on a Sunday — with the possibility of an appropriate homily being heard by full churches, unlike the Solemnity of the Sacred Heart, which is always celebrated on a Friday.

It will take time for the development of a comprehensive evaluation of what Pope John Paul II has meant for promotion of the spirituality of the Heart of Jesus. However, I fully agree with the author that John Paul II already merits the title "Pope of the Sacred Heart."

Frederick J. Power, S.J., Editor,
Canadian Messenger of the Sacred Heart

Introduction

Karol Wojtyla learned devotion to the Sacred Heart of Jesus as a young boy in Poland and retained its practice throughout his life. As cardinal archbishop of Krakow he wrote a pastoral letter to commemorate the two hundredth anniversary of the establishment of the feast of the Sacred Heart of Jesus, which had first been celebrated in Poland. In this letter dated June 11, 1965, he quotes his favorite invocation from his favorite prayer, the Litany of the Sacred Heart: "Heart of Jesus, fountain of life and holiness." It is not surprising that as Pope John Paul II he has said and written so much on the Heart of Jesus, more in fact than any other pope in history. If any pope deserves the title of "Pope of the Sacred Heart" it is Pope John Paul II.

A Personal Note

As far as I can recall I have always had devotion to the Sacred Heart of Jesus. It was therefore a pleasant surprise for me when Cardinal Karol Wojtyla was elected pope on October 16, 1978, the liturgical memorial of St. Margaret Mary Alacoque, Apostle of the Sacred Heart. It could be expected that a pope from Poland, known for its devotion to the Sacred Heart, would have something, and probably much, to say about the Heart of Jesus. Immediately I began to watch for anything the new pope would say about the Heart of Jesus.

Toward the end of the year 1982 I received an assignment to the general curia of the Society of Jesus in Rome as assistant to the procurator general. I arrived in Rome on February 1, 1983, and continued in that position until September 16, 1996. Immediately after my arrival in Rome, I began to collect everything that Pope John Paul II said or wrote on the Heart of Jesus. At the time I had no clear plans as to what I would do with this material, nor did I suspect how extensive it would prove to be. Eventually I gave some talks on the topic in Italy, and when John Paul had been pope for ten years I wrote an article for the Italian *Messenger of the Sacred Heart,* reviewing what he had said and written on the Heart of Jesus during those ten years. It was only later that I decided I would eventually write a book on the topic of Pope John Paul II and devotion to the Heart of Jesus.

It was easy collecting materials when I was in Rome. The daily Vatican newspaper, *L'Osservatore Romano,* became the primary source. But there were other publications as well. After I returned to the United States in 1996 it became a bit more difficult but not an impossible task with modern methods of communication.

Review articles on the pontificate of Pope John Paul II began to appear after he had been pope ten years, fifteen, twenty years. Then came symposia on his thought and biographies. I checked them to see what they had to say about his devotion to the Sacred Heart and was surprised to see how little if anything was ever said about it. From even more recent biographies one would not learn much about what he had said and written on the Sacred Heart. I suppose one might say that since the present Holy Father has said so much on so many topics, it was not possible to refer to everything. But from the size of this book and from the number of documents on the Sacred Heart, it seems there should at least have been some mention of it. Certainly it justifies the appearance of a separate book on the topic.

A Summary of the Devotion

Without wishing to confine devotion to the Sacred Heart or spirituality of the Heart of Jesus within set limits, it may be helpful to begin with a generally acceptable explanation of the devotion as a background for what Pope John Paul II understands as devotion to the Sacred Heart. Against this background we can more easily understand what the pope refers to when he speaks of the devotion or spirituality and how his words accord with or may go beyond what is given in this explanation.

Traditionally, the expression most used in the past has been "devotion to the Sacred Heart," which emphasizes devotedness to the love of Christ as well as devotional practices centered on the love of Christ's Heart. Today the tendency is to use the expression "spirituality of the Heart of Christ," which refers more to a way of life centered on the Heart as symbol of love and the interior life of the Person of Christ.

Spirituality includes devotion but stresses a deeper and more personal aspect in that the relationship to an object of devotion can be considered as having an influence on one's whole life and not just certain devotional practices.

The prayer of the Church venerates and honors the Heart of Jesus as the symbol of the love with which Jesus continually loves his eternal Father and all human beings without exception. This refers both to popular forms of devotions centered on the Heart as well as the celebration of the liturgy. Worship of the Heart of Jesus ultimately is reverence paid to the divine Person of the Incarnate Word.

Devotion to the Sacred Heart is a special form of worship or devotion to the Word Incarnate that focuses attention on the physical Heart of Jesus Christ as the symbol of his love.

Every form of worship rendered to Christ's humanity has for its ultimate object the Second Person of the Blessed Trinity, the God-Man Jesus Christ in his concrete reality. But each particular form of devotion is distinguished from every other by the special object proper to it: that aspect or part of the person on which attention is focused. This special object is usually complex, composed of a psychological or spiritual element and a sensible element that has some intelligible connection with the spiritual element. In devotion to the Sacred Heart the special object is Jesus' physical Heart of flesh as the true natural symbol of his threefold love: the human love, both sensible and spiritual (that is, infused supernatural charity), and the divine love of the Word Incarnate. In and through adoration of the physical Heart the threefold love, and ultimately the Person of the Word, is adored.

To the adoration of this redemptive love are added acts of interior and exterior devotion that spring from the character of this special object, such as imitation of the virtues of Christ's Heart; consecration as dedication to Christ or the gift of self in response to Christ's love; and apostolic reparation for sin as sharing in Christ's redeeming sacrifice of atonement. Specific forms of devotion are celebrating the liturgical feast, the Solemnity of the Sacred Heart of Jesus, on the Friday following the second Sunday after Pentecost with the act of reparation prescribed by Pope Pius XI; observance of the First Friday of the month with the Votive Mass of the Sacred Heart, and Communion of reparation and holy hour; annual renewal of Pope Leo XIII's act of consecration on the feast of Christ the King; Litany of the Sacred Heart; consecration of families and other prayers, and devotional practices, for example, of the Apostleship of Prayer and enthronement of the Sacred Heart in the home.

A remote scriptural foundation for the devotion may be found in the biblical use of "heart" and similar words, referring to the whole inner life of the human person: the rational, emotional, volitional, moral, and religious life.

There is only one scriptural text where Jesus himself refers explicitly to his Heart. It appears in the Gospel of Matthew: "Learn from me for I am meek and humble of heart" (Matt. 11:29). This passage is frequently quoted in referring to the Heart of Jesus.

In the New Testament, on the Jewish feast of Tabernacles commemorating the miracle of the Exodus when Moses saved his people by making water flow from a rock, Jesus promised a fountain of living waters from his Heart, referring to the messianic promise of living waters that he as the new Moses would strike from the rock of his body. For the Evangelist John the living water is the Holy Spirit, whom the risen Christ would send upon his Church. This prediction was fulfilled at Jesus' death, the hour of his glorification, in the piercing of his side. From the time of the first Pentecost onward, the waters of salvation have flowed from the pierced Heart of the Messiah. These two passages, John 7:37–39 joined to John 19:33–37, form the early Christian picture of the Heart of Jesus as the fountain that dispenses the Spirit from the Savior's wounded side.

From this came the image of the Church born from the pierced Heart of Jesus as the new Eve taken from the side of the new Adam.

In the patristic era of the Church attention was fixed on the piercing of the side and Heart of Jesus on Calvary and the symbolism of the blood and water as the source of the sacraments and the Church. In the Middle Ages spirituality evolved in the direction of a greater interiority and affectivity and the symbolism of the Heart of Jesus. With St. John Eudes (1601–1680), called by Pope St. Pius X the "originator, teacher, and apostle of the liturgical worship of the Sacred Heart," and St. Margaret Mary Alacoque (1647–1690), who received revelations from Our Lord at Paray-le-Monial in 1673–1675, we come to the modern phase of devotion to the Sacred Heart of Jesus.

Pope Clement XIII in 1765 approved the feast of the Sacred Heart for the bishops of Poland and the Roman Archconfraternity of the Sacred Heart. In 1856 Pope Blessed Pius IX extended the feast to the universal Church, and in 1899 Pope Leo XIII issued the first encyclical letter on the Sacred Heart, *Annum Sacrum,* and consecrated the human race to the Sacred Heart. Two other important encyclical letters are *Miserentissimus Redemptor* of Pope Pius XI on reparation and *Haurietis aquas* of Pope Pius XII on the nature of the devotion.

An Overview

The thought of Pope John Paul II on the Sacred Heart of Jesus is found in different forms, both oral and written. The pope has spoken of the devotion or spirituality on many occasions and in various ways.

In June 1979, the first "month of the Sacred Heart" after he had become pope, John Paul spoke of the Sacred Heart on four occasions: once at a general audience, once during an Angelus message, and twice in talks to groups of religious, the Priests of the Sacred Heart (the Dehonians) and the Sons of the Sacred Heart (the Comboni Missionaries). There would be many other addresses in the course of his pontificate.

In 1980 the pope visited Paris, where he met with the young people of Paris and then visited the Basilica of Montmartre. He gave a major talk to the polyclinic of the Gemelli University Hospital in Rome in 1981, and a homily at a Votive Mass of the Sacred Heart at Vancouver Airport in Canada on September 18, 1984. At the end of a general audience on January 11, 1984, the pope had special remarks to make to members of the Apostleship of Prayer and to the sick, as he would also do on many other similar occasions.

Pope John Paul II has not issued an encyclical letter on the Heart of Jesus, but over a period extending through three summers, 1985, 1986, and 1989, he gave a series of Sunday Angelus messages on the invocations of the Litany of the Sacred Heart, concluding with the final two invocations in November 1989.

In some of his encyclical letters and in some of his other written documents on other topics, we find references to the Heart of Jesus.

On a visit to Paray-le-Monial in 1986 the pope delivered a letter to the Jesuit superior general on promoting devotion to the Sacred Heart, spoke to the Sisters of the Visitation, delivered a homily on the family in the basilica, and gave a talk before the Angelus.

The pope has spoken of the Heart of Jesus at his general Wednesday audiences and greeted the pilgrims with exhortations to practice the devotion. He has also given other Angelus messages in addition to the series on the Litany of the Sacred Heart. He has visited Roman parishes, including those dedicated to the Sacred Heart, which offered an opportunity to speak of the devotion. At the end of his general audiences and his Angelus messages, the pope has given special greetings to specific groups of pilgrims: members of the Apostleship of Prayer, the sick, newlyweds, and young people. He has spoken of the civilization of love and at times referred it explicitly to the Heart of Jesus. On his pastoral visits throughout the world he has made a point of visiting the sick and prisoners.

The Holy Father has recalled anniversaries of saints devoted to the Sacred Heart, for example, St. John Eudes and St. Margaret Mary Alacoque on the third centenary of her death. Among his numerous beatifications and canonizations, there were many persons devoted to the Heart of Jesus, notably St. Claude La Colombière and St. Faustina Kowalska.

More recently Pope John Paul has sent messages to the world on the centenary of Pope Leo XIII's consecration of the human race to the Sacred Heart. He wrote to the archbishop of Lyons on the same anniversary and earlier to the bishop of Autun, Chalon, and Macon on the third centenary of the death of St. Margaret Mary Alacoque.

The pope celebrated the Votive Mass of the Sacred Heart with a homily at St. Louis, Missouri, in 1999, as earlier he had done at the Vancouver Airport in Canada. He has visited his homeland seven times and especially in more recent visits (in 1991, 1997, and 1999) has spoken at length on devotion to the Sacred Heart.

At the end of each chapter, there is a summary of the Holy Father's words quoted in that chapter. At the end of the book there is a conclusion summarizing what Pope John Paul II has taught on the Sacred Heart of Jesus.

This is a brief overview of what the pope has said and written on the topic of the Heart of Jesus. There can be no doubt that Pope John Paul II, among his many achievements, merits the title "Pope of the Sacred Heart."

Part One

Early Documents
and Messages

Chapter 1

A Candlelight Procession

October 16, 1988

Five thousand of the faithful of the Diocese of Rome gathered on Sunday evening, October 16, 1988, in the Piazza of St. Peter to pray and to express their affection for the pope on the tenth anniversary of his election. Before the conclusion of the event, made even more impressive by a great candlelight procession, Pope John Paul II appeared at the window of his private study to greet the community and to express his appreciation. Replying to the brief greeting of the cardinal vicar Hugo Poletti, who had led the praying of the Rosary and the candlelight procession, the Holy Father spoke to those present in these words.

Dear Brothers and Sisters, ten years ago the Church of Rome received from divine Providence a new bishop who came from afar. This bishop had met you and had greeted you for the first time with the words: Praised be Jesus Christ.

I wish to do that again today after ten years with the same greeting: Praised be Jesus Christ. I wish to greet the Church of Rome, all Romans, and all Christians united in the whole world to the Church of Rome and to its bishop. I thank you from my heart for your presence here today, for this candlelight procession. I thank my dear brother, the cardinal vicar, who truly for ten years has carried with me all the responsibilities of the Diocese of Rome and has not only carried them with me but is for me a loving brother and sure guide in all the problems of this great City and of this great Diocese of Rome in all these problems which we must approach pastorally. I thank him from my heart, as I also thank all my beloved brothers in the episcopate, the auxiliary bishops of Rome.

But I wish to enlarge this my greeting, this my thanks to all the City and all the Diocese to include all the parishes of Rome. I try systematically to visit these parishes, but they are numerous. I hope that perhaps this year, the tenth of my pontificate, I will be able to visit about half of the parishes. By means of the parishes, I greet all the domestic churches, all the families, and all the persons: our brothers and sisters in the faith, as also those who do not share our Catholic faith. All of them, in the ecclesial vision of Vatican II, belong in some way to the same Creator Father, all are redeemed by the same Redeemer Son, and in all of them is mysteriously at work the same Paraclete, the Holy Spirit.

The pope then greets other groups also.

I wish to embrace all. In this embrace today, as in that of the first evening ten years ago and during all these intervening years, I wish to be close especially to those who suffer, who are sick in clinics, in hospitals, in their homes, to all those who are abandoned, who suffer not only physically but also spiritually. We desire that they find a place within our community, that they find by means of this our Christian community, the Petrine community, the Heart of the Savior which is open to all and especially to those who suffer.

I greet and embrace the elderly, the young, children, the newborn, those of every age, all generations, in our City and in our Church.

You have come here for this candlelight procession. Carry in your hands the light, the same light that was carried during the Easter Vigil, the same light that is carried during baptism. The light in your hands symbolizes Christ, who is the Light of the world, who enlightens every person who comes into the world. And so, dear Brothers and Sisters, I greet you from the heart, each and every one of you

Romans, that Christ may ever remain the light of your life, and that we may walk in his light and thus walking in his light we may not lose the way, the way of human life, but may find the way of a profound meaning in human life: in Christ. And finally to find the way that takes us to the House of the Father, of our Father who is in Heaven.

Thank you for your presence.

Summary

This brief message of the pope on the tenth anniversary of his election is noteworthy in giving us not only a brief resume of the past ten years but a preview of the future as well. Throughout his pontificate, Pope John Paul II manifests his love for people, for all people, and especially for the sick and the suffering and the abandoned. His words also illustrate a characteristic that can easily be missed, namely, the ease with which he refers, almost in passing, to the Heart of Jesus even when we would not be expecting it. The Holy Father desires that all may find in the community "the Heart of the Savior which is open to all and especially to those who suffer."

Chapter 2

Month of the Sacred Heart

June 1979 was the first occurrence, after the election of Pope John Paul II to the papacy, of the month traditionally dedicated to the Sacred Heart. During that month the pope spoke of the Heart of Jesus on four occasions.

Wednesday general audience: Let us learn to read the mystery of the Heart of Jesus, June 20, 1979

At the general audience in St. Peter's Square, Pope John Paul II addressed thousands of pilgrims gathered there on the topic of the mystery of the Heart of Christ.

On the day after tomorrow, next Friday, the liturgy of the Church is concentrated with particular adoration and love around the mystery of the Heart of Christ. Today, therefore, anticipating this day and this feast together with you, I wish to turn the eyes of our hearts to the mystery of that Heart. It has spoken to me ever since my youth. Every year I return to this mystery in the liturgical rhythm of the time of the Church.

It is well-known that the month of June is dedicated particularly to the Divine Heart, to the Sacred Heart of Jesus. We express to it our love and our adoration by means of the litany which in the single invocations speaks with particular depth of its theological contents.

Today let the texts of the Friday liturgy speak for us, beginning with the reading of the Gospel according to John. The Evangelist reports a fact with the precision of an eyewitness. [The Holy Father then read the text of John 19:31–34, describing the piercing of the side of Jesus on the cross.]

Not a word about his Heart. The Evangelist speaks only of the piercing of his side with a spear, and the coming out of blood and water. The language of the description is almost medical, anatomical. The soldier's spear certainly penetrated the Heart, to make sure that the condemned Man was already dead. This Heart — this human Heart — has stopped working. Jesus has ceased to live. At the same time, however, this anatomical opening of Christ's Heart after his death — in spite of all the historical "severity" of the text — drives us to think also at the metaphorical level. The Heart is not just an organ that conditions the biological vitality of man. The Heart is a symbol. It speaks of the whole inner person. It speaks of the spiritual interior of a person. And tradition at once reread this meaning of John's description. In a certain sense, moreover, the Evangelist himself gave an inducement to do so when, referring to the attestation of the eyewitness that was himself, he referred, at the same time, to this sentence of Holy Scripture: "They shall look on him whom they have pierced" (John 19:37; Zech. 12:10).

So does the Church look; so does humanity look. And lo, in the One pierced by the soldier's spear all generations of Christians had learned and learn to read the mystery of the Heart of the Crucified Man who was and is the Son of God.

The "riches of Christ" and at the same time that "eternal plan of salvation" of God are addressed by the Holy Spirit to the "inner person," "that Christ may dwell in your hearts through faith" (Eph. 3:16–17). And when Christ, with the strength of the Holy Spirit, dwells through faith in our human hearts, then we will be able "to comprehend" with our human spirit (that is, precisely with this "heart") "what is the breadth and length and height and depth, and to know the love of Christ which surpasses knowledge..." (Eph. 3:18–19).

For such knowledge acquired with the heart, with every human heart, the Divine Heart of the One who was condemned and crucified on Calvary was opened at the end of his earthly life.

Different is the measure of this knowledge on the part of human hearts. Before the power of Paul's words, let each of us question himself on the measure of his own heart. "...[we shall] reassure our hearts before him whenever our hearts condemn us; for God is greater than our hearts" (1 John 3:19–20). The Heart of the God-Man does not judge human hearts. The Heart calls. The Heart "invites." That was the purpose for which it was opened with the soldier's spear.

Christ speaks in the Friday liturgy: "Learn from me; for I am gentle and lowly in heart" (Matt. 11:29).

Only once, perhaps, did the Lord Jesus refer to his own Heart, in his own words. And he stressed this sole feature: "gentleness and lowliness"; as if he meant that it is only in this way that he wishes to conquer man; that by means of "gentleness and lowliness" he wishes to be the King of hearts. The whole mystery of his reign was expressed in these words. "Gentleness and lowliness" cover, in a certain sense, all the "riches" of the Redeemer's Heart, of which St. Paul wrote to the Ephesians. But also that "gentleness and lowliness" reveal him fully.

The beautiful litany to the Sacred Heart of Jesus is composed of many similar words — more, exclamations of admiration for the riches of the Heart of Christ. Let us meditate on them carefully on that day.

Thus, at the end of this fundamental liturgical cycle of the Church — which began with the first Sunday of Advent and passed through the time of Christmas, then of Lent and of the Resurrection up to Pentecost, the Sunday of Holy Trinity, and Corpus Christi — the feast of the Divine Heart, of the Sacred Heart of Jesus, presents itself discreetly. All this cycle is enclosed definitively in it, in the *end of liturgical year*

Heart of the Man-God. From it, too, the whole life of the Church
irradiates every year. *is & the King.*

This Heart is "a fountain of life and holiness."

Angelus Message: The Heart of the Redeemer vivifies the whole Church, June 14, 1979

Four days later on June 24 the pope returned to the same theme, telling
over thirty thousand pilgrims gathered in St. Peter's Square for the Sunday
Angelus that the Heart of the Redeemer vivifies the whole Church and
draws men and women who have opened their hearts to the "unfathomable
riches" of this Heart.

By means of today's meeting and by means of the Angelus of this
last Sunday of the month of June, I wish in a special way to unite
spiritually with all those whose human hearts are inspired by this
Divine Heart. This family is a large one. Not a few congregations,
associations, and communities develop in the Church and in a programmatic way draw the vital energy of their activity from the Heart
of Christ.

This spiritual bond always leads to a great awakening of apostolic
zeal. Adorers of the Divine Heart become men and women with
a sensitive conscience. And when it is granted to them to have
relations with the Heart of our Lord and Master, in them also there
springs up the need of atonement for the sins of the world, for the
indifference of so many hearts and their negligence.

How necessary this host of watchful hearts is in the Church in
order that the love of the Divine Heart may not remain isolated
and unrequited. Among this host special mention deserves to go to
all those who offer their sufferings as living victims in union with
the Heart of Christ, pierced on the cross. Thus transformed with

love, human suffering becomes a particular leaven of Christ's work of salvation in the Church.

On this occasion the pope was ordaining eighty-eight deacons from various countries of the world, many of whom prepared for the priesthood in the "Roman colleges."

Today, conferring Holy Orders on them I wish to unite them even more deeply with the heart of the Church, which beats in union with the Divine Heart of Christ, the Eternal Priest.

May they persevere in this union, bearing the blessed fruits of the evangelical message and the priestly ministry.

I commend to the Divine Heart also the families, dioceses, or religious congregations to which they belong, and finally their Roman colleges and their seminaries. I wish the latter a fervent and truly evangelical life which begins from the Heart of Jesus.

Address to the General Chapter of the Congregation of the Priests of the Sacred Heart of Jesus (Dehonians), June 22, 1979

During the same month of June, Pope John Paul II received in audience two groups of members of religious congregations: On June 22 the General Chapter of the Congregation of Priests of the Sacred Heart of Jesus (the Dehonians) and on June 23 members of Sons of the Sacred Heart of Jesus (the Combonians), and to each he delivered an address.

To the Dehonians, led by their newly elected General Council and by their new superior general, the Holy Father delivered the following address.

This meeting of yours with the pope takes on a further special meaning today because it takes place on the liturgical Solemnity of the Sacred Heart of Jesus, from which your institute takes its name and inspiration. Today the whole Church celebrates the divine and human love of the Word Incarnate and the love that the Father and the Holy Spirit cherish for human beings. This is the feast of the infinite love of God, One and Three; of this, Jesus with his side pierced on the cross is the supreme and definitive revelation.

You are — and must always be — "Priests of the Sacred Heart of Jesus." That is what your founder, the Servant of God Father Léon-Jean Dehon, wanted you to be when he set up a congregation entirely dedicated to the love and atonement of the Sacred Heart....

"The spirit of the congregation," Father Dehon wrote to his sons in a circular letter, "is ardent love for the Sacred Heart, faithful imitation of its virtues, above all, humility, zeal, gentleness, and the spirit of sacrifice; and indefatigable zeal in bringing forth for it friends and atoners, who will console it with their own love." These are words that sum up admirably the whole program of your institute, and they keep intact their strong emotional charge and their perfect relevance today.

Let Jesus Christ, therefore, be the center of your life, your ideals, your interests, and your aims. With conversation, preaching, writings, and the media of social communication, spread "the breadth and length and height and depth" of Christ's love, "which surpasses knowledge" (Eph. 3:18–19). But especially preach and spread it with the example of your priestly and religious life, animated by faith, by the supernatural vision of reality, and strengthened by absolute and jealous faithfulness to the evangelical counsels of poverty, chastity, and obedience, which configure you to Christ. Reproduce in your hearts — according to Father Dehon's happy expression — the "holiness of the Heart of Jesus!"

In particular, in this happy circumstance, I would like to recommend to you two other typical aspects of your founder's spirituality: faithful love of the Apostolic See and filial devotion to the Blessed Virgin....

To the new superior general, to the General Council, to you, capitular fathers, and to all your confreres scatted in all the continents, especially on the missions, my encouragement and the assurance of my prayer that the Priests of the Sacred Heart of Jesus may always be faithful to their original charism and always repeat with joy and enthusiasm: "Vivat Cor Iesu, per Cor Mariae!"

Address to the Sons of the Sacred Heart of Jesus (Combonians), June 23, 1979

The pope spoke to the Combonians on June 23, welcoming the delegates to their General Chapter on the day after a decree was signed reuniting the two branches of the congregation, the Italian and the German, which had been separated since 1923 and were now joined together again, as the pope said, "in the charity of the most Sacred Heart of Jesus," as one religious family.

The Holy Father thanked them for the good missionary work they had accomplished and exhorted them to continue in the spirit of their institute and in imitation of their founder as a zealous priest and tireless bishop. The education of young people, care of the sick, assistance to the poor, instruction of catechumens, and devotion to the Sacred Heart of Jesus "in whom are all the treasures of wisdom and knowledge" were to remain characteristic traits of their religious community.

Summary

In the talk at the general audience, the pope spoke of the two key Scripture texts: John 19:31–34 describing the piercing of the side and Heart of Jesus after his death on the cross, and Matthew 11:29 on learning from Jesus who is "gentle and lowly in heart." The pope concludes: This Heart is "a fountain of life and holiness." The talk during the Angelus message spoke of the Heart of Jesus as vivifying the whole Church, especially the men being ordained deacons and the large number of those who draw inspiration from the Divine Heart.

The Priests of the Sacred Heart of Jesus are very intent on carrying out the directives of their founder, Father Léon-Jean Dehon, in living and promoting devotion to the Heart of Jesus. The Sons of the Sacred Heart of Jesus are thanked for their good missionary work and are praised for the reunion of the Italian and German branches of their original congregation "in the charity of the Sacred Heart of Jesus."

These four talks during the 1979 Month of the Sacred Heart illustrate how the Heart of Jesus is truly "a fountain of life and holiness."

Chapter 3

Encyclical Letters, Apostolic Exhortations, and Other Written Documents

Encyclical Letters

As of the year 2000 Pope John Paul II had written thirteen encyclicals, but he has not written an encyclical on the Sacred Heart. Although from time to time there were rumors that he was working on such an encyclical, the rumors did not materialize. It is understandable why he would not write such an encyclical, considering the nature of an encyclical letter and the fact that we have a magisterial encyclical letter on the Sacred Heart, *Haurietis aquas,* by Pope Pius XII, which could hardly be surpassed. Moreover Pope John Paul has given a series of thirty-three Angelus messages on the invocations of the Litany of the Sacred Heart. The series was spread over three summers and will be discussed in another chapter.

If we look at the encyclical letters Pope John Paul has written, we see that only three of them say anything about the Heart of Jesus. These are the three great encyclicals that form what might be called a trinitarian trilogy, although it seems they were not originally planned to be such a trilogy: (1) *Redemptor hominis,* his inaugural encyclical of March 4, 1979, (2) *Dives in misericordia* of November 30, 1980, and (3) *Dominum et vivificantem* of May 18, 1986.

Redemptor hominis, on the Redeemer of humankind, March 4, 1979

The nature of encyclical letters has developed over the course of time, since their beginning in the eighteenth century. Like the initial encyclical of Pope Paul VI, so *Redemptor hominis* of Pope John Paul II sets the tone of his pontificate. It was published five months after his election as pope. He says he began working on this encyclical immediately after his election. It begins with the words: "The Redeemer of humankind, Jesus Christ, is the center of the universe and of history," indicating that the mystery of the redemption will be the center of his pontificate. This first encyclical explains his Christ-centered humanism.

There are only a few references to the Heart of Jesus in the encyclical. In no. 4 the pope refers to Jesus who is "humble in heart," and in referring to his predecessor Paul VI in footnote 14 he lists the important documents of Paul VI, including *Investigabiles divitias Christi,* but he does not comment on this.

In no. 7, he calls the Eucharist the "fountain of life and holiness" and gives as reference the Litany of the Sacred Heart.

In no. 8 the pope speaks of making contact with the inward mystery of man, which in biblical and nonbiblical language is expressed by the word "heart." Christ, the Redeemer of the world, is the one who penetrated in a unique, unrepeatable way into the mystery of the human person and entered his "heart." He does not develop this further, other than to quote from paragraph 22 of Vatican Council II's Pastoral Constitution on the Church in the Modern World (*Gaudium et spes*), including the words: "For, by his Incarnation, the Son of God, in a certain way united himself with every human person. He worked with human hands, he thought with a human mind. He acted with a human will, and with a human Heart he loved." The pope would frequently quote these words of Vatican II when speaking later of the Heart of Jesus.

Finally in no. 9, speaking of the divine dimension of the mystery of Redemption, the pope says: "The redemption of the world — this tremendous mystery of love in which creation is renewed — is, at its deepest root the fullness of justice in a human heart — the Heart of the first-born Son — in order that it may become justice in the hearts of many human beings, predestined from eternity in the first-born Son to be children of God and called to grace, called to love."

Dives in misericordia, on the mercy of God, November 30, 1980

In Pope John Paul II's second encyclical letter, *Dives in misericordia,* on the mercy of God, we find only one reference to the Sacred Heart, but it is a significant one. In no. 13, explaining the text "he who has seen me has seen the Father," the pope says: "Everything that forms the 'vision' of Christ in the Church's living faith and teaching brings us nearer to the 'vision of the Father' in the holiness of his mercy." He then goes on: "The Church seems in a particular way to profess the mercy of God and to venerate it when she directs herself to the Heart of Christ. In fact, it is precisely this drawing close to Christ in the mystery of his Heart which enables us to dwell on this point — a point in a sense central and also most accessible on the human level — of the revelation of the merciful love of the Father, a revelation which constituted the central content of the messianic mission of the Son of Man." More will be said about this when we speak of Sister Faustina and the devotion to Divine Mercy.

Dominum et vivificantem, on the Holy Spirit in the life of the Church and the world, May 18, 1986

The fifth encyclical in time, but the third in the trilogy dealing with Christ the Redeemer, God the Father, and then the Holy Spirit, is *Dominum et vivificantem,* on the Holy Spirit in the Life of the Church and the World. There is nothing directly on the Sacred Heart. But indirectly there is one reference in no. 21. The pope is speaking of the Trinitarian theophany at the Jordan River, the testimony of the voice from heaven after the baptism of Jesus. He speaks of the testimony coming also from within, from the depths of who Jesus is. He does not even speak directly of the Spirit. "Nonetheless what he says of the Father and of himself — the Son — flows from that fullness of the Spirit which is in him, which fills his Heart, pervades his own 'I,' inspires and enlivens his actions from the depths." The English and the Italian translations use the expression "which fills his Heart" to translate or paraphrase "from within" and "the depths of who Jesus is." Although the word *cor* (heart) does not appear in the original Latin, it clearly can be said to refer to the heart, as the pope himself will explain elsewhere later.

Apostolic Exhortations

There are several other written documents, specifically apostolic exhortation, that touch briefly on the Heart of Jesus.

Familiaris consortio, on the family, after the Synod of Bishops that dealt with issues of family life, November 22, 1981

In no. 61 the pope says that besides public devotions in the church, the Christian family makes use of a wide variety of private prayers. In addition to morning and evening prayers, these include: reading and meditating on the Word of God, preparation for receiving the sacraments, devotion and consecration to the Sacred Heart of Jesus, various forms of devotion to the Blessed Virgin Mary, prayers before meals, and popular devotions. In nos. 65 and 85, the Heart of Christ is mentioned.

Redemptionis donum, to men and women religious on their consecration in the light of the mystery of redemption, March 25, 1984

There are two brief references to the Heart of Jesus. In no. 8 the pope says that the likeness of that love which in the Heart of Christ is both redemptive and spousal is imprinted on the religious profession. And such love should fill each religious from the very source of that particular consecration which, on the sacramental basis of baptism, is the beginning of the new life in Christ and in the Church.

In no. 9 the pope continues speaking of religious profession, which places in the heart of each religious the love of the Father: that love which is in the Heart of Jesus Christ, the Redeemer of the world.

Reconciliatio et paenitentia, on reconciliation and penance in the mission of the Church today, December 2, 1984

In no. 35, a concluding expression of hope, in order that in the not too distant future abundant fruit may come from the pope's call to penance and reconciliation, the Holy Father invites all to turn to the Heart of Christ, the eloquent sign of divine mercy, the "propitiation for our sins," "our peace and reconciliation" (references are to the Litany of the Sacred Heart and the biblical texts), that we may draw from it an interior encouragement to hate sin and to be converted to God, and find in it the divine kindness that lovingly responds to human repentance. In the remaining sections the pope twice refers to the Immaculate Heart of Mary.

Other Written Documents

Pastores dabo vobis, postsynodal apostolic exhortation on the formation of priests in the circumstances of the present day, March 25, 1992

In no. 1, the exhortation begins with the words of the Prophet Jeremiah (referring to God): "I will give you shepherds after my own Heart" (Jer. 3:15). Jesus Christ is the living, supreme, and definitive fulfillment of God's promise: "I am the good shepherd" (John 10:11).

In no. 82, the conclusion, the pope again quotes the opening line of the exhortation and then explains:

> God promises the church not just any sort of shepherds, but shepherds "after his own Heart." And God's "Heart" has revealed itself to us fully in the Heart of Christ, the good shepherd. Christ's Heart continues today to have compassion for the multitudes and to give them the bread of truth, the bread of love, the bread of life (Mark 6:30ff), and it pleads to be allowed to beat in other hearts—priests' hearts: "You give them something to eat" (Mark 6:37). People need to come out of their anonymity and fear. They need to be known and called by name, to walk in safety, along the paths of life, to be found again if they have become lost, to be loved, to receive salvation as the supreme gift of God's love. All this is done by Jesus, the good shepherd—by himself and by his priests with him.

Tertio millennio adveniente, apostolic letter on preparation for the Jubilee of the Year 2000, November 10, 1994

In no. 4 (end), the pope quotes from the Pastoral Constitution on the Church in the Modern World, *Gaudium et spes*, 22: "By his incarnation the Son of God united himself in some way with every human person.

He labored with human hands, thought with a human mind, acted with a human will, and loved with a human Heart."

In no. 7, the pope says that in Jesus Christ God not only speaks to the one who strays from him but also seeks him out. It is a search that begins in the Heart of God and culminates in the Incarnation of the Word of God. God seeks out the human person, moved by his fatherly Heart.

The same line of argumentation continues in no. 8: The religion that originates in the mystery of the Redemptive Incarnation is the religion of "dwelling in the Heart of God," of sharing in God's life.

Holy Thursday letters to priests

From the beginning of his pontificate, Pope John Paul II has issued a letter each year to all the priests of the world on the occasion of Holy Thursday, the anniversary day of the institution of the priesthood. The letters usually speak of the Eucharist and the priesthood in the light of some theme. Only rarely does the pope speak of the Sacred Heart in these letters.

In the Holy Year of the Redemption, 1983, the main theme of the Holy Thursday letter (March 27, 1983) was the sacrament of penance. The pope also spoke of priests, ministers of Penance, and the Eucharist as friends of Christ, but he did not speak of the Sacred Heart.

In 1986, the letter (March 16, 1986) was a reflection on the figure, the life, and the ministry of the Curé of Ars, St. John Mary Vianney, in which the pope urged priests to imitate the saintly confessor.

In no. 4 the pope speaks of the Curé of Ars as a model of priestly zeal for all pastors. The secret of his generosity is to be found in his love of God, lived without limits, in constant response to the love made manifest in Christ crucified. This is where he bases his desire to do everything to save the souls ransomed by Christ at such a great price and to bring them back to the love of God. The pope recalls one of those pithy sayings which the Curé had the knack of uttering: "The priesthood is the love of the Heart of Jesus."

At the end of no. 4 the Holy Father exhorts his brother priests to join St. John Mary Vianney in seeking the dynamism of a pastoral zeal in the Heart of Jesus and in his love of souls. If we do not draw from the same source, our ministry risks bearing little fruit.

The theme of his 1987 letter (April 13, 1987) was the importance of prayer in our lives in relation to our vocation and mission. In no. 5, the pope said that Jesus, who had accomplished this institution in the Upper Room, certainly could not wish to revoke the reality signified by the sacrament of the Last Supper. On the contrary, with all his Heart he desires its fulfillment. He also shows the immensity of the suffering which fills his human Heart. Before the Father he remains in all the truth of his humanity, the truth of a human Heart, oppressed by a suffering which is about to reach its tragic conclusion: "My soul is very sorrowful, even to death."

Summary

Since the documents quoted in this chapter are not primarily speaking of the Sacred Heart, the best approach to reflection would seem to be to read the complete document in which the passage quoted appears, so as to see the context for what the pope says there of the Heart of Jesus. The first encyclical, *Redemptor hominis,* for example, with its emphasis on the Person of Christ throughout can help to deepen devotion to the Sacred Heart even beyond the explicit references to the Heart of Christ. Something similar can be said of *Dives in misericordia* because of the close connection between Divine Mercy and the Sacred Heart, as seen in the conclusion of the apostolic exhortation *Reconciliatio et paenitentia* when the pope calls the Heart of Christ the eloquent sign of Divine Mercy.

Many of these passages also illustrate the point mentioned at the end of chapter 1, namely, the ease with which the Holy Father refers, almost in passing at times, to the Heart of Jesus even when we would not be expecting it.

Chapter 4

Early Messages

June 1, 1980

Vigil with the young people of France at Parc des Princes, Paris: The whole gospel is a dialogue with men and women, June 1, 1980

On Sunday evening, June 1, 1980, the Holy Father met with over ninety thousand young Parisians gathered at the largest stadium in Paris for a prayer vigil. The address the pope actually delivered to the young people was not the one originally prepared for the occasion. The reason for the change was explained to the young people by the pope himself before ending the meeting:

Before concluding I must tell you how I prepared this dialogue, this address-dialogue. I was sent the program and was told that I had to speak to the young people. So then I prepared a speech. Later, the organizers sent me "your" program and the questions you wished to ask the pope. So it was necessary to change the address I had prepared and prepare the one you have just heard. But the "monologue" address, the message, still remains, and I would like to leave it with you so that you can read it and meditate on it. I think the organizers will willingly distribute it to you.

Before the Holy Father actually arrived in Paris, the young people of that city had conducted a survey to draw up a list of questions to be submitted to the pope so that he might answer them in his address to them. The list consisted of twenty-one questions; three of them were eventually chosen as the subject of the Holy Father's talk.

The questions selected were these: (1) If we had not submitted these questions to you, what would you have said to us? (2) Speak to us simply about Jesus Christ. Who is Jesus Christ for you? (3) People frequently speak of a Third World War. What can we young people do to prevent it? The first of these questions was answered by the copy of the originally prepared address distributed to them after the talk. Although only three questions had been chosen, the Holy Father actually wished to give a reply, as complete as possible, to all twenty-one questions. In the address actually given the pope did not speak about the Heart of Jesus, but he did so in the originally prepared address.

Message to the young people of France (originally prepared message): Raise your eyes toward Jesus Christ, June 1, 1980

The pope began by speaking of an existence that is really human. He spoke of the body and mastery of self, of a mind to think and a heart to love. He then developed the idea of openness to God as he spoke of the mystery of Christ's love for us. In speaking of a heart to love he also spoke of the Heart of Jesus.

You are also worth what your heart is worth. The whole history of humankind is the history of the need of loving and being loved. The end of the century — especially in regions of accelerated social change — makes development of healthy emotions more difficult. ... If we are to believe a certain type of advertising, our age is even enamored of what could be called a doping of the heart.

Whatever use human beings make of it, the heart — the symbol of friendship and love — has also its norms, its ethics. To make room for the heart in the harmonious construction of your personality has nothing to do with mawkishness or even sentimentality. The heart is the opening of the whole being to the existence of others, the capacity of divining them, of understanding them. Such a sensitiveness, true and deep, makes one vulnerable. That is why some people are tempted to get rid of it by hardening their heart.

To love is, therefore, essentially to give oneself to others. Far from being an instinctive inclination, love is a conscious decision of the will to go toward others. To be able to love truly, it is necessary to detach oneself from many things and above all from oneself, to give gratuitously, to love to the end. This dispossession of oneself — a long and demanding task — is exhausting and exalting. It is the source of balance. It is the secret of happiness.

Young people of France, raise your eyes more often toward Jesus Christ! He is the Man who loved most, and most consciously, most voluntarily and most gratuitously! Meditate on Christ's testament: "There is no greater proof of love than to give one's life for those one loves." Contemplate the Man-God, the man with the pierced Heart! Do not be afraid! Jesus did not come to condemn love but to free love from its ambiguities and its counterfeits. It was he who changed the heart of Zacchaeus, of the Samaritan woman, and who still operates similar conversions today, all over the world. It seems to me that tonight, Christ is whispering to each one of you: "Give me your heart! . . . I will purify it, I will strengthen it, I will turn it toward all those who need it: toward your own family, your school or university community, your social environment, toward the unloved, toward foreigners living on the soil of France, toward the inhabitants of the world who do not have enough to live on and to develop, toward the most humble of men. Love demands sharing!"

Young people of France, it is more than ever the time to work hand-in-hand at the civilization of love, according to the expression dear to my great predecessor Paul VI. What a gigantic workyard! What a stirring task!

On the plane of the heart, of love, I have something else to confide to you. [The pope then speaks of the possibility of a vocation to the priesthood and to religious life.] Your answer to this call lies along the direct line of Christ's last question to Peter: "Do you love me?"

In the final section, on the Mystery of Christ's love for us, the Holy Father says:

I have spoken of the values of the body, the mind and the heart. But at the same time I have given glimpses of an essential dimension without which men and women become again a prisoner of self or of others: it is openness to God. Yes, without God, we lose the key to self, we lose the key to our history. For, since creation, we have borne within us the likeness of God. This remains in us in the state of an implicit wish and unconscious need, in spite of sin. And we are destined to live with God. There, too, Christ will reveal himself as our way. But this mystery requires, perhaps, greater attention....

I like to repeat here the wish of my first encyclical. "That each person may be able to find Christ, in order that Christ may walk with each person the path of life, with the power of the truth about men and women and the world that is contained in the mystery of the Incarnation and the Redemption and with the power of the love that is radiated by that truth" (*Redemptor hominis*, 13).

If Christ liberates and raises our humanity, it is because he introduces it into the covenant with God, with the Father, with the Son, and with the Holy Spirit. This morning we celebrated the feast of the Holy Trinity. That is the real opening to God to which every human heart aspires even without knowing it and which Christ offers the believer. It is a question of a personal God and not just the God of philosophers and scholars, it is the God revealed in the Bible, the God of Abraham, the God of Jesus Christ, he who is at the heart of our history. He is the God who can seize all the resources of your body, your mind and your heart, to make them bear fruit, in a word, who can seize your whole being to renew it in Christ, now and beyond death.

Visit to the Basilica of the Sacred Heart in Montmartre: Behold the Heart which has loved men so much, June 1, 1980

After the meeting with the young people of Paris, the Holy Father went late at night on Sunday, June 1, 1980, to the Basilica of the Sacred Heart in Montmartre for a pause of prayer and reflection. He gave a brief med-itation, beginning with the words of the disciples of Emmaus: "Stay with us, Lord, for the day is now far spent."

We are at Montmartre, in the Basilica of the Sacred Heart, conse-crated to the contemplation of Christ's love present in the Blessed Sacrament.

We are in the evening of the first of June, the first day of the month particularly dedicated to meditation, to contemplation of Christ's love manifested by his Sacred Heart....

We come here to meet the Heart pierced for us, from which water and blood gush forth. It is the redeeming love, which is at the origin of salvation, of our salvation, which is at the origin of the church.

We come here to contemplate the love of the Lord Jesus: his compassionate kindness to everyone during his earthly life; his predilection for children, the sick, the afflicted. Let us contemplate his Heart burning with love for his Father, in the fullness of the Holy Spirit....

Now still, today, the living Christ loves us and presents his Heart to us as the source of our redemption: "since he always lives to make intercession for us." At every moment we are enveloped, the whole world is enveloped, in the love of this Heart "which loved men so much and which is so little loved by them...."

We are called not only to meditate on, and contemplate, this mystery of Christ's love: we are called to take part in it. It is the mystery of the Holy Eucharist, the center of our faith, the center of our worship of Christ's merciful love manifested in his Sacred Heart....

Dear Brothers and Sisters, my joy is great to be able to end this day in this exalted place of Eucharistic prayer, in your midst, gathered by love for the Divine Heart. Pray to it. Live by this message which, from the Gospel of St. John to Paray-le-Monial, calls us to enter its mystery. May we all "draw water from the wells of salvation with joy," those that spring from the love of the Lord, who died and rose again for us.

Summary

In the talk the Holy Father actually gave, there is no mention of the Sacred Heart, but in the originally prepared message he related the desires of the human heart to the Heart of Jesus, to Jesus the Man with the pierced Heart, and speaks of vocations to the priestly and religious life.

During the pope's visit to the Basilica of the Sacred Heart in Montmartre, he gave a brief reflection on the Sacred Heart of Jesus as related to the mystery of the Eucharist.

Chapter 5

Other Important Early Messages

Homily at the Polyclinic of the Agostino Gemelli University Hospital in Rome: Science that serves the truth prepares for the revelation of God in the school of the Divine Heart of Jesus, June 28, 1984

"Learn from me, for I am meek and humble of heart" (Matt. 11:29). Similar to us in everything, Jesus has a Heart which beats in his breast activating in his veins the vital flow of blood. It is of this Heart that he speaks to us gathered about his altar: Learn from me, for I am meek and humble of heart.

Today, the liturgical Solemnity of the Sacred Heart, in this university and hospital dedicated to the Sacred Heart, we are invited to meditate on the mystery of this Divine Heart.

We meditate on the marvels of the love of God by contemplating the mystery of the Heart of Christ. The word "heart" in biblical language awakens the richness of anthropological resonance. With it are aroused not only sentiments proper to the affective sphere but also memories, thoughts, arguments, projects which constitute the more intimate world of human beings. The heart in biblical culture, and to a great extent also in other cultures, is that essential core of the personality in which the human person stands before God as a totality of body and spirit, as a thinking, willing, loving being, in whom the memory of the past opens itself to plans for the future.

The heart is of interest to many different types of professional people. But the meaning to which the heart refers here transcends such partial considerations to reach up to the sanctuary of the personal self-consciousness in which the concrete essence of the human person is condensed, the center in which individuals decide for themselves before others, before the world, and before God. Only a human being can properly be said to have a heart, obviously not pure spirits, nor animals either. To "return to the heart" from the dispersion of multiple exterior experiences is a possibility reserved to human beings only.

By faith we know that at a determined moment in history, "the Word of God was made flesh and came to dwell in our midst" (John 1:14). From that moment God had begun to love with a human Heart, a Heart truly capable of beating in an intense, tender, and impassioned way. The Heart of Jesus has truly experienced sentiments of joy before the splendors of nature, at the candor of infants, at the sight of a chaste young man, sentiments of friendship toward his apostles, Lazarus, his disciples, sentiments of compassion for the sick, the poor, so many people tested by strife, loneliness, and sin, sentiments of indignation toward the vendors in the temple, toward hypocrites; sentiments of anguish before the prospect of suffering and the mystery of death. There is no authentic human emotion that the Heart of Jesus did not experience.

Today we pause in adoring prayer before this Heart in which the Eternal Word wished to experience directly our misery, "who did not regard equality with God something to be grasped. Rather he emptied himself, taking the form of a slave, coming in human likeness" (Phil. 2:6–7). From the infinite power proper to God, the Heart of Christ did not retain anything except the unarmed power of the love that forgives. And in the radical loneliness of the cross he allowed himself to be pierced with the lance of the centurion, so that from the open wound might flow out upon the filth of the world the inexhaustible torrent of a mercy that washes, purifies, and renews.

In the Heart of Christ is encountered divine riches and human poverty, the power of grace and human fragility, an appeal to God and a human reply. In it the story of humanity has its resting place because "the Father has given all judgment to the Son" (John 5:22). To the Heart of Christ, every human heart, willing or not, must have reference.

The Bible is not sparing in using pessimistic expressions about the human heart, in which deceitfulness is often hidden. Before the deceptive reality of a "stubborn and rebellious heart" (Jer. 5:23), there is only one hope: that of a divine initiative which renews the human heart and makes it again capable of loving God and the brethren with a sincere and generous impulse, as the Lord promised through the mouth of the prophet Ezekiel: "I will sprinkle clean water upon you to cleanse you from your impurities, and from all your idols I will cleanse you. I will give you a new heart and place a new spirit within you, taking from your bodies your stony hearts and giving you natural hearts" (Ezek. 36:25–26).

The promise is realized in Christ. In the meeting with him is offered to human beings the possibility of remaking a new heart, a heart no longer of "stone" but of "flesh." But to arrive at that it is necessary above all to "be born again of water and the Spirit" (John 3:5); then it is necessary to place oneself in the school of Jesus to learn from him how to love concretely. This is precisely what he himself has asked. He has said, in fact: "Learn from me, for I am meek and humble of heart." With the words and example of Christ, he has taught us meekness and humility as indispensable qualities for truly loving; he has taught us that the Son of Man "has not come to be served but to serve and to give his own life as a ransom for many" (Mark 10:45). Authentic love is not served by others but serves them, spending one's self for them even to the total sacrifice of one's self and all one has.

Before concluding the Holy Father speaks to those who are sick and who struggle with infirmities and have need of such moral fortitude so as not to succumb to the temptation of dejection and discouragement. He encourages them to turn to the Divine Heart of Jesus who said: "Come to me, all you who labor and are burdened, and I will give you rest" (Matt. 11:28). Let us go to him, learn from him, trust ourselves to him.

Homily during the Votive Mass of the Sacred Heart of Jesus at the Vancouver Airport (Canada): The Heart of Jesus is a call by God addressed to every human heart, September 18, 1984

The pope begins by quoting from Psalm 103, from the day's liturgy of the Votive Mass of the Sacred Heart: "My soul, give thanks to the Lord; all my being, bless his holy name." He explains that he wishes to address himself to the God of love through the mystery of the Heart of Christ.

The expression "all my being" speaks of our human heart, our whole being, all that is within us, all that forms us from within, in the depth of our being. In this way heart, our heart, meets the Heart of Christ, our heart speaks to the Heart of Christ.

When we say "Heart of Jesus Christ" we address ourselves in faith to the whole Christological mystery: the mystery of the God-Man. This mystery is expressed by St. Paul in a rich and profound way in today's liturgy in the Letter to the Colossians: Christ Jesus is the image of the unseen God and the first-born of all creation. It is also expressed in the Prologue of St. John's Gospel: "In the beginning was the Word..." and is professed every time we say the Creed.

This is our faith, this is the teaching of the church about the divinity of Christ. Here we touch directly on the reality of the Heart of Jesus. For the heart is a human organ belonging to the physical and spiritual make-up of the human person. "And the Word was made flesh." The heart is both a physical organ of the body and its symbolic center which is by nature spiritual.

The Heart of Jesus was conceived beneath the heart of the Virgin Mother and its earthly life ceased at the moment Jesus died on the cross, as attested by the Roman soldier who pierced the side of Jesus with a lance.

During the whole of Jesus' earthly life, the Heart of Jesus was the center in which was manifested in a human way the love of God: the love of the Son and through the Son the love of God the Father.

The greatest fruit of this love in creation, the most magnificent gift of the Heart of Jesus in all of creation is that the human person is born of God, the human person is adopted as son and daughter in the Eternal Son, humanity is given the power to become children of God.

And therefore our human heart "transformed" in this way can and does say to the Divine Heart of Jesus what we hear in today's liturgy, the words of Psalm 103 in the Old Testament: "My soul, give thanks to the Lord." How much more do the Gospels tell us of the Divine Heart of the Son and indirectly of the Heart of the Father.

The Holy Father then quotes three invocations from the Litany of the Sacred Heart:

Heart of Jesus, abode of justice and love! Heart of Jesus, patient and most merciful! Heart of Jesus, fountain of life and holiness!

The Heart of Jesus is a call of God, strong and constant, addressed to all humankind and to every human heart. The words of Paul to the Colossians form the ultimate prospective opened to us by the Heart of Jesus Christ through faith. It is the beginning and the end, the fullness, of all that has been created by God.

The pope concludes with a prayer addressed to the Heart of Jesus:

Lord Jesus Christ, Eternal Son of the Eternal Father, born of the Virgin Mary, we ask you to continue to reveal to us the mystery of God: so that we may recognize in you "the image of the invisible

God"; that we may find in you, in your divine Person, in the warmth of your humanity, in the love of your Heart.

Heart of Jesus in whom dwells the fullness of divinity!
Heart of Jesus, of whose fullness we have all received!
Heart of Jesus, King and center of all hearts, for ever and ever.
Amen!

Homily during the Mass for families at the cathedral of Koekelberg, Belgium: The great prayer of the Sacred Heart: The Church consecrated in the truth and in the unity of Christ, May 29, 1985

"I consecrate myself for them, so that they also may be consecrated in truth" (John 17:19). This is the great prayer of the Sacred Heart of Jesus. "That they may be one just as we are" (John 17:11). The Holy Father calls upon spouses and parents never to forget that their unity and their fidelity, the splendor of their love are graces that come from God, from the Heart of the Trinity. The sacrament of matrimony allows them to reach it constantly. But for this it is necessary for them frequently to ask God, who is love, to help them to live in love. What power there is, what testimony there is, when they have the simplicity to pray as a family, parents and children! Then the family merits the name of domestic church.

Address to participants in the International Symposium on the Alliance of the Hearts of Jesus and Mary at Fatima, September 22, 1986

I am pleased to welcome all of you who have taken part in the International Symposium on the Alliance of the Hearts of Jesus and Mary that was held this past week in Fatima. I wish to greet in a special way Cardinal Sin, the president of your Symposium, and together with him all who were responsible for formulating and carrying out the specific plans of your week of theological study.

The title of your Symposium was taken from my Angelus Address of September 15, 1985, when I made reference to that "admirable alliance of hearts" of the Son of God and of his Mother. We can indeed say that devotion to the Sacred Heart of Jesus and to the Immaculate Heart of Mary has been an important part of the *sensus fidei* of the People of God during recent centuries. These devotions seek to direct our attention to Christ and to the role of his Mother in the mystery of Redemption, and, though distinct, they are interrelated by reason of the enduring relation of love that exists between the Son and his Mother.

Much research has been done on devotion to the Sacred Heart of Jesus. Hence you have made it your specific aim to reflect upon devotion to the Immaculate Heart of Mary in the perspective of Sacred Scripture and Tradition, while at the same time concentrating on the intimate link that unites the Hearts of Jesus and his Mother. Devotion to the Heart of Mary cannot be traced to the early centuries of Christian history, though the Heart of Mary is indeed mentioned in the Gospel of Luke. There are some references to the Heart of the Mother of God in the commentaries upon the Scriptures by the Fathers of the Church, but for the most part it was not until the seventeenth century that under the influence of St. John Eudes this devotion became widespread. In our own century we see that the message of Our Lady at Fatima, the consecration of the world in 1942 to the Immaculate Heart of Mary by my predecessor Pope Pius XII, and theological initiatives such as your own have helped us to appreciate the importance of this devotion.

It is worthy of note that the decree by which Pope Pius XII instituted for the universal Church the celebration in honor of the Immaculate Heart of Mary states: "With this devotion the Church renders the honor due to the Immaculate Heart of the Blessed

Virgin Mary, since under the symbol of this Heart she venerates with reverence the eminent and singular holiness of the Mother of God and especially her most ardent love for God and Jesus her Son and moreover her maternal compassion for all those redeemed by the divine Blood" (S.R.C., May 4, 1944; AAS 37 [1945], p. 50). Thus it can be said that our devotion to Mary's Immaculate Heart expresses our reverence for her maternal compassion both for Jesus and for all of her spiritual children as she stood at the foot of the cross.

I presented this same thought in my first encyclical *Redemptor hominis,* in which I pointed out that from the first moment of the Redemptive Incarnation, "under the special influence of the Holy Spirit, Mary's Heart, the Heart of both a virgin and a mother, has always followed the work of her Son and has gone out to all those whom Christ has embraced and continues to embrace with inexhaustible love" (no. 22).

We see symbolized in the Heart of Mary her maternal love, her singular sanctity, and her central role in the redemptive mission of her Son. It is with regard to her special role in her Son's mission that devotion to Mary's Heart has prime importance, for through love of her Son and of all of humanity she exercises a unique instrumentality in bringing us to him. The act of entrusting to the Immaculate Heart of Mary that I solemnly performed at Fatima on May 13, 1982, and once again on March 25, 1984, at the conclusion of the Extraordinary Holy Year of the Redemption, is based upon this truth about Mary's maternal love and particular intercessory role. If we turn to Mary's Immaculate Heart, she will surely "help us to conquer the menace of evil, which so easily takes root in the hearts of the people of today, and whose immeasurable effects already weigh down upon our modern world and seem to block the paths toward the future" (no. 3).

Our act of consecration refers ultimately to the Heart of her Son, for as the Mother of Christ she is wholly united to his redemptive mission. As at the marriage feast of Cana, when she said, "Do whatever he tells you," Mary directs all things to her Son, who answers our prayers and forgives our sins. Thus by dedicating ourselves to the Heart of Mary we discover a sure way to the Sacred Heart of Jesus, symbol of the merciful love of our Savior.

The act of entrusting ourselves to the Heart of Our Lady establishes a relationship of love with her in which we dedicate to her all that we have and are. This consecration is practiced essentially by a life of grace, of purity, of prayer, of penance that is joined to the fulfillment of all the duties of a Christian, and of reparation for our sins and the sins of the world.

My esteemed friends, I encourage you to continue your scholarly efforts to promote among the People of God a better understanding of devotion to the Hearts of the Son and of his Mother. I thank you for your presence here and I assure you of my prayers for your worthy endeavors. In the love of the Hearts of Jesus and Mary I impart to all of you my apostolic blessing.

Summary

In the first homily reproduced here, given at Gemelli University Hospital, the Holy Father speaks of the meaning of "heart" as the essential core of the human personality and expressly of the mystery of the Heart of Jesus. He speaks of the possibility of remaking a "new heart," of how the human heart "of stone" can be changed into a heart "of flesh." In his homily at the Vancouver Airport in Canada the pope continues speaking of the meaning of the Divine Heart as a call by God addressed to every human heart. He quotes six invocations of the Litany of the Sacred Heart. At the cathedral of Koekelberg, Belgium, the pope connects Jesus' act of consecrating himself in truth to his Sacred Heart and calls it the great prayer of the Sacred Heart.

To these homilies in this chapter we add a message the Holy Father gave to participants in the International Symposium on the Alliance of the Hearts of Jesus and Mary. Since much has been written about the Sacred Heart of Jesus, the symposium participants concentrated on the Immaculate Heart of Mary and the act of entrusting ourselves to the Heart of Our Lady.

Chapter 6

Litany of
the Sacred Heart of Jesus

The Litany of the Sacred Heart of Jesus as we know it consists of thirty-three invocations directed to the Sacred Heart. Its origins date back to the time of St. Margaret Mary Alacoque, who was familiar with a list of invocations honoring the Heart of Jesus composed by Sister Joly of the Dijon Visitation Monastery and another list composed by Mother de Soudeille, superior of the Visitation of Moulins. There was a third list of twenty-three invocations composed by Father Jean Croiset, spiritual director of St. Margaret Mary after St. Claude La Colombière. It was published in the second edition of his book, which was the first treatise on devotion to the Sacred Heart, written during the lifetime of St. Margaret Mary. With ten invocations added later, this third litany had thirty-three invocations in honor of the thirty-three years of the earthly life of Our Lord and was the basis for the litanies approved for the Dioceses of Marseilles and Autun, and for the Visitation Order. The first of these two, with modifications, became the litany approved by Pope Leo XIII for the universal Church on April 2, 1899. Even today it remains as one of six official litanies in the church and is the one commented on by Pope John Paul II in his Angelus messages from 1985 to 1989.

Among traditional practices of the devotion, the Litany of the Sacred Heart is one of the present pope's favorites, which he has recommended on a number of occasions. For example, in a general audience on June 20, 1979, during his first year as pope, he said: "The beautiful Litany of the Sacred Heart of Jesus is composed of many similar words — even more, they are exclamations of admiration for the riches of the Heart of Christ.

Let us attentively mediate on them on this day" (Solemnity of the Sacred Heart of Jesus).

In an Angelus message on July 1, 1984, the pope said: "During the entire month of June, the Church has placed before us the mysteries of the Heart of Jesus, the God-Man. These mysteries are expressed in a penetrating way in the Litany of the Sacred Heart, which can be sung, which can be recited, but above all which ought to be meditated."

On June 27, 1982, the Holy Father devoted a Sunday Angelus message to a reflection on the litany. It is given here in its entirety.

Angelus message: The Litany of the Sacred Heart of Jesus reflects the deepest experiences of human hearts, June 27, 1982

Heart of Jesus, formed by the Holy Spirit in the womb of the Virgin Mary, have mercy on us. So we pray in the Litany of the Sacred Heart of Jesus.

This invocation refers directly to the mystery on which we meditate when we recite the Angelus: by the work of the Holy Spirit, there was formed in the womb of the Virgin of Nazareth the humanity of Christ, Son of the eternal Father.

By the work of the Holy Spirit, the Heart was formed in this humanity. The Heart, which is the central organ of Christ's human organism and at the same time the true symbol of his interior life: his thoughts, his will, his sentiments. Through this Heart, the humanity of Christ is in a particular way the "temple of God" and at the same time, through this Heart, it remains ever open to human beings and to everything human: "Heart of Jesus, of whose fullness we have all received."

The month of June is especially dedicated to the veneration of the Divine Heart. Not just one day, the liturgical feast that usually falls in June, but every day. Connected with it is the devout practice of daily reciting or singing the Litany of the Sacred Heart of Jesus.

It is a marvelous prayer, totally concentrated on the interior mystery of Christ, the God-Man. The Litany to the Heart of Jesus draws abundantly from biblical sources, and at the same time reflects the deepest experiences of human hearts. It is also a prayer of veneration and authentic dialogue.

In it we speak of the Heart, and we also allow our hearts to speak with this unique Heart that is the "fountain of life and holiness" and the "desire of the everlasting hills," with the Heart that is "patient and most merciful," enriching all who call upon him.

This prayer, recited and meditated, becomes a true school of the interior life, the school of the Christian.

The Solemnity of the Sacred Heart of Jesus reminds us above all of the moments when this Heart was "pierced with a lance" and by this piercing was visibly opened to humankind and to the world.

Reciting the litany — and in general venerating the Divine Heart — we learn the mystery of redemption in all its divine and human depth.

At the same time we become sensitive to the need for reparation. Christ opens his Heart to us that we may join him in his reparation for the salvation of the world. The language of the pierced Heart speaks the whole truth about his gospel and about Easter.

Let us try to understand this language ever better.

In November 1989, Pope John Paul II completed a series of Sunday Angelus messages begun in 1985, one of the longest series devoted to a single topic, in this case the Litany of the Sacred Heart of Jesus. The completed series consists of thirty-three meditations on the invocations of the litany: twelve given during the summer of 1985 from June to September, ten given during the summer of 1986 from June to August. The series was then interrupted for two summers for themes dealing with the

Marian Year. Reflections on the litany were resumed with nine talks given during the summer of 1989 from July to September and completed with the final two talks given during November 1989.

After the series of talks was completed by the Holy Father, I gathered together and edited the thirty-three talks along with the earlier Angelus talk of June 27, 1992, which appears above. These meditations were published by the General Office of the Apostleship of Prayer in Rome as a special edition of its regular publication *Prayer and Service.**

To help understand the Litany of the Sacred Heart as a prayer-form in the Church, as editor I added a historical note on litanies in general and specifically on the Litany of the Sacred Heart. These thirty-three messages are not reproduced here, since they are still readily available as a separate book.

The pope's talks are not intended as an exegetical study of the invocations, but he indicates their deeply scriptural basis by incorporating biblical phrases and sources. Since they were given before the Sunday Angelus they also have a clear reference to the mystery of the incarnation and to Mary the Mother of God who leads us to the Heart of her Son.

The Holy Father has quoted invocations from the litany at various times in different talks he has given, for example, toward the end of a homily during a Votive Mass of the Heart of Jesus, celebrated at the Airport of Vancouver, Canada, on September 19, 1984, and in homilies on the Sacred Heart that he gave during his pastoral visits to Poland. His favorite invocation is "Heart of Jesus, fountain of life and holiness." As cardinal archbishop of Krakow, he used this invocation in a pastoral letter, dated June 11, 1965, for the two hundredth anniversary of the establishment of the feast of the Sacred Heart. In his first encyclical letter, *Redemptor hominis,* he quoted the expression "fountain of life and holiness," referring it to the Eucharist but giving as his source the Litany

---

*The meditations were published under the title *Litany of the Heart of Jesus: Angelus Meditations of Pope John Paul II,* edited with an introduction by Carl J. Moell, S.J., and published in three languages, English, Spanish, and French. The English edition was then republished by Our Sunday Visitor as *Angelus Meditations on the Litany of the Sacred Heart of Jesus* and later as *Pope John Paul II Prays the Litany of the Sacred Heart of Jesus.*

of the Sacred Heart. On other occasions he has quoted this invocation more than any other.

Summary

The best way to reflect on the invocations of the Litany of the Sacred Heart would be to take the litany itself and use it for meditation. For convenience, the litany is included as the last chapter in this book. Since the booklet of the Holy Father's reflections on the individual invocations of the litany is still available, the pope's reflections on the individual invocations can be used for a series of meditations on the litany and on the Sacred Heart.

Part Two

Pastoral Visits

Chapter 7

Visits to Parishes Dedicated to the Sacred Heart

Parish of the Sacred Hearts of Jesus and Mary at Tor Fiorenza on the fourth Sunday of Lent, March 17, 1985

The theme of the pope's homily centered on the words: "By grace ... you are saved" (Eph. 2:5).

These words seem to take on a special eloquence during this visit to the parish community dedicated to the Divine Heart of Jesus and the Immaculate Heart of his Mother: these two Hearts united by a holy bond of love, of that love which has in God, One and Three, its eternal and inexhaustible font. God indeed is love, and from this love takes its origin what the Apostle calls "grace" when he says: "By grace you are saved."

The highest and fullest witness of this salvific will of the most Holy Trinity is the Heart of the Redeemer and, united to him, the Heart of the Handmaid of the Lord in whom grace has reached the inexpressible fullness of divine maternity.

The time of Lent asks us to meditate on the mystery of divine grace. Not only the mystery of sin, but also the mystery of grace. In the revealed economy of salvation, one cannot be separated from the other. One cannot separate grace from sin nor sin from grace. They are joined in a mutual relationship, strictly complementary.

This marvelous complementarity properly recalls the mercy of God. The Letter to the Ephesians says this in today's liturgy: "But

God, who is rich in mercy, because of the great love he had for us, even when we were dead in our transgressions brought us to life with Christ" (Eph. 2:4–5).

Rich in mercy — *Rich in mercy* — in a certain sense is the title of the programmatic encyclical of my ministry in the chair of St. Peter.

Mercy means properly this love which is not withdrawn from sin, which does not separate itself from it, but draws near to it. This is properly the love of God, revealed in Jesus Christ.

Dear brothers and sisters, your parish is dedicated to the Sacred Hearts of Jesus and Mary. Today it is granted to me to visit this parish to meditate with you on the mysteries of the grace of God according to the liturgy of the fourth Sunday of Lent.

May our meeting today — in this special time of saving grace that is Lent — renew in you the desire for life in divine grace.

Once again I recall the Heart of our Redeemer, who is the "fountain of life and holiness," and I recall him through the mediation of the Immaculate Heart of the Mother of God!

In the wonderful union of these Hearts which protect your parish, may God be ever manifest in you, the God who is rich in mercy. May he work in you with the power of his grace!

In the pope's meetings with the parish, the first encounter was with the children.

I wish you well, dear boys and girls of the parish of the Sacred Hearts of Jesus and Mary and of the school of the Franciscan Sisters. It is truly a joy for me to meet with you children and students of the elementary school and kindergarten, who are preparing for your First Communion.

Your companion has spoken in the name of all of you and he has spoken very well. He is a good speaker, and you see that his heart too is good because he takes as example the Hearts of Jesus and Mary and he sees everything very clearly. He has also praised your pastor, Don Cesare, and this pleases me very much, because you want to say a good word for your pastor and his associates who teach you religion and catechism and also a good word for the Sisters who direct this school in which you learn so many things. And a good word for your families and for your parents: I want to embrace all of you children and by means of you to embrace your whole family because that is what Jesus did who drew children to himself, embraced them and thus showed them his Heart.

It is important for children to know the heart: the heart says love. Behold, Jesus lets you know the greatest love of all possible loves, and his Mother lets you know her motherly love close to the Heart of Jesus. It is important to be able to know love in life, to be able to know the human heart, and to be able to learn from the heart, from love, how to love. This is the most important thing in life. There are many persons, even young persons, who have learned to hate, and this is very dangerous and destructive: it destroys the good, it creates evil. You ought to learn to love, learn love, because it is only love that creates good, brings love into life in different surroundings. And so in your classes, if it is there, love brings good in your different contacts among yourselves; in the family, if there is love, you live well; and the same things apply to other surroundings, to society, even to all of humankind.

This is my message for you in this parish under the patronage of the Sacred Hearts: that the Heart of Jesus and the Heart of Mary may be manifest and that by means of these Hearts you learn to have a heart, that is, to love; and that this heart, this love, may become a program of love for boys and girls. This message I confide to you and with these simple words I present it. I hope that you wish to love, because your youthful hearts are open to love, wish to love and not to hate, wish to build good and not build evil, wish to build and not to destroy. Behold, I am convinced that your hearts are like that.

Finally, I also want to greet all those who teach you and catechize you, your parents who are here with you. I wish all of you well and offer you my blessing.

To the parishioners in reply to the greeting of the pastor:

May Jesus Christ be praised. I wish to thank you for those words which your pastor has made in the name of the entire parish. I greet you in the name of the Sacred Hearts of Jesus and Mary, to whom your parish is dedicated. I greet all here present, who I see are very numerous.

The pope too wishes all of you well: when you are under the patronage of the Sacred Hearts of Jesus and Mary you cannot but be well, because the human heart is for good, for love. I wish that love may reign in this your family, in your environment, in your community; that it may dominate, may give a direction to your life, love: heart means love, the Heart of Jesus means love, the Heart of Mary means love. Finally, I wish you a happy Easter: A Happy Easter to all!

To catechists and parish members of Caritas:

You are part of "the parish of the Hearts," the Heart of Jesus and the Heart of Mary: heart means love, it means charity, it means mercy, it means grace, just as I said in our meditation during Mass.

I cannot but thank you and I thank the Lord because it is here in the Heart of Jesus and in the Heart of Mary that you find the inspiration for your own heart to be a heart for others. And with this I bless you and all your dear ones.

Parish of the Sacred Heart of Jesus at Pontemammolo on the Feast of the Anniversary of the Dedication of the Lateran Basilica, November 9, 1986

"God is in his Church — Let us adore the Lord in his holy dwelling."

I am very happy to be with you, dear brothers and sisters of the Roman Parish of the Sacred Heart, to adore the Lord in the midst of this Eucharistic Assembly, on the day the liturgy recalls the Dedication of the Lateran Basilica, the cathedral of Rome.

In the homily the Holy Father greeted the pastor and his associate pastors of the religious order of Friars Minor Conventual, the Sisters of the Daughters of the Sacred Heart of Jesus, and various groups such as Third Order Franciscans, Caritas, Young Franciscans, Catholic Action, Apostleship of Prayer, and Confraternity of the Sacred Heart.

For my part I wish to exhort you to a great confidence inspired by devotion to the Heart of Jesus and the imitation of St. Francis, to whom you are particularly devoted.

I repeat also to you what I said at Paray-le-Monial a month ago, during the Eucharistic celebration in the Basilica of the Sacred Heart: "Above all, in society, in our villages, in our regions, in our factories and in our offices, in our encounters among peoples and races, the 'heart of stone,' the dried-up heart should transform itself into 'a heart of flesh,' open to brothers and sisters, open to God. Peace demands this. The survival of the human race demands it. This surpasses our forces. It is the gift of God, a gift of his love. We have the certainty of his love."

In appearing to St. Margaret Mary Alacoque, Jesus wished to manifest his infinite love for humankind and his desire to make himself loved. Therefore you ought to pledge yourself to love Jesus Christ totally and constantly, so that devotion to the Sacred Heart draws you and serious religious culture enlightens you; I recommend also consecration of your families to the Heart of Jesus and the practice of the First Friday of the month. I heartily desire that your parish be a center of fervent spirituality. Work diligently and confidently that the Sacred Heart of Jesus reign in every family in your parish.

To the young and to the children of the community:

I am very happy to greet you. And I join my applause to yours for you young people of this parish which is made alive by various groups. Your parish is dedicated to the Sacred Heart of Jesus. Behold a key word: "heart." We know well that it is a key word. It is a key word in life, in the personality of each of you, and I would say expressly in the life and personality formation of young people.

This word "heart" synthesizes all that we know and express by another key word, which is the word "love." These two words go together: heart and love. The Sacred Heart of Jesus is near to you, to all and especially to the young. The Sacred Heart of Jesus is the synthesis of all that Jesus was and that Jesus is. Where can we find the story of this Heart of Jesus? We can find it in the Gospels, especially in the Gospels of John and of Luke. Then you will find the answer to what it means to understand the story of the Heart of God. The Heart of Jesus has opened a new chapter in the history of salvation. For this the Church venerates with great love the Heart of Jesus. We direct to this Heart our worship. We pray to the Heart of Jesus by reciting the litany.

But we must pass from the worship of the Heart of Jesus to the culture of the human heart. The Gospel teaches us the profound culture of the human heart. The saints are those persons who have acquired and who acquire a supreme culture of the heart: The Virgin Mary has done this with her Immaculate Heart. Behold all of us must acquire from the Heart of Jesus and from the Heart of Mary a deep culture of our hearts. It is here that Christianity stands, lived as experience and as witness. To all you young people I wish you to acquire this culture which embraces Christianity but also humanity. The Heart of Christ is the Heart of the Son of God, but also a heart that is profoundly human. You cannot think of anything more human, any reality more human than the Heart of Christ.

To the parish council:

Since I am in your parish dedicated to the Sacred Heart of Jesus, I invite you to find in devotion to the Sacred Heart the counsels useful for your spiritual growth, for that of your families and also for that of your pastor who has the important responsibility for all of you.

Parish of the Sacred Heart in Castro Pretorio (via Marsala) on the first Sunday of Advent, November 29, 1987

The text of the homily was: "You, pastor of Israel, listen" (Ps. 79:2).

The experience of a "hardened heart" in people of our times makes this question more urgent: What is the vocation and the mission of a parish dedicated to the Heart of Christ in one of the more dynamic centers of Rome, crossroad of hope and culture, of institutions and initiatives? [The pope spoke of Don Bosco and the building of this basilica]...a church which, by means of the message of the Heart of Christ, is made a house of brothers because it is a house of the Father.

From the basilica to the parish community: In the midst of a residential population of three thousand persons, with a nucleus of a thousand families, your pastoral presence is conceived of and realized ever more as a service to the Heart of Christ, who seeks the human heart of those living concretely in this territory. A sublime and difficult mission!

For this you are charged to present on every occasion, by old means and by new, the good news of his love, the projects of his Heart.

Christ who has opened the unfathomable mystery of his Heart to little ones gives to each the victory over "hardness of heart" in order to welcome each other with a "mind humble and generous."

Parish of the Sacred Heart of Jesus in Prati, February 1, 1988

On this day the Holy Father inaugurated the phase of the City Mission called the "Visit to Families." At the end of Mass he himself would visit a family in the community and in the coming weeks, over thirteen thousand missionaries would visit Roman families and invite them to make room in their lives for Christ, the one Redeemer of humankind. He asked everyone to welcome them with joy. He addressed his brothers and sisters of Sacred Heart of Jesus Parish in Prati, the Missionaries of the Sacred Heart of Jesus, and the parish workers.

Dear faithful of this parish of the Sacred Heart of Jesus, be witnesses to the Gospel of love. Spread God's love among everyone who lives, works, studies, or spends his free time in this neighborhood. Serve Christ's truth with tenacity, courage, and fidelity. May the Lord, who promised to remain with his disciples always, accompany you on your way. Turn your gaze to him.

Parish of St. John the Baptist at Castel San Giovanni, June 5, 1988

This is not a parish dedicated to the Sacred Heart, nor was the homily centered on the Heart of Jesus. It is included here because during the homily the Holy Father spoke to the sick on the Heart of Jesus.

To my dear sick people, sharers in the Passion of our Lord, I desire that you see in the cross of Jesus the beginning of the resurrection.

May the most Sacred Heart of Jesus, rich in love and mercy, give you the strength to live your faith intensely even in the test of illness. "Of all of you who suffer we ask you to support us. Precisely of you who are weak we ask that you become a source of strength for the Church and for humanity" [a quotation from the pope's apostolic letter *Salvifici doloris* on the Christian meaning of human suffering].

Parish of Holy Mary of Graces at Fornaci, January 26, 1992

This is not a parish dedicated to the Sacred Heart, and the Holy Father did not give a homily on the Sacred Heart, but he did speak to the pastoral council on devotion to the Sacred Heart.

You are very near to this parish, you are within this parish. This "being within" has two dimensions.

The first dimension is to be within Christ himself, in his person, in his Heart. We are among the privileged because we have before us the opened Heart of Christ. And this allows us to be in his thought, in his affections, in his joys, and in his sorrows. There is also a second dimension which is the Church, and which shows how these two dimensions meet because the Church is the Body of Christ.

Naturally this communitarian dimension represents the continuation of the mystery of Christ. You are in a special way within the sentiments of Christ, his sufferings; and you are also within his redemptive power, within his mission. This belongs to our identity as Christians, to participate in the mission of Christ, King and Lord of the universe and of time.

I wish that this meeting will stir up in all of you an awareness of being near, beyond being near in terms of space, above all being near in spirit to the mystery of Christ by means of the Church. This is the profound meaning of what you are and of how you work with your pastors.

I thank you again and I wish you an ever greater awareness of that to which you are called, that is, of your vocation.

Parish of St. Maria Josefa of the Heart of Jesus on Gaudete Sunday, December 16, 2001

This parish is included because of St. Maria Josefa's devotion to the Sacred Heart and the significance of the pope's three-hundredth visit to a Roman parish. In a letter to his cardinal vicar for Rome, dated two days before the visit, the pope wrote:

On Sunday, December 16, God willing, I will visit the Roman parish of St. Maria Josefa of the Heart of Jesus. With this visit I will have visited three hundred parishes since I began this spiritual pastoral pilgrimage in 1978.... Spontaneously I feel the desire to give thanks to God as I reach this significant goal....

I am most grateful, because for me the visit to the Roman parishes has always been an enjoyable task.... If today I can say that I feel fully "Roman," it is thanks to the visits to the parishes of this extraordinary and beautiful City.

In the homily during the Mass, the Holy Father said:

Dear brothers and sisters of the Parish of St. Maria Josefa of the Heart of Jesus! The joy of being with you today is particularly strong. It is the delight of being able to visit the three hundredth parish community of the beloved Church of Rome. From the beginning of my pontificate, I have made a priority of exercising the ministry of bishop of Rome, even by visiting the parish communities of the diocese....

I wish to thank the Institute of the Servants of Jesus, who, with a genuine ecclesial spirit, made possible the construction of this new church, consecrated last January 27, which is dedicated to their foundress, St. Maria Josefa of the Heart of Jesus.

May the example of this saint, who was animated by an intense love of the Eucharist and for her neighbor in difficulty, be a stimulus for you, dear Sisters, to grow in devotion to the Eucharist and in the care of their older sick and needy neighbors.

Summary

In his visits to these parishes the Holy Father gave a homily at the Eucharistic celebration and later spoke to various parish groups. To the parishioners of the Sacred Hearts of Jesus and Mary Parish, he spoke of "having a heart" as meaning "to love" and of grace and mercy as symbolized by the Heart of Jesus.

To the parishioners of the Sacred Heart of Jesus Parish, the pope referred to his recent visit to Paray-le-Monial and contrasted a "heart of stone" or "dried-up heart" with a heart modeled on the Heart of Jesus. He urged his hearers to see "heart" and "love" as conjoined and to find in the Gospels the way to imitate the Heart of Jesus and the Heart of God.

To the Sacred Heart Parish in Castro Pretorio, the pope urged victory over a "hardened heart" by the unfathomable mystery of the Heart of

Jesus. In Sacred Heart Parish in Prati the Holy Father inaugurated the phase of the City Mission called "Visits to Families" and urged the people to be witnesses to the Gospel of love and to spread God's love to everyone.

Two of the parishes visited are not dedicated specifically to the Sacred Heart, but in one of them in his homily the pope spoke to the sick on the Heart of Jesus and in the other he spoke to the pastoral council on devotion to the Sacred Heart.

The visit to the Parish of St. Maria Josefa of the Heart of Jesus marked a significant milestone for the Holy Father, since it was his three-hundredth visit to a Roman parish.

Chapter 8

Visit to Paray-le-Monial

October 5, 1986

Letter to Father Peter-Hans Kolvenbach, superior general of the Society of Jesus, October 5, 1986

As part of my pilgrimage to Paray-le-Monial, I wanted to come and pray in the chapel where the tomb of Blessed Claude La Colombière is venerated. He was the "faithful servant," whom the Lord in his providential love gave as spiritual director to St. Margaret Mary Alacoque. This is how he was led to be the first to spread her message. In just a few years of religious life and intense ministry, he revealed himself an "exemplary son" of the Society of Jesus and to him, as St. Margaret Mary herself bears witness, Christ entrusted the mission of spreading the devotion to his Divine Heart. I know with what generosity the Society of Jesus welcomed this admirable mission and with what zeal it has sought to accomplish it as perfectly as possible in the course of the last three centuries: but on this solemn occasion I want to exhort every member of the Society to promote with even greater zeal this devotion which corresponds more than ever to the expectations of our day.

In the seventeenth century, on the very threshold of the modern age, the Lord in his Providence wanted a powerful movement in favor of devotion to the Heart of Christ, in the ways indicated in the revelations received by St. Margaret Mary, to spread out from Paray-le-Monial; but the essential elements of this devotion belong permanently to the spirituality of the Church throughout its history.

From the very beginning the Church has contemplated the pierced Heart of the crucified Christ from which came blood and water, the symbols of the sacraments which constitute the Church; and in the Heart of the Word incarnate, the Fathers of the Christian East and West saw the beginning of the whole work of our salvation, the fruit of the love of the divine Redeemer, whose pierced Heart is a particularly expressive symbol.

The desire to "know the Lord intimately" and to "speak heart to heart with him" is, thanks to the Spiritual Exercises, characteristic of Ignatian spiritual and apostolic dynamism, totally at the service of the love of the Heart of God.

While recalling that Christ, the Word incarnate, "loved with a human heart," Vatican II assures us that "his message, far from diminishing the human person, serves his progress by bringing light, life and liberty, while apart from him nothing can satisfy the human heart" (*Gaudium et spes,* 22, 21). In the Heart of Christ the human heart comes to know the true and only meaning of life and destiny, to understand the value of an authentically Christian life, to protect itself from certain perversions, to unite filial love for God with love for the neighbor. In this way — and this is the true meaning of the reparation demanded by the Heart of the Savior — on the ruins accumulated through hatred and violence can be built the civilization of love so greatly desired, the kingdom of the Heart of Christ.

For these reasons I am most anxious that you pursue with perseverance the diffusion of true devotion to the Heart of Christ and that you be ever ready to bring effective help to my brothers in the episcopate in order to promote this devotion everywhere, taking care to find the most suitable means of presenting and practicing it, so that contemporary men and women, with their own particular mentality and sensitivity, may discover there the true answer to their questions and expectations.

As last year on the occasion of the Congress of the Apostleship of Prayer, I entrusted very especially to Father General this work so intimately linked to devotion to the Sacred Heart, today again during my pilgrimage to Paray-le-Monial, I beseech you to deploy every possible effort to accomplish ever more perfectly the mission which Christ himself entrusted to the Society, the spreading of the devotion to his Divine Heart.

The abundant spiritual fruits which come from devotion to the Heart of Jesus are widely recognized. Expressing itself in particular through the practice of the Holy Hour, confession, and Communion on the first Friday of the month, it has encouraged generations of Christians to pray more and to participate more frequently in the sacraments of reconciliation and the Eucharist. Those are ways still appropriate for proposing to the faithful of today.

May the maternal protection of the Virgin Mary help you: it was on the occasion of her feast of the Visitation that this mission was entrusted to you in 1688; and in all your apostolic efforts, may the apostolic blessing which I give with all my heart from Paray-le-Monial to the whole Society of Jesus be a source of strength and comfort to you!

Homily in the basilica at Paray-le-Monial:
What will separate us from the love of Christ?
October 5, 1986

The Holy Father began his homily with the words of the prophet Ezekiel: "I will give you a new heart" (Ezek. 36:26).

[The words of Ezekiel are confirmed in this place] by a poor and hidden handmaid of the Divine Heart of Our Lord: St. Margaret Mary. Many times in the course of history the truth of this promise has been confirmed by revelations in the Church through the experience of saints, mystics, and souls consecrated to God. The entire history of Christian spirituality testifies to it: the life of a person who believes in God stretches toward the future by means of hope, called to a communion of love; this life is that of the heart, that of the "interior" person. It is illuminated by the marvelous truth of the Heart of Jesus who offers himself for the world.

"I will give you a heart": God says this through the prophet. And the meaning is clarified from the context. "I will sprinkle clean water upon you to cleanse you" (Ezek. 36:25). God purifies the human heart. The heart created to be the hearth of love has become the hearth of the refuse of God, of the sin of human beings who distance themselves from God to cling to every sort of "idol." In this case the heart is "impure." But when this interior "hearth" of the human person opens itself to God, it finds again the purity of the image and likeness impressed upon it by the Creator in the beginning.

The heart is also the central hearth of that conversion which God desires from and for the human person, to enter into his interior, into his love. God has created the human person so that it may be, not indifferent or cold, but open to God. How beautiful are the words of the prophet: "I will take from your bodies your stony hearts and give you natural hearts" (Ezek. 36:26)! A heart of flesh, a heart that has a human sensitivity, and a heart capable of allowing itself to be conquered by the breath of the Spirit. This is what Ezekiel says: "I will give you a new heart and place a new spirit within you, . . . I will put my spirit within you" (Ezek. 36:26–27).

May each of you allow yourselves to be purified and to be converted by the Spirit of the Lord! May each of you find in him inspiration for your own life and light for your own future, to purify your own desires!

Today, I wish to announce especially to families the good news of a wonderful gift: God gives you purity of heart, God permits you to live true love.

But how will the Spirit come into human hearts? It will be the work of Jesus Christ, the eternal Son whom God has not spared but has given for all of us to give us every grace along with him, to offer ourselves completely with him!

It will be the wonderful work of Jesus. So that it may be revealed it will be necessary to await until the end, until his death on the cross. And when Christ "has handed over" his own spirit into the hands of his Father, then this event will be verified: "So the soldiers came.... But when they came to Jesus and saw that he was already dead ... one soldier thrust his lance into his side, and immediately blood and water flowed out" (John 19:32–34).

The event seemed "ordinary." On Golgotha comes the final gesture of a Roman executioner: verification of the death of the condemned. He is dead, he is really dead!

And in his death he has revealed himself until the end.... The pierced Heart is the final testimony. The Apostle John at the foot of the cross has understood it; in the course of centuries, the disciples of Christ and the teachers of the faith have understood it. In the seventeenth century a religious of the Visitation received anew this testimony at Paray-le-Monial: Margaret Mary transmitted it to the entire church at the dawn of modern times.

Through the Heart of his Son, pierced on the cross, the Father has freely given all. The Church and the world have received the Consoler, the Holy Spirit. Jesus said: "But if I go, I will send him to you" (John 16:7). His pierced Heart testifies to the fact that he has gone. He finally sends the Spirit of truth. The water which flows from his pierced side is the sign of the Holy Spirit: Jesus had announced to Nicodemus the new birth "of water and the Spirit" (John 3:5). The words of the prophet have been fulfilled: "I will give you a new heart, I will place a new spirit within you."

St. Margaret Mary knew this wonderful mystery, the disturbing mystery of divine love. She has known all the depths of the words of Ezekiel: "I will give you a heart." During her hidden life in Christ she was marked by the gift of this Heart which offered itself without limit to all human hearts. She was completely taken by this divine mystery, as the wonderful prayer of today's psalm expresses it; "Bless the Lord, my soul; all my being, bless his holy name!" (Ps 102/103:1). "All my being" means "all my heart."

For all her life, St. Margaret Mary burned with the living flame of this love that Christ had come to inflame in human history. Here at Paray-le-Monial, as once the Apostle Paul did, the humble handmaid of God seemed to cry out to all the world: "What will separate us from the love of Christ?" (Rom. 8:35).

Paul addressed himself to the first generation of Christians. He knew what was "distress, anguish, famine, nakedness," he knew what was peril and the sword! In the seventeenth century the same question put by Margaret Mary to the Christians of her time resounded from Paray-le-Monial. In our time the same question is addressed to each one of us, to each one of us in particular when we examine our own experience of family life. What breaks the bond of love? What extinguishes the love that burns in the hearth?

The family, thanks to the sacrament of matrimony, in alliance with divine wisdom, in the infinite love of the Heart of Christ is given to develop in each of your members the richness of the human person, its own vocation to love of God and fellow human beings.

With Paul of Tarsus, with Margaret Mary, we proclaim the same certainty: neither death nor life, neither the present nor the future, neither any force nor any other creature, nothing can separate us from the love of God which is in Jesus Christ. Before the open Heart of Christ, we seek to obtain from him the true love of which our families have need. The family cell is the foundation for building the civilization of love.

Above all, in society, in our villages, in our regions, in our factories, and in our offices, in our encounters among peoples and races, the "heart of stone," the dried-up heart should transform itself into a "heart of flesh," open to brothers and sisters, open to God. Peace demands this. The survival of the human race demands it. This surpasses our forces. It is the gift of God, a gift of his love. We have the certainty of his love.

Prayer in the Basilica at Paray-le-Monial, October 5, 1986

See below p. 273.

Angelus Message at Paray-le-Monial, October 5, 1986

At the end of the morning, as he was accustomed to do on Sundays and feast days in Rome, the Holy Father prayed the Angelus with the people for the needs of the world.

On this occasion, the pope prayed for the first world day of the environment organized for the following day, October 6, by the United Nations to find suitable housing for the millions of homeless people worldwide. This day prepares for the international year of homeless persons. Invoking the Blessed Mother the pope said:

Mary, Mother of mercy, show your children the Heart of Jesus which you saw opened to be ever the fountain of life.

Mary, who in this place had shown to Margaret Mary the Heart of your Son, grant that we may follow your example of humble faithfulness to his love.

Talk to the Visitation Sisters of the Monastery in Paray-le-Monial: Help people to uncover the love of the Savior, October 5, 1986

"Behold this Heart which has so loved men and women as not to spare itself anything but to exhaust and consume itself as a testimony of its love." With emotion I wish to give thanks for this message received and transmitted here by St. Margaret Mary. Near her tomb I ask her to help people constantly to open themselves to the love of the Savior and to allow themselves to be permeated by it.

We give thanks for the development of this monastery, recalling what St. Francis de Sales had said about the Daughters of the Visitation: "They have the Heart of Jesus their crucified spouse as their dwelling place in this world." I know that there is a group of souls here dedicated to the Heart of Jesus.

We give thanks for the mystical experience of St. Margaret Mary. To her was given, with a particular light but in a hidden existence, to know the power and the beauty of the love of Christ. In Eucharistic adoration, she had contemplated the Heart pierced for the salvation of the world, wounded by the sins of men and women, but also the "fountain of life," as witnessed by the light that shone from the wounds of his risen body.

We give thanks for the intimacy of this humble religious with the Savior. The sufferings which had afflicted her in so many ways she generously offered in union with the passion of Christ, in reparation for the sins of the world. At the same time, she was known as a witness to the salvation effected by the Son of God and called to unite herself by means of the offering of herself to the work of divine mercy.

We give thanks for the privileged meeting of this holy religious with Blessed Claude La Colombière. The support of this faithful disciple of St. Ignatius permitted Margaret Mary to overcome her doubts and to discern the authentic inspiration of her extraordinary experience. Their conversation is a model of sound judgment in spiritual advice. Father La Colombière himself received illumination from her whom he counseled. We give thanks for the great development of adoration and Eucharistic Communion which has taken a new impulse here, thanks to devotion to the Sacred Heart promoted especially by the Visitation and by the Jesuit Fathers, approved by the popes. The particular devotion of the First Fridays of the month has borne much fruit, thanks to the urgent message received by Margaret Mary. And I cannot forget that the bishops of Poland had obtained from Clement XIII the office and Mass of the Sacred Heart almost a century (1765) before the feast was extended to the universal Church (1856).

We give thanks for the many pastoral initiatives and religious foundations which have found here a decisive fount of inspiration.

With you gathered with me in this Chapel of the Apparitions, the Sisters of the Visitation united with other contemplative religious of the diocese, with Monsignor Guidon and the chaplains of the sanctuary, we invoke for all humanity, consecrated to the Sacred Heart by my predecessor Pope Leo XIII, the inexhaustible grace of redemptive love which gushes from the Heart of Jesus.

Summary

In the letter the Holy Father gave to the superior general of the Society of Jesus, several things should be expressly noted. The purpose of the letter was to urge all Jesuits to be faithful to the commission already given to them of promoting devotion to the Sacred Heart of Jesus, "which corresponds more than ever to the expectations of our day." The Holy Father also gives his definition of the reparation associated with the devotion. "This is the true meaning of the reparation demanded by the Heart of the Savior — on the ruins accumulated through hatred and violence can be built the civilization of love so greatly desired, the kingdom of the Heart of Christ." The pope also mentioned the practices associated with devotion to the Sacred Heart from the time of St. Margaret Mary: the Holy Hour and confession and Communion on the First Friday of the month. He also mentioned the Apostleship of Prayer, which he had particularly recommended just a year previously.

In his homily given in the Basilica of the Sacred Heart in Paray-le-Monial, the Holy Father spoke of the new heart prophesied by

Ezekiel and given especially to families, a gift from the pierced Heart of Christ. Nothing can separate us from the love of Christ. Once again the pope mentions the civilization of love, of which the family cell is the foundation.

The prayer of the pope in the Basilica in Paray-le-Monial is given in chapter 28 with other prayers to the Sacred Heart. The pope gave a short message before the Angelus and a talk to the Visitation Sisters of the Monastery urging them to continue the work of St. Margaret Mary in promoting devotion to the Heart of Jesus.

Chapter 9

Fourth Visit to Poland

June 2, 1991

Pope John Paul II has made seven pastoral visits to Poland. During his second visit in 1983 he beatified Sister Urszula Ledochowska, foundress of the Ursuline Sisters of the Sacred Heart of Jesus in Agony. There were a few brief references to the Sacred Heart but no distinct talk on the topic of the Sacred Heart. These pastoral visits to Poland were usually made during the month of June. During three of them the Holy Father spoke at length of the Sacred Heart: in 1991, 1997, and 1999. In this chapter we will consider the talks the pope gave on June 2, 1991, during his fourth visit and in the next chapter his talks given during that same visit on June 7, 1991, the Solemnity of the Sacred Heart of Jesus. Separate chapters will be given to the talks of 1997 and 1999.

On Sunday, June 2, 1991, on the esplanade behind Sacred Heart Church in Rzeszow, the Holy Father celebrated Mass with a vast crowd of faithful attending. During the sacred liturgy the pope beatified Bishop Jozef Sebastian Pelczar, who had been the diocesan bishop of Przemysl from 1900 to 1924. The pope did not speak about the Sacred Heart in this homily.

Angelus message in Rzeszow: Hail Jesus, Son of Mary!
June 2, 1991

At the end of the Eucharistic celebration the Holy Father led the recitation of the Angelus. As an introduction to the prayer, he gave a short address.

In how many places in your land, in how many Marian shrines, is this redeeming moment of the Annunciation now happening? How many lips are repeating the words of the Virgin Mother of God. "Hail Jesus, Son of Mary, you are true God in the Holy Host" — in that Eucharist which we have celebrated here.

Hail Jesus! Hail Divine Heart of the Son of Man. This house of God in the city of Rzeszow is dedicated to you, alongside of which the beatification of a son of your land has taken place — a priest and bishop of your Church, Jozef Sebastian Pelczar.

Blessed be this house of God as devoted to the Divine Heart as was Blessed Jozef Sebastian.

Christ spoke to him as he is speaking to us: "Learn from me, for I am meek and humble of heart" (Matt. 11:29). So many times did this priest, and later bishop, of Przemysl, repeat "make my heart like yours" — this supplication externalized the mystery of his progress in holiness, the source of which is the Heart of Jesus, "the fountain of life and holiness."

Blessed are you, Mother of God's Son! Blessed are you, Mother of Christ's Heart! Bring us closer to your Son, to that Heart which is "propitiation for our sins" (Litany of the Sacred Heart of Jesus; see also 1 John 2:2; Rom. 3:25).

Visit to the tomb of Blessed Jozef Sebastian Pelczar in Przemysl, June 2, 1991

Early Sunday afternoon on June 2, 1991, the Holy Father left Rzeszow and went to the cathedral in Przemysl to visit the tomb of Blessed Jozef Sebastian Pelczar. He first prayed at the tomb of the new Blessed and then addressed the faithful gathered in the cathedral, among whom were many sisters of the Handmaids of the Sacred Heart of Jesus, the congregation founded by Blessed Pelczar. He began his remarks with the text: "Every high priest is taken from among men and made their representative before God, to offer gifts and sacrifices for sins" (Heb. 5:1).

A particular legacy because also a particular gift of the Heart of the Redeemer is the charism of the religious vocation, of consecrated life which remains in the midst of the Church and of the world the living testimony of that love which never dies. Blessed Jozef Sebastian Pelczar read in the Heart of Jesus the importance of that cause according to the exigencies of his times. So too you must learn to find the same importance according to the exigencies of the new times, of the new possibilities, but also of the new difficulties and challenges of the millennium which is just ending.

I would say that your congregation takes its origin in a certain sense from Mary and finds its proper fullness in the Heart of Jesus. It is born in fact from the Fraternity of the Most Holy Virgin Mary Queen of Poland. Your blessed founder was a great devotee of the Mother of God, which he made visible in his episcopal coat of arms and his motto "Ave Maria."

May this Marian characteristic be joined in your spiritual life with love of the Divine Heart. With the word of life, mediating the attitude of service in regard to all those who have need of spiritual, moral, or material help, proclaim the glory of the Divine Heart. Learn from the Heart of God to embrace every human person with your heart.

May your blessed founder obtain for you the grace of creative fidelity to the charism of your congregation, may he help you in the imitation of the First Handmaid of the Heart of Christ, may he call to your community qualified young people to serve the same saving cause.

Address to Byzantine-Ukrainian Rite Catholics, June 2, 1991

Dear brothers and sisters, Bishop Ignacy Tokarczak, pastor of the Latin-rite diocese of Przemysl, in his concern for solving the problem regarding the cathedral of your rite, in the spirit of the agreements signed in February of this year, is handing over to me this church dedicated to the Sacred Heart of Jesus.

Your Excellency, it is with great joy and gratitude that I accept this gift from your diocese and from the entire Church of the Latin rite. I in turn hand it over as an everlasting possession to you, dear brothers and sisters of the Greek-Catholic, now called Byzantine-Ukrainian Rite, in place of the church which was to have been built according to the agreements. I establish this church today as the cathedral of the diocese and of the bishop of your rite. I greatly desire that this temple — where until recently lay the mortal remains of Bishop Jozef Sebastian, beatified today, a great apostle of reconciliation and harmonious collaboration between the two rites — may challenge every generation to build together, regardless of the rite to which they belong. The Church is one, holy, universal, and apostolic.

Heart of Jesus, patient and rich in mercy, fount of life and holiness, bless this beloved city, which history has not spared painful experiences, but which has also known magnificent signs of Christian brotherhood and solidarity.

Heart of Jesus, source of all consolation, I entrust to you the continuation of my pilgrimage in this land, in faith, love, and hope for the generations to come. Praised be Jesus Christ!

Summary

There is nothing particularly noteworthy in these three brief messages. The first is a message given before the Angelus and refers to the Divine Heart of Jesus in the Eucharist. The second speaks of the new Blessed and his devotion to the Heart of Jesus in relation to the congregation founded by him. The third donates the Church of the Sacred Heart to the Catholics of the Byzantine-Ukrainian Rite to be their cathedral.

Chapter 10

Fourth Visit to Poland

Solemnity of the Sacred Heart, June 7, 1991

During his 1991 pastoral visit to Poland, Pope John Paul II had as a program or theme the Ten Commandments. During the principal homilies throughout the trip he spoke on one or another of the Ten Commandments. In the two homilies given here, both delivered on the Solemnity of the Sacred Heart, in addition to speaking of the Divine Heart of Jesus, he also spoke of the Ninth Commandment (at Wloclawek) and the Tenth Commandment (at Plock). These sections of the homilies are omitted here.

Homily during the Mass at the Aeroclub in Wloclawek: One of the soldiers pierced his side with a lance (John 19:34), June 7, 1991

The Church returns today to the mystery of Good Friday. The feast of the Sacred Heart of Jesus is a great epilogue and a profound commentary on the events of Good Friday. The Gospel according to St. John refers to the very climax of these events. The soldiers sent by Pilate check whether the condemned at Golgotha are already dead. Christ is already dead. In order to check this, one of the soldiers pierces Christ's side. From the pierced side "there came blood and water" (John 19:34). That was a proof of his death.

The evangelist does not mention the Heart, but it is the human Heart of the Crucified One which has been pierced. It is from this Heart that flows the blood and water which signifies that Jesus

89

of Nazareth is no longer alive. This took place on the afternoon of Good Friday; the ritual law required that the bodies of those crucified not remain on the cross on the Passover, which was the greatest religious feast in Israel.

The evangelist adds two sentences to this account which attest to the fulfillment of the prophecy described in the Old Testament. The Old Testament says: "Not a bone of it shall be broken" (John 19:36, as opposed to what happened to the other two who were crucified). The Old Testament reads thus: "They shall look on him whom they have pierced" (John 19:37; Zech. 12:10).

They will look upon the Crucified One. They will look into his Heart. The key to the mystery which constitutes the central point of today's celebration is contained in these words. But not only the key to this mystery, but also to the spiritual history of many people, who, through this visible open wound in the side of the crucified Christ, penetrate through to that which is invisible. They look upon his Heart. They fix their gaze on his Heart.

How many people gazing on the Heart of the Redeemer have passed through this land on the banks of the Vistula, through this diocese? [The pope lists a number of these people.] All these people fixed their gaze on this Heart, pierced on the cross, and from it drew superhuman strength to witness to this Heart in life and death: to this Heart, which is a fountain of life and holiness.

This Heart contains, in a form able to be understood by people, the mystery of God's eternal Love. This is the mystery which the apostle proclaims in his Letter to the Ephesians, "the unsearchable riches of Christ ... the fulfillment of the secret plan, hidden for ages in God, who created all things" (3:8 – 9).

What kind of plan is this? And what kind of riches? Today's liturgy answers in the words of the prophet Hosea. First of all, it answers through this one phrase: "love," or rather, "I loved": When Israel was a child, I loved him ... I taught Ephraim to walk, I took them up in my arms ... I led them with cords of compassion, with the bands of love (Hos. 11:1, 3 – 4). Divine love, human hands; the human expression of this divine love couched in terms of the image of a father or a mother. "I took them up in my arms ... and I bent down to them and fed them" (Hos. 11:3 – 4).

The Heart of the only Son, the Heart pierced on the cross, is the mature fruit of God's eternal love for human beings. The truth of St. John's letter is inscribed in this Heart: God loved human beings first. "God loved us and sent his Son to be the expiation for our sins" (1 John 4:10). There is no greater love than this. No greater love has a person than this, that one lay down his life for his friends (John 15:13). There is no greater love than that which, at the end, is manifested in the Heart pierced by the lance of a centurion on Golgotha.

"My heart recoils within me, my compassion grows warm and tender. I will not execute my fierce anger, I will not again destroy Ephraim" (Hos. 11:8 – 9). Yes. His fierce anger flared up and consumed the Heart of the Son. And in the Heart of the Son this flame remained not as a flame of destructive punishment for humankind, but as a flame of renewing love.

In this way the divine Love reigns in the history of humankind — and in the spiritual lives of every one of us. "I, the Holy One, am in your midst and I will not come to destroy" (Hos. 11:9). The Heart of Jesus, expiation for our sins, is a fountain of life and holiness.

As we follow in the footsteps of so many sons and daughters of this land of Kujawy, this cathedral town, we should fix our gaze upon the Divine Heart. From this Heart flows "the strengthening with power in the inner self," as the apostle teaches in his Letter to the Ephesians (3:16).

The section of the homily dealing with the Ninth Commandment is omitted here.

"Jesus, meek and humble of Heart, make our hearts like yours." We can speak in this way to God, that God who became man, and in this human Heart bears the entire fullness of the divinity and the whole, immeasurable depths of the human vocation in God. He also bears in this human Heart, which ended up being pierced by a lance, the entire mystery of the price, the value of human beings, the whole mystery of the redemption....

The mystery of the Heart that was pierced, the mystery of the Heart of the one whom they looked upon....

The Solemnity of the Sacred Heart of Jesus is the celebration of the redemption of Europe, of the redemption of the world, of the redemption of Europe for the world. The world needs a redeemed Europe....

At the end of the Mass and before the final blessing, the Holy Father said a few words.

Today we give thanks to the Divine Heart for this difficult but rich past of the Church in Kujawy.

Your diocese has paid an enormous price for its fidelity to God and the Apostolic See.... In this diocese has been poured out abundantly the blood and water from the pierced side of Christ....

I recommend to the Divine Heart the entire future of the Diocese of Wloclawek. I place you in the maternal hands of the Mother of God.

Act of Consecration to the Sacred Heart of Jesus in Wloclawek, June 7, 1991

See below p. 275.

Homily during the Mass in Plock: Learn from me; for I am meek and humble of heart! (Matt. 11:29), June 7, 1991

Today the whole Church is listening to the words in which Christ discloses the secret of his Heart. "Learn from me," he says. This means that he is our Teacher and our Master. He is our Teacher and Master not only because of what he said and did, but because of who he was. We find out who Jesus Christ was through his Heart, first and foremost.

Who he was is an unfathomable secret. "No one...knows the Son but the Father," says Jesus (Matt. 11:27). At the same time, "whoever has seen the Son has seen the Father" (John 14:9), because "only the Son knows the Father" (Matt. 11:27). Everyone to whom the Son chooses to reveal him will know the Father (Matt. 11:27). So Christ, the Son of God and the Son of Man, is the key to our knowledge of God. His Heart is at the center of that knowledge.

Today, the entire Church celebrates that Heart in her liturgy. I am overjoyed that I am able to visit Plock today, one of the Piast capitals of our country and an ancient diocese.

How many people — sons and daughters of Polish Mazovia — have over the centuries learned the divine and human truth from contact with the inner secret of the Heart of Christ? There were many of these in centuries past, such as St. Stanislaus of Rostkow, for example, and many in the twentieth century, which has carefully recorded the deeds of martyrs and the faithful.

"Learn from me."

The truth which we must learn from Christ is the truth of love, first and foremost. The Heart of the Redeemer reveals to us the truth of love that is "from God" (John 4:7). God's love manifested itself in the fact that God "sent his only-begotten Son into the world that we might live through him" (1 John 4:9). The love which comes from God is life-giving. "Every one that loves is born of God...for

God is love" (1 John 4:7–8). He was born; God gave him life. He lives God's life. And only then does he "know God" because there is no other way of coming to know love other than through love itself. That is why "whoever does not love does not know God" (1 John 4:8).

That life-giving love comes from God, not from us: "not that we loved God, but that he loved us" (1 John 4:10).

So God is the first. All creatures not only follow from him, but the love of all living things does so as well. All the love that is in our human hearts! Love has its source in God. This everlasting source revealed itself fully when God the Father "sent his Son to be the propitiation for our sins" (1 John 4:10). Sin must be overcome so that love, which is the gift of God himself, may become part of the human heart. Only love has the power and might to attain this because it is the redeeming love which is present in the Heart of the Son.

John the Apostle and Evangelist, who speaks through today's liturgy, explains what we must learn from the Son who is the Redeemer of the world. We must "believe the love God has for us" (1 John 4:16). This faith not only signifies coming to know God; it is also new life — life in God. St. John writes, "and he that dwells in love dwells in God, and God in him" (1 John 4:16). Life in God permits us to experience the fact that God is love.

That is what we are to learn from the Sacred Heart of Christ the Redeemer.

Jesus, our Lord, finds particular joy in revealing this most profound truth about God. He says, "I thank you, Father, Lord of heaven and earth, that you have hidden these things from the wise and understanding and revealed them to babes; yea, Father, for such is your gracious will" (Matt. 11:25–26).

Who are those "babes"? Can the "wise and understanding" be "babes" as well? After all, we live in an era of scientific progress and the spread of knowledge. One must say, therefore, that many wise and scholarly people are responsive to the revelation of God who is Love.

God's love means being chosen and responding to being chosen by him, who loved first. This is the core of the covenant God made with man. The history of that covenant is first connected with the annals of Israel (as the first reading of today's liturgy reminded us). God let the descendants of Abraham come to know him as the God of the covenant in an exceptional way by delivering the sons and daughters of the chosen people from slavery in Egypt. "The smallest nation" was chosen, we hear, in order to make it plain that it was love, not human greatness, that had prompted the choice, because "the Lord loved you" (Deut. 7:8).

God's covenant with the chosen people is merely an image of that everlasting choice with which God embraces humankind through his only-begotten Son. The Heart of the Son — the Heart of Jesus — pierced with a spear at Golgotha is a manifestation of that universal choice and at the same time a manifestation of a new and everlasting covenant. God reveals himself as Love through Jesus' Heart. He reveals himself as the one who is faithful in love despite the sins of man, despite all the sins and evidence of infidelity which fill the annals of humankind.

"He is God, the faithful God, who keeps his covenant and stead-fast love" (Deut. 7:9). The human Heart of the God-man is the proof, the fullest proof, the irreversible proof of God's faithful love.

The section of the homily dealing with the Tenth Commandment is omitted here.

"Learn from me." Christ says, "Learn from me." And the beloved disciples adds, "Beloved, let us love one another ... if God so loved us, we also ought to love one another" (1 John 4:7–11).

And then Christ says, "Come to me, all who labor and are heavy laden, and I will give you rest. Take my yoke upon you, and learn from me . . . and you will find rest for our souls. For my yoke is easy and my burden is light" (Matt. 11:26–30). Amen.

Act of Devotion to the Sacred Heart of Jesus, Plock, June 7, 1991

An Act of Devotion to the Sacred heart of Jesus was celebrated by Pope John Paul II on Friday evening, June 7, Solemnity of the Sacred Heart, in the cathedral of Plock, dedicated to the Assumption of the Blessed Virgin Mary. Excerpts of the pope's talk which refer explicitly to the Heart of Jesus are translated here.

Heart of Jesus, King and center of all hearts! Your Synod is a contribution to the common treasure of the universal Church. The bishop and pastor of the Church of Plock has given me a copy of the documents of the Synod of your Diocese. . . .

Let us thank the Divine Heart of Jesus for this work of the community of the People of God in Mazovia, directing to him this invocation: King and center of all hearts, accept our contribution toward building up the Body of your Church in the perspective of the Third Millennium of Christianity.

Heart of Jesus, King and center of all hearts. The Church — according to the words of the Council — in Christ, is in the nature of a sacrament, a sign and instrument, that is, of communion with God and unity among all human beings (*Lumen gentium,* 1). Consequently, the mystery exalts the character of the Church as an interhuman "community" which is a particular reflection of the Trinitarian unity in God: Father, Son, and Holy Spirit (*Lumen gentium,* 4).

In virtue of this communion, the Divine Heart of the Redeemer of the world is an inexhaustible source of the union of all hearts. The Church — and in it also your Church of Plock — wishes to be and to experience itself here on the Vistula like a sacrament and servant of that union. All the definitive synodal decisions and recommendations reflect this. All of them — like the universal Church — "draw from the fullness of this Heart," draw from the "treasures of wisdom and knowledge" which dwell in the Divine Heart of the Redeemer — to serve the "union of hearts" for human beings.

In what way ought you to become a servant of this "union of all hearts" in the Divine Heart of the Redeemer?

As bishop of Rome, Successor of the Apostle Peter, I wish to thank you for this contribution to the common treasure of the universal Church...important for the postconciliar period at the dawn of the year 2000 from the birth of Christ.

He is for all "the way, the truth and the life" (John 14:6).

To him also — to the Heart which is the source and the unity of all hearts — I recommend the very ancient Church of Plock in its way toward new times and new tasks. I recommend all of you and the synodal work of your Church to Christ, Redeemer of the world, through the Heart of his Mother, who is the Mother of the Church. May all the Holy Patrons of this land — in particular young Stanislaus (Kostka) of Rostkow — obtain that Christ will ever be "the way, the truth, and the life" for all, for generations of the present and of the future.

Summary

Of the two homilies given on the Solemnity of the Sacred Heart, the first centers around the text of the piercing of the side of Jesus on the cross and the second on learning from the Heart of Jesus, the two principal texts on the Sacred Heart. The Act of Consecration of the Diocese of Wloclawek is included with the prayers to the Sacred Heart in chapter 28 but the Act of Devotion to the Sacred Heart at Plock is included here. This homily was based on the text "Heart of Jesus, King and Center of all hearts" and speaks of the Heart of Jesus as the source and unity of all hearts.

Chapter 11

Sixth Visit to Poland

June 1997

Homily at Mass for the Beatification of Mother Maria Bernardina Jablonska and Mother Maria Karlowska on the Solemnity of the Sacred Heart of Jesus in Zakopane, Poland, June 6, 1997

Mother Maria Bernardina Jablonska (1878–1940) served most of her life as superior general of the Congregation of the Sisters Servants of the Poor of the Third Order of St. Francis (the Albertines), a Franciscan community that cares for the very poor founded by St. Albert Chmielowski.

Mother Maria Karlowska (1865–1935), was the foundress of the Sisters of the Good Shepherd of Divine Providence, who work for the moral and social rehabilitation of prostitutes and care for those suffering from venereal diseases.

We meet today in this great liturgical assembly at the foot of the cross on Mt. Giewont, on the Solemnity of the Sacred Heart of Jesus. I thank divine Providence for enabling me to celebrate this solemnity in my homeland, with you — beneath the "Krokiew" in the land of Podhale — who faithfully preserve in your religious devotion veneration for the mystery of the Heart of Jesus. The Church in Poland made a great contribution to the introduction into the liturgical calendar of the Solemnity of the Sacred Heart of Jesus. It was the expression of a deep desire that the extraordinary fruits produced by this devotion should be multiplied in the life of the faithful throughout the Church. And so it happened. How we should thank God for all the graces which we experience through his Son's Heart. How thankful we are for today's meeting! We have long waited for it. For a long time you have been inviting the pope, an invitation made on various occasions, especially during your frequent pilgrimages to the Eternal City. You certainly remember how I then used to say that we have to be patient and leave to divine Providence the visit to Zakopane. During my visit to Slovakia, at Levoca, I read the placard which you had prepared: "Zakopane is waiting! Zakopane welcomes you!" And today we can say that Zakopane has managed it and I have too. God has so arranged it: Our Lady of Levoca has brought the pope to Zakopane.

I greet you all, especially the people of Zakopane. I greet the mountaineers from Podhale so dear to my heart. I address words of particular greeting to Cardinal Franciszek, and to the bishop of Torun, who today rejoices at the beatification of a member of his diocese, to all the Polish bishops led by the cardinal primate and to all the foreign bishops who are taking part in this celebration. I greet the clergy, the women religious, and especially the Albertine Sisters and the Good Shepherd Sisters, for whom this day has a particular significance. I address words of greeting to the mayor of Zakopane and to the local authorities of Podhale. I am grateful for this eloquent homage of Podhale, ever faithful to the Church and the nation. You can always be counted on! Let us thank God for this day which he has made for us. In a spirit of gratitude I wish, together with you — dear brothers and sisters — to meditate on the great mystery of the Sacred Heart of Jesus. It is good that we can do this in the course of my pilgrimage occasioned by the Eucharistic Congress in Wroclaw. In fact, all devotion to the Heart of Jesus and all its manifestations are profoundly Eucharistic.

"They shall look on him whom they have pierced" (John 19:37). These are the words which we have just heard. With this prophetic quotation St. John ends his description of Christ's passion and death on the cross. We know from it that on Good Friday, before the feast of Passover, the Jews asked Pilate that the legs of those crucified might be broken and their bodies taken away (John 19:31). The soldiers did this to the two criminals crucified with Jesus. "But when they came to Jesus and saw that he was already dead, they did not break his legs. But one of the soldiers pierced his side with a spear, and at once there came out blood and water" (John 19:33–34). It was the proof of death. The soldiers were able to assure Pilate that Jesus of Nazareth had ceased to live. But St. John the Evangelist sees at this point the need for a special authentication. He writes thus: "He who saw it has borne witness — his witness is true." And at the same time he affirms that in this piercing of Christ's side the Scripture had been fulfilled. For it says: "Not a bone of him shall be broken," and elsewhere "They shall look on him whom they have pierced" (John 19:35–37).

This Gospel passage is at the foundation of the whole tradition of devotion to the Divine Heart. It developed in a special way from the seventeenth century onward, in connection with the revelations to St. Margaret Mary Alacoque, a French mystic. Our own century testifies to an intense development of devotion to the Heart of Jesus, attested to by the magnificent "Litany of the Sacred Heart" and linked to it, "The Act of Consecration of the Human Race to the Sacred Heart" with the added "Act of Reparation to the Sacred Heart." All this has profoundly pervaded our Polish piety; it has become part of the life of many of the faithful who feel the need to make reparation to the Heart of Jesus for the sins of humanity and also of individual nations, families, and people.

"They shall look on him whom they have pierced" — these words guide our gaze toward the holy cross, toward the tree of the cross on which was hung the Savior of the world. "For the word of the cross is folly to those who are perishing, but for us it is the power of God" (1 Cor. 1:18). The people of Podhale understood this very well. And as the nineteenth century was drawing to a close and the

new one was beginning, your forebears planted a cross on the top
of Giewont. It is there and remains there still. The cross is a silent
but eloquent witness to our time. It can be said that this Jubilee
cross looks in the direction of Zakopane and Krakow, and beyond:
in the direction of Warsaw and Gdansk. It embraces all our land
from the Tatra to the Baltic. Your fathers wanted the cross of Christ
to reign in a special way in this beautiful corner of Poland. And
thus it happened. This city of yours extended, one can say, to the
foot of the cross; it lives and develops in its radius both Zakopane
and Podhale. The beautiful little wayside chapels, carefully carved
and tended, speak of this fact. This Christ accompanies you in your
daily work as well as on your walks through the mountains. The
churches of this city speak of it, both the ancient and monumental
ones, which contain the whole mystery of faith and human piety,
and also recent ones, built thanks to your generosity, as for example,
the parish church of the Holy Cross in the parish of Our Lady of
Fatima which is offering us hospitality.

Do not be ashamed of this cross. Try every day to accept it and
to return Christ's love. Defend the cross; do not offend God's name
in your hearts, in family or social life. We thank divine Providence
that the crucifix has returned to the schools, public offices, and
hospitals. May it ever remain there! May it remind us of our Christian dignity and national identity, what we are and where we are
going and where our roots are. May it remind us of God's love for
humanity, which on the cross found its deepest expression.

Love is always associated with the heart. The Apostle Paul linked
it precisely to that Heart which on Golgotha was pierced by the
centurion's lance. In this gesture there was revealed the depth of
the love with which the Father has loved the world. He has loved it
so intensely "that he gave his only Son" (John 3:16). In this pierced
Heart that dimension of love which is greater than any created
love whatever has found its external expression. In it saving and
redemptive love has manifested itself. The Father has given "his

only Son, that whoever believes in him should not perish but have eternal life" (John 3:16). And therefore Paul writes: "I bend my knees before the Father, from whom every family in heaven and on earth is named" (Eph. 3:14–15); I bend them to express the gratitude which I feel before the revelation which the Father has made of his love in his Son's redeeming death. At the same time I bend my knees so that God "according to the riches of his glory may grant you to be strengthened with might through his Spirit in the inner man" (Eph. 3:16). The heart is precisely "the inner man." The Heart of God's Son becomes, for the Apostle, the source of strength for all human hearts. All this has been wonderfully rendered in many of the invocations of the Litany of the Sacred Heart.

The Heart of Jesus became the source of strength for the two women whom the Church is raising today to the glory of the altars. Thanks to this strength they reached the heights of holiness. Maria Bernardina Jablonska — spiritual daughter of St. Albert Chmielowski, his helper and one who continued his work of mercy. Living in poverty, she consecrated herself to the service of the poorest of the poor. The Church places this devout religious before us today as an example. Her motto of life was the words: "To give, eternally to give." With her gaze fixed on Christ she followed him faithfully, imitating his love. She wanted to satisfy her neighbor's request, to dry every tear, to console at least with a word every suffering soul. She always wanted to be good to everyone, but even better to those most tried by fate. She used to say: "My neighbor's suffering is my suffering." Together with St. Albert she founded hospices for those who were sick and homeless as a result of war.

This great and heroic love matured in prayer, in the silence of the nearby hermitage of Kalatowski, where she stayed for some time. In life's most difficult moments — in keeping with the suggestions of the one who guided her soul — she entrusted herself to the Sacred Heart of Jesus. To him she offered everything she possessed, especially her inner sufferings and physical torments. All for the love of

Christ! As superior general of the Congregation of the Sisters Servants of the Poor of the Third Order of St. Francis — the Albertines — she ceaselessly gave her sisters the example of that love which flows from the union of the human heart with the Sacred Heart of the Savior. Jesus' Heart was her solace in her service of the most needy. It is good that she is beatified in Zakopane, because she is a saint of Zakopane. Even if she was not born in these parts, it was here that she developed spiritually to reach holiness through the experience of the hermitage of Brother Albert at Kalatowski.

At the same time in the territories under Prussian occupation, another woman, Maria Karlowska, worked as a true Samaritan among women suffering great material and moral deprivation. Her holy zeal quickly attracted a group of disciples of Christ, with whom she founded the Congregation of the Sisters of the Good Shepherd of Divine Providence. For herself and her sisters she set the following goal: "We must proclaim the Heart of Jesus, that is, so to live from him, in him and for him, as to become like him so that in our lives he may be more visible than we ourselves." Her devotion to the Savior's Sacred Heart bore fruit in a great love for people. She felt an insatiable hunger for love. A love of this kind, according to Blessed Maria Karlowska, will never say "enough," will never stop midway. Precisely this happened to her, who was as it were transported by the current of love of the divine Paraclete. Thanks to this love she restored to many souls the light of Christ and helped them to regain their lost dignity. It is good that she too is beatified in Zakopane because the cross of Giewont looks over all Poland, it looks to the north, to Pomerania, and to the city of Plock, to all the places where the fruits of her holiness live on, her sisters and their service to the needy.

Both these heroic women religious, carrying forward their holy works in extremely difficult conditions, showed in all its fullness the dignity of woman and the greatness of her vocation. They showed that "feminine genius" which is revealed in deep sensitivity to human suffering, in tact, openness, and readiness to help, and in other qualities proper to the feminine heart. Often this is shown without drawing attention to itself and therefore is sometimes undervalued. How much today's world, our generation, needs this! How badly needed is this feminine sensitivity in the things of God and man, that our families and all of society may be filled with heartfelt warmth, goodwill, peace, and joy! How much this "feminine genius" is needed, that today's world may esteem the values of life, responsibility, and faithfulness, that it may preserve respect for human dignity! For God, in his eternal plan, has established such a role for women, by creating the human being "man and woman" in his own "image and likeness."

In his Letter to the Ephesians St. Paul makes as it were a personal confession. He writes: "To me, though I am the very least of all the saints, this grace was given, to preach to the Gentiles the unsearchable riches of Christ, and to make all men see what is the plan of the mystery hidden for ages in God who created all things" (3:8–9). In this way, through the Heart of Jesus crucified and risen, we read God's eternal plan for the salvation of the world. The Divine Heart becomes, in a sense, the mysterious and life-giving center of this plan. In this Heart the plan is fulfilled. As the Apostle writes: "that through the Church the manifold wisdom of God might now be made known.... This was according to the eternal purpose which he has realized in Christ Jesus our Lord, in whom we have boldness and confidence of access through our faith in him" (Eph. 3:10–12).

All is contained here. Christ is the fulfillment of the divine plan of redemptive love. By virtue of this plan men and women have access to God, not only as a creature to its Creator, but as a son and daughter to one's father. Christianity therefore means a new creation, a new life — life in Christ through which we can say to God: Abba — my Father, our Father. The Solemnity of the Sacred Heart of Jesus is thus in a sense a magnificent completion of the

Eucharist, and the Church, guided by a profound intuition of faith, therefore celebrates this feast of the Divine Heart on the day after the end of the octave of Corpus Christi.

We praise you, Christ our Savior, who from your Heart on fire with love pour out upon us fountains of grace. We thank you for these graces through which the hosts of the saints and blessed have been able to bring to the world the witness of your love. We thank you for the blessed sisters — Maria Bernardina and Maria — who found the source of their holiness in your loving Heart.

Most Sacred Heart of Jesus, have mercy of us!

Heart of Jesus, Son of the eternal Father, Heart of Jesus formed in the womb of the Virgin Mother by the Holy Spirit, Heart of Jesus, united substantially with the Word of God, Heart of Jesus in whom are all the treasures of wisdom and knowledge, have mercy on us!

Address at the Shrine of Divine Mercy in Krakaw, June 7, 1997

The Shrine is located in the former convent chapel of the Sisters of the Blessed Virgin Mary. The pope prayed at the tomb of Blessed Faustina Kowalska and then addressed those present. Only once, near the beginning, does the pope mention the Heart of Christ; because of the close connection between the Sacred Heart and Divine Mercy this part of the address is included here.

"The mercies of the Lord I will sing forever" (Ps 89:1).

Here I come to this shrine as a pilgrim to take part in the unending hymn in honor of Divine Mercy. The psalmist of the Lord had intoned it, expressing what every generation preserved and will continue to preserve as a most precious fruit of faith. There is nothing that we need more than Divine Mercy — that love which is benevolent, which is compassionate, which raises us above our weakness to the infinite heights of the holiness of God. In this place we become particularly aware of this. From here, in fact, went out the Message of Divine Mercy that Christ himself chose to pass on to our generation through Blessed Faustina. And it is a message that is clear and understandable for everyone. Anyone can come here, look at this picture of the merciful Jesus, his Heart radiating grace, and hear in the depths of his own soul what Blessed Faustina heard: "Fear nothing. I am with you always" (*Diary*, q. II). And if this person responds with a sincere heart: "Jesus, I trust in you," he will find comfort in all his anxieties and fears. In this dialogue of abandonment, there is established between the human person and God a special bond that sets love free. And "there is no fear in love, but perfect love casts out fear" (1 John 4:18).

Summary

Two beatifications took place on the Solemnity of the Sacred Heart in Zakopane. Both Mother Maria Bernardina Jablonska and Mother Maria Karlowska were devoted to the Sacred Heart of Jesus as well as foundresses of religious congregations, and so the pope can easily weave their lives into his reflections on the Sacred Heart along with some history of the territory.

The gospel text (John 19:35–37) is the foundational text of the tradition of devotion to the Sacred Heart, the piercing of the side and Heart of Jesus on the cross. The pope notes that all devotion to the Heart of Jesus and all its manifestations are profoundly Eucharistic. The pope relates the piercing of the side to the tree of the cross in Christian spirituality and to the devotional practices of the litany and Acts of Consecration and Reparation. The second reading speaks of the love symbolized in the pierced Heart and leads into a consideration of the lives of the two new Blesseds noting the "feminine genius" exemplified in them. The homily ends where it began, relating the Eucharist and the Heart of Jesus.

At the Shrine of Divine Mercy in Krakow, the Holy Father prayed at the tomb of Blessed Faustina and gave an address on Divine Mercy. The beginning of that address is included here because it mentions the Sacred Heart of Jesus. Divine Mercy is an important characteristic of devotion to the Heart of Jesus.

Chapter 12

Seventh Visit to Poland

June 1999

Homily during Sacred Heart devotions, including Act of Consecration of the Human Race to the Sacred Heart of Jesus, at the Aviation Club in Elblag, June 6, 1999

"We honor your Heart, O Jesus..."

I thank divine Providence that together with all of you here present I am able to give praise and glory to the Most Sacred Heart of Jesus, the most complete revelation of the paternal love of God. I am glad that the devout practice of reciting or singing the Litany of the Sacred Heart of Jesus every day during the month of June is very much alive in Poland and continues to be followed.

I greet everyone gathered here this Sunday afternoon. [The pope mentions a number of those he wishes to greet in a special way.]

"Heart of Jesus, fountain of life and holiness, have mercy on us."

Thus we invoke Jesus in the litany. Everything that God wanted to tell us about himself and about his love he placed in the Heart of Jesus, and by means of that Heart he has told us everything. We find ourselves before an inscrutable mystery. In Jesus' Heart we read the eternal divine plan of the world's salvation. It is a plan of love. The litany we have sung marvelously expresses this whole truth.

We have come here today to contemplate the love of the Lord Jesus, his goodness which is compassionate toward every person; to contemplate his Heart blazing with love for the Father, in the fullness of the Holy Spirit. Christ loves us and reveals his Heart to us as a fountain of life and holiness, the source of our redemption. In order to have a deeper understanding of this invocation, we must turn perhaps to Jesus' meeting with the Samaritan woman in the little town of Sychar, at the well which had been there since the time of the patriarch Jacob. She had come to draw water. Jesus said to her: "Give me a drink," and she answered him: "How is it that you, a Jew, ask a drink of me, a woman of Samaria?" The Evangelist then adds that the Jews had no dealings with Samaritans. She then received Jesus' response: "If you knew the gift of God, and who it is that is saying to you, 'Give me a drink,' you would have asked him, and he would have given you living water.... The water that I shall give will become a spring of water welling up to eternal life" (John 4:1–14). Mysterious words.

Jesus is the source, it is from him that divine life in men and women finds its beginning. To have this life, we need only approach him and remain in him. And what is this life if not the beginning of human holiness, the holiness which is in God and which we can reach with the help of grace? All of us wish to drink from the Divine Heart, which is a fountain of life and holiness.

"Blessed are they who observe justice, who do righteousness at all times" (Ps. 106:3).

Meditating on God's love, revealed in the Heart of his Son, requires a consistent response on our part. We have not been called only to contemplate the mystery of Christ's love, but to take part in it. Christ says: "If you love me, you will keep my commandments" (John 14:15). He thus places before us a great calling and at the same time a condition: if you want to love me, keep my commandments, keep God's holy law, walk in the ways God has shown you, and I have shown you by the example of my life.

Most of the next sections on the Ten Commandments and sin have been omitted, since they do not speak of the Sacred Heart.

Today's liturgical celebration dedicated to the Most Sacred Heart of Jesus reminds us of God's love, for which we yearn intensely. It shows us that the practical response to this love is the keeping of God's commandments in our daily lives. God does not intend that they should grow dim in our memory but that they should remain forever impressed on people's consciences so that, knowing and keeping the commandments, they "might have eternal life."

Let us contemplate the Sacred Heart of Jesus, which is the fountain of life, since by means of it victory over death was achieved. It is also the fountain of holiness, since in it sin — the enemy of man's holiness, the enemy of his spiritual development — is defeated. The Heart of the Lord Jesus is the starting point of the holiness of each one of us. From the Heart of the Lord Jesus let us learn the love of God and understanding of the mystery of sin — the mystery of iniquity.

Let us make acts of reparation to the Divine Heart for the sins committed by us and by our fellow human beings. Let us make reparation for rejecting God's goodness and love. Let us draw close each day to this fountain from which flow springs of living water. Let us cry out with the Samaritan woman: "Give me this water," for it wells up to eternal life.

> Heart of Jesus, burning flame of love,
> Heart of Jesus, fountain of life and holiness,
> Heart of Jesus, expiation for our sins — have mercy on us.
>
> Amen.

Homily during Sacred Heart devotions and beatification of Father Stefan Wincenty Frelichowski, at the Aviation Club in Torun, June 7, 1999

"Heart of Jesus, our peace and reconciliation, have mercy on us."

We bow in faith before the great mystery of the love of the Divine Heart and we give it honor and glory. Hail, O Jesus; hail,

O Heart Divine of the Son of Man, which has so loved men and women.

I give thanks to God for granting today that I should visit this young Diocese of Torun and that I should, together with you, praise the Most Sacred Heart of the Savior. With joy I thank divine Providence for the gift of a new Blessed, the priest and martyr Stefan Wincenty Frelichowski, heroic witness to the love of which a pastor is capable. I cordially greet all those present at this month of June celebration. In a special way I greet Bishop Andrzej, pastor of the Church of Torun, his auxiliary Jan, the clergy, consecrated men and women, and all the People of God in this land. I greet Torun, a city dear to my heart, and beautiful Pomerania on the Vistula. I am pleased to be in your city made famous by Nicolaus Copernicus. Torun is also known because of the efforts for peace undertaken in the course of history. In fact, on two occasions peace treaties were concluded here, treaties which history has dubbed the Peace of Torun. It was also in this city that there took place the meeting of Catholic, Lutheran, and Calvinist representatives which received the name Colloquium Charitativum, that is, the "Fraternal Colloquium." Here the words of the Psalmist take on a particular eloquence: "For my brethren and companions' sake I will say, 'Peace be within you!' For the sake of the house of the Lord our God, I will seek your good" (Ps. 122:8 – 9).

"Heart of Jesus, our peace and reconciliation."

This is the Heart of the Redeemer — the tangible sign of his invincible love and the inexhaustible source of true peace. In him "the whole fullness of deity dwells bodily" (Col. 2:9). The peace that Christ brought to earth comes precisely from this fullness and from this love. It is the gift of a God who loves, who has loved humankind in the Heart of the only-begotten Son. "He is our peace" (Eph. 2:14), exclaims St. Paul. Yes, Jesus is peace, he is our reconciliation. He was the one who put an end to the enmity which arose after we had sinned, and who reconciled all people with the Father through his death on the cross. On Golgotha Jesus' Heart was pierced by a lance as a sign of his total self-giving, of that sacrificial and saving love with which he "loved us to the end" (John 13:1), laying the foundation of the friendship between God and man.

This is why the peace of Christ is different from the peace envisaged by the world. In the Upper Room before his death, speaking to the Apostles, Jesus stated clearly: "Peace I leave with you; my peace I give to you; not as the world gives do I give to you" (John 14:27). While men understand peace primarily at the temporal and external level, Christ says that it springs from the supernatural order; it is the result of union with God in love.

The Church lives ceaselessly by the Gospel of peace. She proclaims it to all peoples and nations. Tirelessly she indicates the paths of peace and reconciliation. She ushers in peace by breaking down the walls of prejudice and hostility between people. She does this first of all through the sacrament of penance and reconciliation: bringing the grace of divine mercy and of forgiveness, she arrives at the very roots of human suffering, she heals consciences wounded by sin so that the person experiences inner comfort and becomes a peacemaker. The Church also shares the peace that she herself experiences every day in the Eucharist. The Eucharist is the culmination of our peace. In it is accomplished the sacrifice of reconciliation with God and with our brothers and sisters, in it resounds the word of God announcing peace, in it is raised without end the prayer: "Lamb of God, you take away the sins of the world, have mercy on us." In the Eucharist we receive the gift of Christ himself, who offers himself and becomes our peace. So with particular clarity we experience the fact that the world cannot give this peace, for it does not know this peace (John 14:27).

We praise today the peace of our Lord Jesus Christ, the peace that he gave to all those who met him during his earthly life. The peace with which he joyously greeted the disciples after his resurrection.

"Blessed are the peacemakers, for they shall be called sons and daughters of God" (Matt. 5:9).

This is what Christ tells us in the Sermon on the Mount. From the depths of his Heart filled with love he expresses his desire for our happiness. Christ knows that our greatest happiness is union with God, which makes us sons and daughters of God. Among the paths that lead to fullness of happiness, he indicates the one that involves working on behalf of peace and sharing peace with others. Men and women of peace are worthy of being called children of God. Jesus calls such people "blessed."

"Blessed are the peacemakers." The dignity of such a designation rightly belongs to Father Stefan Wincenty Frelichowski, raised today to the glory of the altars. His whole life, in fact, is a kind of mirror reflecting the light of that teaching of Christ according to which true happiness is attained only by those who, in union with God, become men and women of peace, peacemakers who bring peace to others. This priest of Torun, whose pastoral service lasted less than eight years, offered a very clear witness of his giving himself to God and to others. Drawing his sustenance from God, from the very first years of his priesthood, with the wealth of his priestly charism he went wherever the grace of salvation needed to be brought. He learned the secrets of the human heart and adapted pastoral methods to the needs of every person he met. He had picked up this ability from the school of scouting, where he had acquired a particular sensitivity to the needs of others, a sensitivity which he constantly developed in the spirit of the parable of the Good Shepherd who searches out the lost sheep and is ready to give his own life to save them (John 10:1–21). As a priest he was always aware of being a witness of the Great Cause, and at the same time he gave himself with deep humility to the service of others. Thanks to his goodness, meekness, and patience he won many souls over to Christ, even in the tragic circumstances of the war and the occupation.

During the tragedy of the war his life was like a written record, one chapter following another, of service on behalf of peace. The so-called Fort Seven, then Stutthoff, Grenzdorf, Oranienburg-Sachsenhausen, and finally Dachau are the list of stations on a path of suffering, but a path on which he was always the same: courageous in fulfilling his priestly ministry. He would minister especially to those who were most in need of his services, to those who were part of the masses dying of typhus, to which he himself fell victim. He gave his priestly life to God and to others, bringing peace to the victims of war. He generously shared peace with others because his soul drew strength from the peace of Christ. And that strength was so great that not even death as a martyr was able to crush it.

Without inner renewal and without a commitment to overcome evil and sin in our hearts, and especially without love, we will never achieve inner peace. Such peace will be lasting only when it is rooted in the highest values, when it is based on moral norms and is open to God. Otherwise, when built on the shifting sands of religious indifference and arid pragmatism, it can only be short-lived. Inner peace comes to birth in the human heart and in the life of society as a result of moral order, ethical order, the observance of God's commandments.

Let us share this peace of God with others, as did the blessed priest and martyr Wincenty Frelichowski. Thus we will become a source of peace in the world, in society, in the environment in which we live and work. I make this appeal to everyone without exception, and particularly to you, dear priests. Be witnesses of God's merciful love! Proclaim joyfully the Gospel of Christ, dispensing God's forgiveness in the sacrament of reconciliation. Through our service seek to bring everyone closer to Christ, the giver of peace.

I also address these words to you, dear parents, who are the first educators of your children. Be for them an image of love and divine forgiveness, striving with all your might to build a united and harmonious family. In fact, it is the family that has been entrusted with a mission of primary importance: to participate in the building of peace, of the well-being that is indispensable for development and for the respect of human life.

I ask you, educators, who are called to impart authentic life values to the younger generations: teach children and young people tolerance, understanding, and respect for every human being; educate the younger generations in a climate of true peace. It is their right. It is your duty.

You, young people, who cherish great hopes in your hearts, learn to live in harmony and mutual respect, lending assistance by your solidarity with others. Sustain in your hearts the aspiration to good works and the desire for peace (see the Message for the 1997 World Day of Peace, no. 8).

Societies and nations need men and women of peace, authentic sowers of harmony and mutual respect; men and women who fill their own hearts with Christ's peace and bring this peace to others, to their homes, offices, institutions, workplaces, to the entire world. Both history and the events of our own day show that the world cannot give peace. The world is often powerless. That is why it is necessary to point to Jesus Christ, who by his death on the cross has left his peace to humankind, assuring us of his presence for all times (John 14:7–31). How much innocent blood has been shed in the twentieth century in Europe and throughout the world because certain political and social systems forsook the principles of Christ that guarantee a just peace. How much innocent blood is being shed under our very eyes. The tragic events in Kosovo have demonstrated this and are demonstrating it in a very painful way. We are witnesses to how strongly people cry out for and yearn for peace.

I speak these words in a land that in its history experienced the tragic effects of the lack of peace, having been victim of a cruel and ruinous war. Our memory of the Second World War is still vivid; the wounds inflicted by that cataclysm of history will need much time to be completely healed. May the cry for peace spread out from this place to the entire world! I wish to repeat the words I spoke this year in the Easter Urbi et Orbi Message: "Peace is possible, peace is a duty, peace is a prime responsibility of everyone! May the dawn of the third millennium see the coming of a new era in which respect for every man and woman and fraternal solidarity among peoples will, with God's help, overcome the culture of hatred, of violence, of death."

With deep gratitude we welcome the witness of the life of Blessed Wincenty Frelichowski — a modern-day hero, priest, and man of peace — as a call to our generation. I wish to entrust the gift of this beatification in a particular way to the Church in Torun, so that she may preserve and make known on an ever wider scale the memory of the great works which God accomplished in the short life of this priest. I entrust this gift above all to the priests of this diocese and of all Poland. Father Frelichowski, at the beginning of his priestly journey, wrote: "I must be a priest after the Heart of Christ." If this beatification is a great act of thanksgiving to God for his priesthood, it is also an act of praise to God for the marvels of grace which are accomplished through the hands of all priests, through your hands too. I wish to address a few words also to the family of Polish scouts, with whom the Blessed shared a profound bond. May he become your patron, teaching you nobility of spirit and interceding for peace and reconciliation.

In just a few days it will be the hundredth anniversary of the consecration of the human race to the Most Sacred Heart of Jesus. This took place in all dioceses through the work of Pope Leo XIII, who, to that end, published the encyclical *Annum sacrum*. In that encyclical he wrote: "The Divine Heart is the symbol and living image of Jesus Christ's infinite love, which invites us to respond in turn with love" (no. 2). A little while ago we renewed together the act of consecration to the Most Sacred Heart of Jesus. We thus expressed our utmost homage and our faith in Christ, the Redeemer of humankind. He is "the Alpha and the Omega, the beginning and the end" (Rev. 21:6), to him belong this world and its destiny.

Today, in adoring the Sacred Heart, le us pray fervently for peace. First of all for peace in our hearts, but also for peace in our families, in our nation, and in all the world. Heart of Jesus, our peace and reconciliation, have mercy on us!

Homily at a Mass for the closing of the Polish national synod in Warsaw's cathedral, June 11, 1999

The pope had opened the Polish national synod during his 1991 visit to Poland. Since June 11 was the Solemnity of the Sacred Heart and the hundredth anniversary of Pope Leo XIII's consecration of the human race to the Sacred Heart of Jesus, Pope John Paul II refers to this in the conclusion to his homily. Only this conclusion is reproduced here.

Divine Providence has surely decreed that the closure of the synod should fall on the Solemnity of the Sacred Heart of Jesus, instituted by the Apostolic See in the eighteenth century following insistent requests from the Polish bishops. Today the whole church ponders and venerates in a special way the ineffable love of God, which found its human expression in the Savior's Heart pierced by the centurion's lance. Today we also recall the hundredth anniversary of the consecration of the entire human race to the Sacred Heart of Jesus, a great event in the Church which contributed to the development of the devotion and produced saving fruits of holiness and apostolic zeal.

"God is love" (John 4:8), and Christianity is the religion of love. While other systems of thought and action seek to construct the human world on the basis of wealth, power, force, science, or pleasure, the Church proclaims love. The Sacred Heart of Jesus is precisely the image of this infinite and merciful love which the heavenly Father has poured out upon the world through his Son, Jesus Christ. The goal of the new evangelization is to lead people to encounter this love. Only love, revealed by the Heart of Christ, can transform the human heart and open it to the whole world, making the world more human and more divine.

A hundred years ago, Pope Leo XIII wrote that in the Heart of Jesus "we need to place all our hope. In him we must seek and from him we must expect the salvation of all people" (*Annum sacrum,* 6). I too exhort you to renew and nurture devotion to the Sacred Heart of Jesus. To this "fountain of life and holiness" draw individuals, families, parish communities, and all elements of the Church that they may obtain from him "the unsearchable riches of Christ" (Eph. 3:8). Only those who are "rooted and grounded in love" (Eph. 3:17) can oppose the civilization of death and upon the ruins of hatred, contempt, and force build a civilization which springs from the Heart of the Savior.

To conclude my meeting with you on this solemnity so loved by all the Church, I entrust the entire work of the second plenary synod, its implementation, and its outcome in Poland to the Sacred Heart of Jesus and to the Immaculate Heart of his mother, who in speaking her fiat was totally united to the redeeming sacrifice of her Son.

Reflections on the recent pastoral visit to Poland at a general audience, Rome, June 23, 1999

Today I would like to reflect again on the pilgrimage to Poland which I had the joy of making from the 5th to the 17th of this month. My seventh and longest pastoral visit to my country took place twenty years after my first journey from June 2 to June 10, 1979. On the eve of the Great Jubilee of the Year 2000, I shared with the Church in Poland in celebrations to mark the millennium of two events which are at the root of her history: the canonization of St. Adalbert and the establishment of the country's first metropolitan see: Gniezno, with its three suffragan dioceses of Kolobrzeg, Krakow, and Wroclaw. I was also able to conclude the nation's Second Plenary Synod and to proclaim a new saint, as well as numerous new Blesseds, exemplary witnesses of God's love.

"God is love" was the theme of my apostolic journey, which became a great hymn of praise to the heavenly Father and to the wonderful works of his mercy. For this reason I never stop thanking him, the Lord of the world and of history, who once again allowed me to cross the land of my ancestors as a pilgrim of faith and hope, and in particular, as a pilgrim of his love.

In the third section of his talk, the pope spoke of the Sacred Heart and the Blessed Virgin Mary. Only this section is reproduced here.

In Poland faith was nourished and greatly supported by devotion to the Sacred Heart and to the Blessed Virgin Mary. Veneration of the Divine Heart of Jesus had special prominence in this pilgrimage: in the background was the consecration of the human race to the Sacred Heart, which my revered predecessor Leo XIII performed for the first time exactly one hundred years ago. Humanity needs to enter the new millennium with trust in God's merciful love. However, this will be possible only if we turn to Christ the Savior, the inexhaustible source of life and holiness.

And then what can we say of my compatriots' filial affection for their queen, Mary most holy? In Licheri I blessed the large new shrine dedicated to her, and in some cities, including my birthplace, I crowned revered images of the Blessed Virgin. In Sandomierz I celebrated the Eucharist in honor of the Immaculate Heart of the Blessed Virgin Mary.

Summary

Two of the three homilies were given during Sacred Heart devotions in Elblag and in Torun, the latter also with the beatification of Father Stefan Wincenty Frelichowski. The text of the first homily was "Heart of Jesus, fountain of life and holiness, have mercy on us." The text of the second was "Heart of Jesus, our peace and reconciliation, have mercy on us." The pope spoke of efforts for peace historically connected with the city of Torun and related both peace and reconciliation to the priestly ministry of Father Frelichowski. In the third homily the Holy Father referred to Pope Leo XIII's consecration of the human race to the Sacred Heart of Jesus. The anniversary of this consecration occurred on the day itself when the pope gave the homily for the closing of the Polish national synod, which he spoke of in the conclusion of his homily. Upon his return to Rome, the Holy Father reviewed his pastoral visit to Poland at the general audience of June 23, 1999.

Chapter 13

Visit to St. Louis, Missouri

January 27, 1999

In January 1999, Pope John Paul II spent five days in Mexico. At the Basilica of Our Lady of Guadalupe, he formally presented the apostolic exhortation *Ecclesia in America,* a document based on and responding to the 1997 Special Assembly for America of the Synod of Bishops, a document he had signed the evening before in Mexico City, January 22, 1999. In speaking of the Church in America, the pope refers to North, Central, and South America and the Caribbean as one continent.

Before returning to Rome, the pope made a two-day visit (thirty hours) in St. Louis, Missouri. In addition to his message after arrival and his farewell message before departing, the pope presented a written message to sick children, a homily at a prayer service with young people at Kiel Center the first evening, and a homily at another prayer service at the cathedral basilica on the second evening. The central event was the Votive Mass of the Sacred Heart he celebrated in the Trans World Dome stadium with a homily on the Sacred Heart and life issues, such as abortion, violence, hunger, euthanasia and assisted suicide, and the death penalty, in the presence of over a hundred thousand people. Here is the text of this important homily.

"In this way the love of God was revealed to us: God sent his only Son into the world so that we might have life through him" (1 John 4:9).

In the incarnation, God fully reveals himself in the Son who came into the world (*Tertio millennio adveniente,* 9). Our faith is not simply the result of our searching for God. In Jesus Christ, it is God who comes in person to speak to us and to show us the way to himself.

The incarnation also reveals the truth about the human person. In Jesus Christ, the Father has spoken the definitive word about our true destiny and the meaning of human history (ibid., 5). "In this is love: not that we have loved God, but that he loved us and sent his Son as an expiation for our sins" (1 John 4:10). The apostle is speaking of the love that inspired the Son to become man and to dwell among us. Through Jesus Christ we know how much the Father loves us. In Jesus Christ, by the gift of the Holy Spirit, each one of us can share in the love that is the life of the Blessed Trinity.

St. John goes on: "Whoever acknowledges that Jesus is the Son of God, God remains in him and he in God" (1 John 4:15). Through faith in the Son of God made man we abide in the very Heart of God: "God is love, and whoever remains in love remains in God and God in him" (1 John 4:16). These words open to us the mystery of the Sacred Heart of Jesus: The love and compassion of Jesus is the door through which the eternal love of the Father is poured out on the world. In celebrating this Mass of the Sacred Heart, let us open wide our own hearts to God's saving mercy!

In the Gospel reading which we have just heard, St. Luke uses the figure of the Good Shepherd to speak of this divine love. The Good Shepherd is an image dear to Jesus in the Gospels. Answering the Pharisees, who complained that he welcomed sinners by eating with them, the Lord asks them a question: Which of you, "having a hundred sheep and losing one of them would not leave the ninety-nine in the desert and go after the lost one until he finds it? And when he does find it, he sets it on his shoulders with great joy and, upon his arrival home, he calls together his friends and neighbors and says to them: 'Rejoice with me because I have found my lost sheep'" (Luke 15:5–6).

This parable highlights the joy of Christ and of our heavenly Father at every sinner who repents. God's love is a love that searches us out. It is a love that saves. This is the love that we find in the Heart of Jesus.

Once we know the love that is in the Heart of Christ, we know that every individual, every family, every people on the face of the earth can place their trust in that Heart. We have heard Moses say, "You are a people sacred to the Lord, your God.... The Lord set his Heart on you and chose you... because the Lord loved you" (Deut. 7:6–8). From Old Testament times, the core of salvation history is God's unfailing love and election, and our human answer to that love. Our faith is our response to God's love and election.

Three hundred years have passed since December 8, 1698, when the holy sacrifice of the Mass was offered for the first time in what is now the city of St. Louis. It was the feast of the Immaculate Conception of our Blessed Mother, and Father Montigny, Father Davion, and Father St. Cosme set up a stone altar on the banks of the Mississippi River and offered Mass. These three centuries have been a history of God's love poured out in this part of the United States and a history of generous response to that love.

In this archdiocese, the commandment of love has called forth an endless series of activities for which — today — we give thanks to our heavenly Father. St. Louis has been the Gateway to the West, but it has also been the gateway of great Christian witness and evangelical service. In fidelity to Christ's command to evangelize, the first pastor of this local church, Bishop Joseph Rosati — who came from the town of Sora, very near Rome — promoted outstanding missionary activity from the beginning. In fact, today we can count forty-six different dioceses in the area which Bishop Rosati served. With great affection I greet your present pastor, dear Archbishop Rigali, my precious collaborator in Rome. In the love of the Lord I greet the entire Church in this region.

In this area, numerous religious congregations of men and women have labored for the Gospel with exemplary dedication, generation after generation. Here can be found the American roots of the evangelizing efforts of the Legion of Mary and other associations of the lay apostolate. The work of the Society for the Propagation of the Faith, made possible by the generous support of the people of this archdiocese, is a real sharing in the church's response to Christ's command to evangelize.

From St. Louis, Cardinal Ritter sent the first *fidei donum* priests to Latin America in 1956, giving practical expression to the exchange of gifts which should always be a part of the communion between the churches. This solidarity within the Church was the central theme of last year's Special Assembly for America of the Synod of Bishops, and it is the central idea of the apostolic exhortation *Ecclesia in America* — the Church in America — which I have just signed and issued at the Shrine of Our Lady of Guadalupe in Mexico City.

Here, by the grace of God, charitable activities of every kind have been a vibrant part of Catholic life. The St. Vincent de Paul Society has had a privileged place in the archdiocese from the beginning. Catholic Charities have for years performed exceptional work in the name of Jesus Christ. Outstanding Catholic health care services have shown the human face of the loving and compassionate Christ.

Catholic schools have proven to be of priceless value to generations of children, teaching them to know, love, and serve God, and preparing them to take their place with responsibility in the community. Parents, teachers, pastors, administrators, and entire parishes have sacrificed enormously to maintain the essential character of Catholic education as an authentic ministry of the church and an evangelical service to the young. The goals of the strategic pastoral plan of the archdiocese — evangelization, conversion, stewardship, Catholic education, service to those in need — have a long tradition here.

Today American Catholics are seriously challenged to know and cherish this immense heritage of holiness and service. Out of that heritage you must draw inspiration and strength for the new evangelization so urgently needed at the approach of the third Christian millennium. In the holiness and service of St. Louis's own St. Philippine Duchesne, and of countless faithful priests, religious and laity since the Church's earliest days in this area, Catholic life has appeared in all its rich and varied splendor. Nothing less is asked of you today.

As the new evangelization unfolds, it must include a special emphasis on the family and the renewal of Christian marriage. In their primary mission of communicating love to each other, of being co-creators with God of human life, and of transmitting the love of God to their children, parents must know that they are fully supported by the church and by society. The new evangelization must bring a fuller appreciation of the family as the primary and most vital foundation of society, the first school of social virtue and solidarity (*Familiaris consortio,* 42). As the family goes, so goes the nation!

The new evangelization must also bring out the truth that "the Gospel of God's love for man, the Gospel of the dignity of the person and the Gospel of life are a single and indivisible Gospel" (*Evangelium vitae,* 2). As believers, how can we fail to see that abortion, euthanasia, and assisted suicide are a terrible rejection of God's gift of life and love? And as believers, how can we fail to feel the duty to surround the sick and those in distress with the warmth of our affection and the support that will help them always to embrace life?

The new evangelization calls for followers of Christ who are unconditionally pro-life: who will proclaim, celebrate, and serve the Gospel of life in every situation. A sign of hope is the increasing recognition that the dignity of human life must never be taken away, even in the case of someone who has done great evil. Modern society has the means of protecting itself, without definitively denying criminals the chance to reform (*Evangelium vitae,* 27). I renew the appeal I made most recently at Christmas for a consensus to end the death penalty, which is both cruel and unnecessary.

As the new millennium approaches, there remains another great challenge facing this community of St. Louis, east and west of the Mississippi, and not St. Louis alone, but the whole country: to put an end to every form of racism, a plague which your bishops have called one of the most persistent and destructive evils of the nation.

The Gospel of God's love, which we are celebrating today, finds its highest expression in the Eucharist. In the Mass and in Eucharistic adoration we meet the merciful love of God that passes through the Heart of Jesus Christ. In the name of Jesus, the Good Shepherd, I wish to make an appeal — an appeal to Catholics throughout the United States and wherever my voice or words may reach — especially to those who for one reason or another are separated from the practice of their faith. On the eve of the Great Jubilee of the two thousandth anniversary of the incarnation, Christ is seeking you out and inviting you back to the community of faith. Is this not the moment for you to experience the joy of returning to the Father's house? In some cases there may still be obstacles to Eucharistic participation; in some cases there may be memories to be healed; in all cases there is the assurance of God's love and mercy.

The Great Jubilee of the Year 2000 will begin with the opening of the Holy Door in St. Peter's Basilica in Rome: This is a powerful symbol of the Church — open to everyone who feels a need for the love and mercy of the Heart of Christ. In the Gospel Jesus says, "I am the door, whoever enters through me will be saved, and will come in and go out and find pasture" (John 10:9).

Our Christian life can be seen as a great pilgrimage to the house of the Father, which passes through the door that is Jesus Christ. The key to that door is repentance and conversion. The strength to pass through that door comes from our faith and hope and love.

For many Catholics, an important part of the journey must be to rediscover the joy of belonging to the Church, to cherish the Church as the Lord has given her to us, as mother and teacher.

Living in the Holy Spirit, the Church looks forward to the millennium as a time of far-reaching spiritual renewal. The Spirit will truly bring about a new springtime of faith if Christian hearts are filled with new attitudes of humility, generosity and openness to his purifying grace. In parishes and communities across this land holiness and Christian service will flourish if "you come to know and believe in the love God has for you" (1 John 4:16).

Mary, mother of mercy, teach the people of St. Louis and of the United States to say yes to your son, our Lord Jesus Christ!

Mother of the Church, on the way to the great jubilee of the third millennium, be the star which safely guides our steps to the Lord!

Virgin of Nazareth, two thousand years ago you brought into the world the incarnate Word: Lead the men and women of the new millennium to the one who is the true light of the world! Amen.

At the end of Mass, the pope made the following remarks.

Peace — the peace of Christ — to all: to my brother cardinals and bishops — so many here today — the pastors of the Church in America.

A special greeting to the priests, who carry forward with love the daily pastoral care of God's people.

My thanks to you all for this beautiful liturgy!

I appreciate very much your enthusiastic participation and your spirit of prayer.

Again, I express my gratitude to Archbishop Rigali, our pastor, and to everyone who cooperated in preparing this great event.

[In Polish] I cordially greet my fellow Poles in America, particularly those living in St. Louis. I thank you for remembering me in your prayers. God bless you all!

A special word of affection goes to the sick, those in prison, and all who suffer in mind and body.

My gratitude and esteem go also to our brothers and sisters who, in a spirit of ecumenical friendship, have shared this wonderful moment with us.

Summary

During his visit to St. Louis the Holy Father celebrated the Votive Mass of the Sacred Heart with a homily on the Heart of Jesus and life issues, such as abortion, violence, hunger, euthanasia and assisted suicide, and the death penalty. The pope renewed his appeal made the previous Christmas for a consensus to end the death penalty, "which is both cruel and unnecessary." He also singled out "another great challenge ... to put an end to every form of racism." The Gospel reading was that of the Good Shepherd. The pope traced the history of the Church in the United States and specifically in the Archdiocese of St. Louis. The homily was not a theoretical one on the Sacred Heart but spoke of the practical life issues related to the love and mercy of the Heart of Christ.

Part Three

Various Messages

Chapter 14

Talks to Groups of Religious: Men

Pope John Paul II has given a number of audiences to groups of religious, usually on the occasion of their general chapters or of a historical anniversary of the religious community, such as the date of its founding, or of a significant date in the life of the founder or foundress. The talks refer to the occasion of the audience and the pope speaks of topics of interest to the religious. Usually the religious are devoted to the Sacred Heart of Jesus and frequently have "Sacred Heart" in the title of their congregation.

In this chapter are collected excerpts from these talks of the pope. At times the talks are devoted in great part to the Sacred Heart, at other times to the spirit of the congregation. At times very little is said of the Sacred Heart. These excerpts usually refer only to what the pope has said about the Sacred Heart.

Priests of the Sacred Heart of Jesus (Dehonians): To the Seventeenth Ordinary General Chapter, June 22, 1979

See above p. 28

Priests of the Sacred Heart of Jesus (Dehonians): To the Eighteenth Ordinary General Chapter, June 14, 1985

In the spirituality of Father Dehon, the basis and center of your institute is worship of and devotion to the Heart of Jesus. That must determine your theological reflection and ascetical formation as well as your pastoral and missionary activity. We could affirm that he always had before him the dramatic and sublime scene of Calvary, described by the Evangelist John: "When [the soldiers] came to Jesus and saw that he was already dead, they did not break his legs, but one soldier thrust his lance into his side, and immediately blood and water flowed out" (John 19:33–34).

Recalling the message and apparitions of Paray-le-Monial, Father Dehon saw in the pierced side the Heart of Jesus, symbol of the love of God for humankind, from which flowed sanctifying "grace," the sacraments, the Church, and from this Heart, bloodied and crowned with thorns he arrived at his apostolic ardor and profound Eucharistic and reparatory piety. In the final booklet of his well-known "diary," when he was already old and ill, he noted: "I assist at the great perpetual Mass of heaven: Jesus who offers himself to the Father as the Lamb immolated from the beginning: the Heart of Jesus, victim of love for the glory of God and the salvation of men and women."

On September 6, 1888, Father Dehon was received in private audience by Pope Leo XIII; a little before that he had received the "Decree of Praise" and the pope, manifesting his satisfaction, said to him, "Your intention is very good; because reparation is very necessary.... Preach my encyclical, where contemporary errors are refuted: it is necessary moreover to pray for priests." These words were the program of his priestly life and of the congregation, which from the time he was a young priest he intended to found: an ardent and affectionate love for Christ, to make reparation for the sins of the world; a restless and courageous love of Christ, also social, to make the Divine Redeemer known and loved; and finally a scrupulous attention to the magisterium of the Church, in order to have the guarantee of the truth announced and to give authentic help to the formation and to the perseverance of priests. He, as secretary of the Vatican Council I and of various encounters with the Conciliar Fathers, had deeply understood the meaning and the mission of the Church and of the papacy in the salvific design of Providence; besides in his pastoral ministry and during his journeys he had been able to evaluate at first hand that the "social question" could be resolved in a concrete and positive way only in the light of the message of Christ.

"As far as we are concerned," he said. "we must all be on fire to make the good Master known and loved, as the admirable love that his Divine Heart has witnessed to us in all his mysteries and that still manifests itself every day in the Holy Eucharist."

From 1887 on he had written: "...the study according to the spirit of Rome and reparation to the Sacred Heart of Jesus, truth and charity, are the two great passions of my life, and I only desire that these two should be what attracts to the work I will leave behind."

More than a century has passed from that humble and hidden beginning of the "Dehonian" congregation: but the message and the "charism" of the founder are ever actual because the society of today is still in greater need to encounter the Heart of Jesus, in order to find peace, serenity, comfort, and pardon.

Therefore, preach with ardor the love of God, presenting the Heart of Christ, symbol and center of such divine reality. In fact, "God so loved the world that he gave his only Son" (John 3:16). "In this way the love of God was revealed to us: God sent his only Son into the world...as expiation for our sins" (1 John 4:8–10). To the human person torn by such tribulations and by such questions, indicative in Christ crucified and risen of the supreme certitude of the love of God!

With particular solicitude and ecclesial sense take care of the apostolate of the press, which takes up no small part of your ecclesial service. This is very important for the diffusion of Christian principles and for the defense of Catholic values. I trust that there will not be lacking on your part in this area a renewed commitment of fidelity and of vigilance to contribute to the true good of souls and the edification of the Church. Form Christian consciences, presenting with clarity the truth that should guide life and eliminate all that disturbs or confuses it. Be completely faithful to the magisterium and the Apostolic See.

Witness your love for Christ with Eucharistic adoration and with a penitential life, in reparation for the evil that weighs on the world. "Study, action, prayer!" — Father Dehon often repeated — "We have need of learned men, apostles, saints!" But he also added: "God does not know what to do with our knowledge and our works, if he does not have our hearts."

Dearly beloved! At Christmas in 1921, Father Dehon wrote from Brussels: "I ask all of you to renew your fervor. We are in difficult times...; but I repeat to you the encouraging words of Our Lord: 'Have confidence! I have overcome the world!' " I too in the solemn circumstances of your General Chapter address to you and to all "Dehonians" the same words: Trust in the Heart of Christ and in Holy Mary, renewing every day your fervor and carrying on with courage and serenity on the road indicated by your founder. Immense is the work to be done and we must not lose time!

Priests of the Sacred Heart of Jesus (Dehonians): To the Nineteenth Ordinary General Chapter, May 31, 1991

I thank and bless the Lord for all the good you are doing; I thank him for the growth of your institute which from the distant 1878, date of its foundation, until today goes on extending the sphere of its religious presence. I ask the Lord, who is ever constant in his love, to keep you faithful to the particular apostolic charism which urged on Father Dehon to found the Congregation of the Priests of the Sacred Heart.

The Chapter now in progress, besides electing a new superior general and his Council, seeks to promote in our times in a concrete way the "Dehonian values" by means of an efficacious work of spiritual updating.

Your dominant preoccupation is that of keeping in a balanced unity the spiritual life and the apostolic social commitment, in the light of your specific charism which is "Love-Oblation-Reparation" to the Sacred Heart of Jesus by following the teaching of the Church.

Wishing to base every activity on silent listening to God, but at the same time desirous of making your work respond to modern needs, you try to determine how to develop your apostolate without separating it from the indispensable spirit of contemplation. And you outline for your entire religious family certain ideal perspectives which are intended to guide you faithfully for the present and for the future. I refer, as is obvious, above all to the "heart" of the charismatic intuition of Father Dehon, that is, "to the profound and supernatural intimacy of his message and to the courage of his social work."

Embracing with enthusiasm the directives of the encyclical *Rerum novarum* of Leo XIII, he underlined: "Saints are needed to solve the social problem. Without holiness man is a wolf to his fellow man."

In one of his writings, published in the review founded by him and with the title "The Reign of the Heart of Jesus in Souls and in Society," we read: "This century will be democratic. People want great liberty, civil, political, and communal. Workers want a reasonable share in the fruit of their labors. But this democracy will either be Christian or it will not be democratic. . . . Only the gospel can make justice and charity reign. Every effort at social reform from outside Christianity will flounder in egoism and domination by force. Nations will fluctuate between the tyranny of one man only and that of an oligarchy. . . . "

As a response to the challenge of the modern era, Father Dehon promoted, as he himself left in writing in his "Records-Testimony," two great enterprises: to lead priests and the faithful to the Heart of Jesus and to offer him a daily tribute of adoration and of love; to contribute to the uplifting of the masses of the people by working for the coming of Christian justice and charity. It is an apostolate to be continued, to spread abroad and to intensify.

"Firmness and gentleness": this apostolic method which was that of your founder should be that of all of you. It should be so, especially today, in a society that is restless and in search of certitude and authenticity. Be faithful to your Spiritual Father! He is a master who has suffered and who has loved! May that "penitent love, grateful, confident, and devoted" that Father Dehon promised to the Heart of Jesus be alive in each one of you.

In union with Mary, be apostles of the love of Christ, following the example and the teaching of your venerated teacher and founder!

Priests of the Sacred Heart of Jesus (Dehonians): To the Twentieth Ordinary General Chapter, May 30, 1997

Christian life, and even more the consecrated life is a life of self-giving love (*Vita consecrata*, 75). Father Dehon was thoroughly convinced of this: while still a young priest, he felt called to respond to the love of the Heart of Christ with a consecration of missionary and reparatory love.

Continue generously on this path, aware that to be faithful to the founder's charism, it is first necessary to foster in yourselves that docility to the Holy Spirit which enabled him to adhere fully to divine inspiration. The vitality of your religious family depends precisely on the intensity of your spiritual life, expressed primarily in prayer. The Heart of Jesus is the focal point of your consecration. That Jesus, on whom the whole Church fixes her gaze especially this year, the first phase of the three-year preparation for the Jubilee of the Year 2000, shows contemporary men and women his Heart, the fountain of life and holiness. King and center of all hearts, Christ asks consecrated persons not only to contemplate him, but to enter into his Heart, to be able to live and work in constant communion with his sentiments.

The radicalism of following Christ, fidelity to your vows, brother-hood, apostolic service, ecclesial communion — everything derives from this inexhaustible source of grace.

Father Dehon's charism is a fruitful gift for building the civilization of love, since the soul of the new evangelization is the witness of divine charity: "God so loved the world that he gave his only Son..." (John 3:16).

In a few day's time we will be celebrating the Solemnity of the Sacred Heart: the Church's liturgy offers you the richest source of inspiration for your Chapter. I pray that the Lord, through the intercession of Mary most holy, will fill each one of you with his wisdom, so that your assembly may produce the fruits for which you hope. To this end, I cordially impart to you and to all the Priests of the Sacred Heart of Jesus a special apostolic blessing, which I willingly extend to the whole Dehonian Family.

Sons of the Sacred Heart of Jesus (Comboni Missionaries), Month of the Sacred Heart, June 23, 1979

See above p. 30.

Sons of the Sacred Heart (Comboni Missionaries): To the Fourteenth General Chapter, September 20, 1991

Every missionary, according to [Bishop Daniel] Comboni, should be "motivated by the impetus of that ardent charity fired with the divine blaze on the slopes of Golgotha and issuing from the wound in the side of Christ crucified" (Daniel Comboni, *Scritti,* no. 138 2742).

Sons of the Sacred Heart (Comboni Missionaries): To the Fifteenth General Chapter, September 25, 1997

The Fifteenth General Chapter takes place between two significant moments in the life of your institute: the first is the beatification of your founder, Bishop Daniel Comboni, whom I had the joy of raising to the glory of the altars last year; the second is the celebration of the Great Jubilee of the Year 2000, whose preparation involves every member of the People of God. These two events encourage your religious congregation to deepen its own charism, to throw itself with renewed zeal into the work of evangelization, in view of the third Christian millennium.

Congregation of the Sacred Hearts of Jesus and Mary and of Perpetual Adoration of the Most Blessed Sacrament (PICPUS): To the General Chapter, September 21, 2000

While the Revolution was raging around them, your founders understood that true freedom was only to be found in the pierced Heart of Christ (John 19:34) and that those who, like Mary, shared in his passion and had their souls pierced through by a sword (Luke 2:35), could attain it. Throughout their lives in those turbulent times, they proclaimed the truth of the cross of Jesus Christ.

Today as always the Church is called to proclaim the power of the cross to the world. It is a power that has no need of "eloquent wisdom" (1 Cor. 1:17), nor of "philosophy and empty deceit" (Col. 2:8) nor even less of deceptive ideologies. What it demands of you is that like Christ himself you open your heart to be converted through a reflection of the source of living water (John 4:10), the only One that can quench the thirst of the human heart. For this, each of you must imitate the Apostle in his wish to participate in Christ's sufferings "becoming like him in his death" so that others may know him and "the power of his resurrection" (Phil. 3:10).

You must therefore continue to follow the path of contemplation, since your mission requires a profound union with the Lord. Before sending you out, Christ calls you to himself; and if every day you do not seek him in prayer, you will lack the strength to carry on as missionaries filled with the power of the Holy Spirit. Only in the depths of contemplation can the Holy Spirit transform your hearts; and only if your own hearts are transformed will you be able to fulfill the great task of helping others so that the Spirit may guide them "into all truth" (John 16:13), which is the essence of the Christian message. Social structures will never be able to be perfected or improved without a genuine conversion of hearts. Both of these must go together, because if structures are changed without hearts being converted the structural changes might camouflage evil but without overcoming it. This is why mission without contemplation of the Crucified One is condemned to frustration, as the founders very opportunely realized. This is also the reason why they insisted especially on the commitment to adoration of the Eucharistic mystery, since it is in the sacrament of the altar that the Church contemplates uniquely the mystery of Calvary, from whose sacrifice flows all the grace of evangelization. Learn in contemplation of the Eucharistic mystery to imitate the One who makes himself bread shared and blood poured out for the world's salvation.

Sacred Heart Missionaries (MSC), congregation of priests and brothers founded by Jules Chavalier in 1854: To the General Chapter, September 8, 1987

Your founder, Father Jules Chavalier, was fully aware of the implications of the beautiful name he gave you: Sacred Heart Missionaries. This name was full of meaning for him, and his desire was that it should also recall to you the style of life and mission of your congregation.

I, too, wish to propose to you again with great warmth this great ideal: your life and your apostolic work should clearly show your convinced and fervent participation in one of the greatest mysteries of our faith: that of the mercy of God who loves men and women, and who gave himself for their salvation. Our Lord is Love, and has revealed this love in Jesus Christ by means of his human Heart. Jesus himself invites us: "Come to me, all you who labor and are burdened, and I will give you rest" (Matt. 11:28).

Jesus Christ is the way, the truth, and the life. We must again and always invite men and women "to look upon him whom they have pierced" (John 19:37; see also Zech. 12:10). This opened Heart from which flowed blood and water, symbol of the sacramental life of the Church, is an inexhaustible fountain of life. Your founder saw a new world that flowed from the Heart of our Savior, pierced on Calvary. People today above all desperately desire a new world and a new heart to animate and guide them.

Speaking of the Sacred Heart on an earlier occasion, I indicated the value and the practice of reparation as an essential element of this devotion, strictly bound to the desire and to the necessary conditions for the building of a new world: "In this way — and this is the true meaning of the reparation demanded by the Heart of the Savior — on the ruins accumulated through hatred and violence can be built the civilization of the Heart of Christ [the civilization of love so greatly desired, the kingdom of the Heart of Christ] (letter to Father Peter-Hans Kolvenbach, S.J., October 5, 1986).

Several times over in the past, I have expressed my conviction that the devotion to the Sacred Heart corresponds more than ever to the expectations of our day and I have underlined the fact that the essential elements of this devotion "belong permanently to the spirituality of the Church throughout its history" (ibid.).

I desire to ask you to continue to carry out your worldwide missionary work with confidence and generosity. May your apostolate be filled with strength and mercy, always following in the footsteps of Christ, the Good Shepherd, who did not come "to judge the world, but that the world might be saved through him" (John 3:17) and who did not come to be served, "but to serve and to give his life as a ransom for many" (Matt. 20:28). Follow him! Imitate him! Make his sentiments yours.

I would also emphasize your special competence, in that you are present in so many countries so diverse among themselves in customs and culture: the work of evangelizing the culture and the cultures. It is my conviction that an integral spirituality, founded on a prayerful and fervent opening to the Heart of the Lord, is of capital importance for this work of evangelization of cultures and of human behavior, from which to make them conformable to the dictates of the gospel. I insist on the expression "a prayerful and fervent opening to the Heart of the Lord," given the impossibility of laboring as missionaries if you do not live as his disciples, close to his Heart.

In the course of these important days dedicated to your General Chapter, I desire that you remain united in prayer, in a special way in prayer to Mary our Mother, to whom your founder gave the beautiful title, so significant and inspired: "Our Lady of the Sacred Heart."

Society of Jesus: Letter given to the superior general at Paray-le-Monial, October 5, 1986

See above p. 75.

Priests of the Sacred Heart of Betharram:
Written message to the superior general on the occasion of the two hundredth anniversary of the birth of the founder, St. Michael Garicoits, July 5, 1997

After St. Michael's example, the priests of the Sacred Heart of Betharram are called to turn to the Lord, to show him their love and their total availability. Through prayer, particularly mental prayer, an intimate encounter with the Sacred Heart, and through recourse to the sacraments, they find the strength to live their priesthood in the heart of their religious community and in the different ecclesial services entrusted to them. In fact, contemplation and union with Christ are the sources of all apostolates; "it is altogether impossible to enumerate the heavenly gifts which devotion to the Sacred Heart of Jesus has poured out on the souls of the faithful, purifying them, offering them heavenly strength, rousing them to the attainment of all virtues" (Pius XII, *Haurietis aquas,* 2), and the encounter with Jesus in prayer enlarges the human heart to the dimensions of the world. Today, by living the spirituality of the Heart of Jesus "consumed by love for us," the priests of your institute are following an admirable school for their personal life and for their missions. They will let themselves be led by the Spirit, in order to serve the Church according to the Heart of God, by giving themselves totally, through love, for the salvation of their brothers and sisters. May everyone remember that "to lose something for God is to find it several times over" (Origen, *Homily on Genesis,* 7,6).

Rogationist Fathers of the Heart of Jesus:
To the superior general on the first centenary
of their foundation, May 16, 1997

The festive occasion of the first centenary of the foundation of the congregation of Rogationist Fathers of the Heart of Jesus offers me the welcome opportunity to address to you and to all the sons of Blessed Annibale Maria Di Francia, the Daughters of Divine Zeal, and all who share the same ideal, a word of congratulations and good wishes and especially of thanks to God for the gift he has wished to give his Church, enriching her with the "Rogationist" religious charism.

"Pray [Rogate] the Lord of the harvest to send out laborers for his harvest" (Matt. 9:38): here is the joyful discovery of Blessed Annibale Maria Di Francia. As he meditated on these words of Jesus, he understood the apostolic anxiety of his Divine Heart at the sight of the crowds "tired and helpless, like sheep without a shepherd" (Matt. 9:36), and he made it his own, basing his whole life and apostolate on it. Your founder was already dedicating himself with all his strength, as he himself says, to the spiritual and temporal relief of the most neglected....

In making them his own, he made his own the Heart of Christ: his compassion for the scattered children of God who must be led back to the unity of a single family (John 11:52).

In the footsteps of Blessed Annibale Maria Di Francia, the Rogationists have inherited the vocation of imitating Christ, the Heart of the world; a Heart filled with understanding and brimming with love for the brothers and sisters waiting for the Word of salvation and the bread of life; a Heart which, with trusting perseverance, never tires of praying the Father to "send laborers into his harvest."

The very prayer of the "Rogate" ("Pray, then ... "), source of an original form of apostolic life, is not merely a prayer addressed to God, but a prayer lived in God: for it is conceived in union with the merciful Heart of Christ, motivated by the "sighs" of the Spirit (Rom. 8:26) and addressed to the Father, the source of all good.

Blessed Annibale Maria Di Francia, docile to the divine Master's teachings and inwardly guided by the impulse of the Spirit, highlighted the conditions and characteristics of that prayer which make it an ecclesial work par excellence, yielding abundant fruit for the Church and for the world.

The first condition is to put the Blessed Eucharist at the center of personal and community life, in order to learn from it how to pray and love according to the Heart of Christ, indeed, to unite the offering of his own life with the offering Christ makes of his, continuing to intercede with the Father on our behalf (Heb. 7:25; 9:24). After the founder's example, may every member of the Rogationist family be a profoundly Eucharistic soul!

The second condition is the unanimity of hearts that makes prayer acceptable to God: "If two of you agree on earth about anything they ask, it will be done for them by my Father in heaven. For where two or three are gathered in my name, there am I in the midst of them" (Matt. 18:19–20).

The third condition on which the founder insisted is intimate association with the suffering of the Most Sacred Heart of Jesus through the practice of meditation and the generous acceptance, day after day, of exterior and interior suffering, one's own and that of others, especially that endured by Holy Church, the Bride of Christ.

Finally, Blessed Annibale Maria stressed the need to conform one's life to that of Mary most holy, who in her Immaculate Heart bore "engraved in golden letters all the words spoken by Jesus Christ our Lord," and who therefore could not but bear within herself "those words which issued from the divine zeal of the Heart of Jesus: 'Pray the Lord of the harvest. . . .' " (*Scritti,* vol. 54, p. 165).

Service to the young and the poor, in the spirit of your Father Founder, is not only the necessary test of the sincerity of your prayer, but stems from deep penetration into the sentiments of the Heart of Christ who blessed the Father because he hid the secrets of the kingdom from the wise and understanding and revealed them to children (Matt. 11:25).

Sons of Merciful Love: Letter to the superior general on the fiftieth anniversary of their institute, August 11, 2001

From the pierced Heart of the Redeemer streams the infinite source of merciful love. God is "rich in mercy": may your whole life be a hymn of praise to this sublime mystery of salvation. Make everyone you meet in your daily apostolate feel that the Heavenly Father is always "particularly close to men and women, especially when they are suffering, when they are under threat at the very heart of their existence and dignity" (*Dives in misericordia,* 2).

Brothers of the Sacred Heart: Letter to the superior general on the 175th anniversary of their institute, June 14, 1996

To mark your institute's 175th anniversary in this month specially dedicated to the Sacred Heart of Jesus, a "treasure of tenderness" (St. Thérèse of the Child Jesus, *Poesie,* no. 23, 6), I willingly join in the joy and thanksgiving of the Brothers spread across the continents and of all those who have benefited from their apostolate. In 1821, Father Andre Coindre of the Archdiocese of Lyons, who became vicar general of the Diocese of Blois, founded the Institute of the Brothers of the Sacred Heart, approved as a pontifical institute on July 22, 1894, after he had previously founded the Institute of the Religious of Jesus and Mary with St. Claudine Thevenet. The two foundations were inspired by the same concern to give the poor young people of that time a Christian education.

The region of France where your institute began is a crucible of spiritual life; in the seventeenth century, thanks to St. Margaret Mary Alacoque and St. Claude La Colombière, devotion to the Sacred Heart, which offers "numerous graces of purification, supernatural consolation, encouragement for the practice of all virtues" (Pius XII, *Haurietis aquas*), was already widespread. In living the spirituality of the Heart of Jesus today, the Brothers will be following a wonderful school for their personal life and for their missions. They should let themselves be guided by the Spirit, so as to serve in the Church according to God's Heart, giving themselves totally through love.

By community prayer, by listening to and meditating on the Word which Father Coindre "made his most constant and dearest study," and by sharing in the Eucharist, the Bothers are united with each other around Christ and contribute to building up their community and the entire Church. Heart-to-heart conversation with Jesus widens the human heart to world dimensions, for prayer brings us closer to God and to human beings. "Through our faith in him, Christ increases our love for God and neighbor" (St. Ignatius of Lyons, *Demonstration of the Apostolic Preaching,* no. 87). Thus, as your *Rule of Life* says, "Love of God and neighbor enables us to discover the ways of prayer" (no. 134).

I therefore urge the Brothers to draw from a life of intimacy with Christ the graces to respond to their specific Christian and apostolic vocation (*Rule of Life,* 119, 150). Our contemporaries need witnesses if they are to discover the love which comes from Christ, in order to know God and to know themselves, "a love which spurs us to love one another" (Leo XIII, *Annum sacrum*), so as to participate in building the civilization of love.

Summary

This chapter gives excerpts from messages of Pope John Paul II to various groups of religious priests and brothers. The excerpts vary considerably in length and in number. The most extensive are the words of the Holy Father to the Priests of the Sacred Heart, four distinct excerpts and most of them long. The Dehonians are very active in practicing and in promoting devotion to the Sacred Heart and keeping a balanced unity of the spiritual life and apostolic social commitment. In their extensive publishing they also produce books on the Sacred Heart.

But even a relatively unknown group may have something important to contribute to our growth in knowledge and understanding of the Heart of Jesus.

There are different ways that this chapter can be used. If one has a connection with any of the groups of religious quoted, those quotations will have priority. In the contents of any quotation strikes one, that may be an incentive to learn more about the charism of that particular congregation.

Chapter 15

Talks to Groups of Religious: Women

**Missionaries of the Sacred Heart, congregation of
Sisters founded by St. Frances Xavier Cabrini in 1888:
Letter to the superior general on the 150th anniversary
of Mother Cabrini's birth, May 31, 2000**

Mother Cabrini's tireless apostolic work was more and more inspired by her desire to bring salvation to all, and in a hurry. She
used to say: "The Heart of Jesus does things in such a hurry that I
can barely keep up with him."

Seeking the will of the divine Bridegroom should also be the
center of your lives. At the school of Jesus' Heart, you can learn to
hear the cries of the poor, in order to respond in the best way to
their material and spiritual problems. This is the mission that your
Mother is entrusting to you at the beginning of a new millennium,
so full of expectation and hope, but also marked by the bleeding
wounds in the living body of humanity, especially in the poorest
countries of the world.

I pray to the Lord that, through your example, many young
people will be attracted by the missionary ideal of Mother Cabrini,
which is so timely in our day. May the celebration of the Holy
Year 2000 and the providential anniversaries you are commemorating be beneficial occasions for each member of the institute to
grow in fidelity and love for the Sacred Heart of Jesus. May each of
you often repeat throughout your lives these words of the Apostle
which were so dear to your holy foundress: "I can do all things in
him who strengthens me" (Phil. 4:13).

Apostles of the Sacred Heart of Jesus:
To over seven thousand participants in a pilgrimage organized by the Apostles of the Sacred Heart of Jesus, October 5, 1994

Your charism in the Church is to adore and make known the Sacred Heart of Jesus, and to strive for the perfect love of God, giving a very special witness of charity among men and women as a gift of the heavenly Father's abundant concern for all his children.

This is a demanding vocation, but one that is always necessary in the Church, because it is from contemplating the love of Christ that every apostolic action must spring, in the awareness that "the plan of the Lord stands forever; the design of his Heart through all generations. To deliver them from death and preserve them in spite of famine" (Ps. 33:11, 19).

As we have just been reminded, the Institute of the Apostles of the Sacred Heart was founded on May 30, 1894 through the initiative of the Servant of God Mother Clelia Merloni, with the aim of bringing assistance to orphans, to the poor, the sick, and to young people, while working for "the glory of the Sacred Heart of Jesus, spreading devotion to it, and seeking to atone for the outrages that he receives from sinners" (Dir. Man., no. 1, p. 8).

The decision to give the congregation a specific charitable stamp is to be sought in the intense devotion she had to the Heart of Christ — "the first and most beloved of devotions," as she used to say — so much so that she wished to call the new foundation the Institute of the Apostles of the Sacred Heart of Jesus. Under this title the Servant of God Bishop Giovanni Scalabrini of Piacenza welcomed it into his diocese, and on June 10, 1900, gave his approval to its regulations and way of life.

From its very beginnings, your community felt a pressing desire to go out in the world to announce and witness to the love of Christ and the infinite treasures of his Heart.

"Let anyone who thirsts come to me and drink. From within him rivers of living water shall flow" (John 7:37–38). This is the very timely invitation that the Redeemer entrusts to all, but especially to you, dear Apostles of the Sacred Heart, in order that everyone may know and experience that it is only in Christ, Son of God and Son of man, that the desires and truest aspirations of every human person find total fulfillment.

With these wishes, I gladly bless the statue of the Sacred Heart intended for the Albanian village of Dajc, where your sisters are working. I also bless the cornerstone for the Church of the Sacred Heart of Jesus, which you will build in Rocca di Papa as a gift to the Diocese of Frascati in memory of your centenary.

Apostles of the Sacred Heart Secular Institute:
To participants in an Extraordinary Congress to update its Constitutions, January 2, 1998

You have met to reflect on the path traveled thus far and to plan the next stages. The Sacred Heart of Jesus, placed at the center of your spirituality, shows you the high road to a witness that is humble and often ignored by men, but precious and appreciated in the eyes of God. You wish to participate in the apostolic mission of the Lord: it is not by chance that you call yourselves "Apostles of the Sacred Heart."

Look then to him: he "delivered himself" for the life of the world. He willingly obeyed the Father until death, death on a cross, so that the new life of God's children might triumph in history. Thus you too are called to be the leaven of liberation and salvation for humankind and all creation (Rom. 8:18–21), by sharing from within, in your secular condition, the living situation of your many brothers and sisters.

I invoke on your persons, on your loved ones, and on the entire Institute of the Apostles of the Sacred Heart the constant assistance of the Lord, so that, scattered like little seeds throughout the world, without giving in to its allurements, you may be for everyone who approaches you an occasion for meeting Jesus and the inexhaustible wealth of love that flows from his blessed Heart.

Little Servants of the Sacred Heart of Jesus: On the occasion of the 125th anniversary of their foundation and the 25th anniversary of the beatification of their foundress Blessed Anna Michelotti, December 2, 1999

Visit the sick in a spirit of poverty, with only the wealth of God to whom you are consecrated, and bring them your motherly love. As your foundress liked to recommend: "Do not say, 'I go to the sick,' but 'I go to console the Heart of the suffering Jesus.' If you go with this spirit of faith, be calm and certain that you are serving them well" (*Parole vissute,* p. 43). May visiting the sick be your first and most demanding pilgrimage, especially in the Jubilee Year.

Handmaids of the Sacred Heart of Jesus Dying: To the Fourteenth General Chapter, January 5, 2001

Each institute of consecrated life is a precious gift of the Lord for the Church and for the world. The Handmaids of the Sacred Heart of Jesus Dying have been so for over a hundred years in Italy and in other countries.

Contemporary men and women need more than ever to draw from the springs of the Sacred Heart of Christ. Only in his Heart can they find peace in the moments of anguish which today's secular culture makes less and less bearable. Spiritual poverty is very widespread today, even at times becoming misery. That is why the true remedy is the rediscovery of Christian prayer. This is not an escape from reality and its trials, but rather a spiritual watchfulness and confident union with the divine will, in the certainty that this is always a will of love seeking to give men and women full and eternal life.

What better witness can this trusting abandonment find than that of a life wholly consecrated to the service of God, known and loved in the Heart of his Son Jesus Christ, who "is in agony until the end of the world" (Blaise Pascal)? And how can this consecration be expressed other than in generous and faithful service to our brothers and sisters, especially the neediest, for love of whom Christ willingly drank the bitter cup of the passion?

Handmaids of the Child Jesus: On the centenary of their foundation, August 30, 1990

The entire charism of your religious community is expressed in its name: Handmaids of the Child Jesus. With this service, to use the words of your founder, you would merit that "God will mercifully open to you his wounded Heart," in which you will find a "fountain of life and holiness."

Daughters of St. Joseph of Caburlotto: Written message given at the end of the general audience to the Sisters preparing for their General Chapter and the 150th anniversary of their foundation, June 30, 1999

You will not fail to make an explicit reference to the mystery of the Incarnation contemplated at Nazareth, from which stems your characteristic "devotion of the heart," summing up your specific style of prayer.

May the constant love that flows from Christ's Heart reign among you, sisters of various backgrounds and ages. May you always be an eloquent sign of this divine love in your life and daily activities. Never turn your gaze from Christ, who in his paschal mystery reveals the heavenly Father's mercy to us. To each one he says again: "Fear not, for I have redeemed you: I have called you by name, you are mine" (Isa. 43:1). And then, having experienced that you are loved by him with a boundless love, be ready and eager to share this same spiritual treasure with others. May the love of Christ, which inspired your founder 150 years ago and has sustained you and your sisters until now, always be the center of your life.

Cloistered Cistercian Benedictine Sisters, June 15, 1985

The pope's first visit upon arriving at Vittorio Veneto was to the monastery of the Sisters. In the written text of his talk to them, he did not refer to the Sacred Heart, but after that he spoke spontaneously on the Sacred Heart.

To what I have said in the talk I handed to you, I want to add a few words, taking my inspiration from the liturgical feast which we observed yesterday and which we are still living today: the Solemnity of the Sacred Heart of Jesus, today as it were completed by the commemoration — I would say also by the feast — of the Immaculate Heart of Mary. Therefore I salute you in this Heart, in the Heart of Jesus by way of the Heart of Mary, the Immaculate Heart, and I approach all of you by this Heart of Mary which knew how to learn — in an unusual way — from the Heart of her Son. Normally it is the children who learn from the heart of their mothers. But, with time, it is also the mothers who begin to learn from the hearts of their children. This is verified in an exceptional, supernatural, divine way between the two Hearts of Jesus and Mary, of Mary and Jesus. Behold, we have an experienced Heart, profoundly expert in the mysteries of the Most Blessed Trinity, of the divine plans, a Heart expert in the mystery of creation in the light of the mystery of the Redemption. A most experienced Heart. No human heart, aside from that of the Redeemer, which is a Divine Heart, is so expert in the mystery of the Redemption as that of Mary, her Immaculate Heart. It had to be immaculate to be able to be perfectly sensitive to all that came from the Divine Heart of her Son, to all that came — we may say — also from the eternal Heart of the Most Holy Trinity, Father, Son, and Holy Spirit. For this reason it had to be immaculate.

Behold the liturgical mystery of the day on which we meet. Dear Sisters, I wish to meet you in this mystery. Naturally, without pretending to be able to explain it in its fullness, in its profundity, I wish at least to touch this mystery of yesterday and today, both of them profoundly bound together. Thus we are profoundly united in the Church of Christ, we are united by means of the mystery of Christ and of Mary, as the Second Vatican Council has also taught us, above all in the Constitution *Lumen gentium,* which concludes with a chapter on the presence of the Blessed Virgin and Mother of Christ in the Church, in the mystery of the Church.

Summary

In this chapter we have excerpts from messages of the Holy Father to eight different groups of religious women, all of them of approximately the same length, relating the specific charism of that congregation to the Heart of Jesus. Suggestions similar to those given in the preceding chapter would apply here.

Chapter 16

Messages to Members of the Apostleship of Prayer

To a group of the Apostleship of Prayer at the parish of the Holy Canadian Martyrs, November 2, 1980

Two different though very similar groups: both with a Christocentric nature. One, the Apostleship of Prayer, centered mainly on the mystery of the Heart of Jesus; the other, the adorers, centered on the Most Holy Sacrament. We are grateful for these two fundamental forms of apostolate because prayer is the fundamental apostolate.

To a group of the Apostleship of Prayer after a general audience, June 23, 1982

I also cordially greet the group of the Apostleship of Prayer of the combined dioceses of Macerata, Tolentino, Recanati, Cingoli, and Treia.

Dearly beloved, I encourage you to collaborate in this fine form of apostolate, achieved through each person's daily offering of oneself and of one's daily life, in union with the Eucharistic Sacrifice, for the needs of the Church and the salvation of all men and women, according to the pope's intentions. May the Heart of Jesus continue to be the center of inspiration for all your apostolic activity.

I bless you and thank you, since today the diffusion of the spirit of the Apostleship of Prayer and your solicitude in spreading

155

the knowledge and love of the Heart of Jesus are more precious than ever for the Church. And they are particularly appreciated by the pope.

To diocesan directors of the Apostleship of Prayer in Italy after a general audience, January 11, 1984

It is with particular affection that I greet the diocesan directors of the Apostleship of Prayer who are assembled for a study congress on the relationship between the Divine Heart of Jesus and the Holy Spirit, in connection with a catechesis of prayer and the diffusion of the spirituality of the Heart of Jesus.

My dear priests, you are committed to keeping the flame of the torch of prayer alive through membership of this type of apostolate, which involves special devotion to the Most Holy Heart of Jesus and the daily offering of prayers and actions according to the intentions of the Church and the Supreme Pontiff. I would like to express my lively satisfaction for this diocesan responsibility and exhort you to persevere in this activity of such importance for the Church with courage and ardor.

To a group of the Apostleship of Prayer after a general audience, March 31, 1984

Finally, I would like to express my warm appreciation and satisfaction to the members of the Apostleship of Prayer and speak at greater length and more fully than I can in these few minutes, in view of the fundamental importance of this apostolate for the Church in general and for the individual life of each believer.

On this occasion of the Jubilee pilgrimage of the Holy Year of the Redemption, referring to the message of the Sacred Heart of Jesus to St. Margaret Mary and to the great encyclicals of my predecessors Leo XIII (*Annum sacrum,* May 25, 1899), Pius XI (*Miserentissimus Redemptor,* May 8, 1928), Pius XII (*Haurietis aquas,* May 15, 1956), Paul VI (*Investigabiles divitias Christi,* February 6, 1965, and *Diserti interpretes facti,* May 25, 1965), as well as my own two encyclicals *Redemptor hominis* and *Dives in misericordia,* I exhort you to constantly extend and intensify the range of your apostolate in every parish, community, and diocese, fostering prayer and daily offering for the conversion of sinners, for the needs of the Church, for the governors and civil authorities that they may govern with a true and upright conscience; and stimulating authentic devotion to the Sacred Heart through the consecration of families and above all through the heartfelt celebration of the First Friday of each month with sacramental confession and participation in the Eucharist.

To a group of the Apostleship of Prayer at the parish of Our Lady of the Visitation, January 20, 1985

I am very happy to meet this group. We all know that every person must pray, but we possibly do not reflect sufficiently on the fact that prayer is also an apostolate — the fundamental apostolate in fact — since it is through prayer that we remain in Christ, since without him we can do nothing.

Through prayer we are rooted in his Heart; or rather rooted in his prayer. I believe that what is essential in this apostolate is that we become rooted in Christ's prayer, just as he always prays for the whole world, for the entire cosmos, for the whole of humanity and — as St. Paul says — "with a loud cry." This prayer rises up from the cross to the Father for the redemption of the world. Therefore you are part of this prayer.

To the World Congress of National Secretaries of the Apostleship of Prayer in Rome, April 13, 1985

The World Congress of National Secretaries of the Apostleship of Prayer gives me the happy opportunity to greet you; you who have come to Rome from the five continents, and in particular the Very Reverend Father Peter-Hans Kolvenbach, superior general of the Society of Jesus and director general of the Apostleship of Prayer, to whom goes my sincere thanks for this initiative.

In this Congress, you propose to study the way to proceed with this work, which for more than a century has rendered such great service in the apostolate of the Church, as a particularly well adapted and efficacious instrument.

The Apostleship of Prayer — which I have known and appreciated for many years — wants to highlight the apostolic value of prayer in the Church. This is based on the exhortation of St. Paul, who recommended prayers for all men as something "good and acceptable in the sight of God our Savior" (1 Tim. 2:3); on the efficaciousness of prayer in the name of Jesus (John 16:23ff.), in common (Matt. 18:19ff.), with Mary Most Holy (Acts 1:14). By instilling the spirituality of the "offering" in union with Christ's oblation in the Mass, the Apostleship of Prayer is right in the line of conciliar teaching which presents the Eucharistic Sacrifice as the foundation, center, and culmination of all Christian life (*Lumen gentium,* 11; *Presbyterorum ordinis,* 5; *Ad gentes,* 9) and puts a just value on "the prayer of the faithful," which the Church has given back to the Eucharistic celebration and the Liturgy of the Hours (*Sacrosanctum concilium,* 53).

The Apostleship of Prayer has always distinguished itself by its commitment to spread the devotion and the spirituality to the Heart of the Redeemer. In this you have followed the teachings and exhortation of my predecessors: Leo XIII, who, in the encyclical *Annum sacrum* (May 25, 1899), consecrated the whole human race to the

Sacred Heart; Pius XI, who, in the encyclical *Miserentissimus Redemptor* (May 8, 1928), inculcated consecration to the Heart of Jesus and the duty of reparation; Pius XII, who wrote in the encyclical *Haurietis aquas* (May 15, 1956): "The Heart of Jesus is the Heart of a divine Person, that is, of the Word Incarnate, and continues to put before our eyes all the love that he had and continues to have for us. For this reason, the cult of the Most Sacred Heart of Jesus must be held in such high esteem as to be considered as the most complete expression of the Christian religion.... Therefore, it is easy to conclude that, in substance, the cult of the Sacred Heart of Jesus is the cult of love with which God has loved us through Jesus, and is the practice of our love for God and for others" (*AAS* 48 [1956], 344ff.).

I wish also to recall my great predecessor, Paul VI, who, in the apostolic letter *Investigabiles divitias,* stressed the centrality of the devotion to the Heart of Jesus:

> Since the Ecumenical Council strongly recommends the pious exercises of the Christian people... especially when they are accomplished in accordance with the Apostolic See, this form of devotion seems to be above all other devotions. In fact... it is a cult that consists essentially in the adoration and reparation due to Christ Our Lord and it is founded principally on the august Eucharistic Mystery from which — as from the other liturgical actions — derive the sanctification of people and the glorification of God in Christ, to which converge, as to their end, all the Church's activities. (*AAS* 57 [1956], 300ff.)

Continue, therefore, to be evangelizers of him who is rich in mercy, because "the Church professes, in a particular manner, God's mercy and venerates it by turning to the Heart of Christ" (*Dives in misericordia,* 13).

Today I wish to express my sincere appreciation to the Society of Jesus throughout the world for its great effort to spread and

keep alive in all the faithful the "spirit of the redemption," that sacred fire that must inflame the hearts of all Christians. The vitality
of the spirit of offering, of immolation of Christian life, the awareness of collaborating in the work of redemption are attributed in
large part to the Apostleship of Prayer. So also are the strength of
the spirituality centered in the Heart of Christ. The various editions
of the *Sacred Heart Messengers,* the organ of the Apostleship of
Prayer, have been and are a great and precious instrument for the
diffusion in all languages of the spirituality of "consecration" and
"reparation," essential for an authentic living of the mystery of the
Heart of Christ.

This Congress of the National Secretaries of the Apostleship of
Prayer occurs at a significant moment in the life of the Church,
twenty years after the Second Vatican Ecumenical Council.

From the beginning of my pontificate, I have urged the faithful
to adhere totally to Christ, Redeemer of man and of the world (encyclical *Redemptor hominis*); to live the merciful love of God for
sinful humanity (encyclical *Dives in misericordia*). It is in this spirit
that I wished to celebrate the extraordinary Holy Year of the Redemption, presenting the Crucified Christ as the definitive answer
to the mystery of our humanity (apostolic letter *Salvifici doloris*) to
obtain the fruits of the Redemption and to collaborate in the work
of this same Redemption.

The Apostleship of Prayer can bring a meaningful and concrete
contribution to the diffusion, at all levels, of the great and consoling truth that all Christians can be intimately united to Christ the
Redeemer by offering their own life to the Heart of Christ. I do not
doubt that the Society of Jesus will continue to put its strength, its
talents, its organization, and its obedience at the service of such
a high spiritual end. Again today, I entrust this commitment to the
zeal of the superior general, urging him to seek, in fidelity to the
spirit of the Association, for more efficacious means adapted to our

times to spread among all the faithful this awareness of collaborating with Christ the Redeemer through the offering of their own lives united and lived with the Heart of Christ in total consecration to his love and in reparation for the sins of the world. All this through the Immaculate Heart of Mary Most Holy, that Heart which "is met spiritually in the Heart of the Son opened by the soldier's lance," that Heart which "was opened by the same love for man and for the world, with which Christ has loved man and the world, offering himself on the cross even unto that stroke of the soldier's lance" (*Insegnamenti di Giovanni Paolo II,* V, 2 [1982], pp. 1573–82).

The promotion and vivification of this essential spirit must continue to be the reason d'être of the whole organization, structure, and activity of the Apostleship of Prayer at this time. Special attention must be given to children and the young who constitute the "Youth Eucharistic Movement," formerly known as the "Eucharistic Crusade," and also to the sick who, by their willingness to unite their sufferings to the Passion of Christ (apostolic letter *Salvific doloris,* 23–27) are powerful and privileged elements of the Association.

Moreover, you must strive to form Christians that are shaped by the Eucharist, which gives them the strength to commit themselves generously to embrace all the dimensions of their own life in service of their brothers and sisters as the offered body of Christ and his blood which was shed (Luke 22:19ff.).

In this perspective, continue, with ever renewed commitment, to recommend and spread the pious practice of the First Friday. Reconciled with God, the Church, and their brothers and sisters through the sacrament of penance, Christians are united and nourished in the sacrament of the Eucharist, by the Heart of Jesus, and participate in his work of offering and reparation.

You feel particularly bound to the Vicar of Christ and pray for him every day as the mother Church of Jerusalem did for Peter (Acts 12:4); and you wish to deepen and make known to Christians the concrete problems that trouble the universal Church, especially those of the missions. They are the object of attentive reflection which inspires knowledgeable and responsible prayer in the People of God. The prayer that you promote does not consist in the mere repetition of a formula but must rise from the hearts of the faithful, in awareness of their own situation as creatures, but also as beloved children of God, and in the consciousness of their own participation in the priestly, prophetic, and royal function of Christ, by virtue of their union with him (*Lumen gentium,* 30–38). May your members be conscious of the sanctifying and apostolic value of their daily work which is seen as a collaboration in the work of God, Creator and Redeemer (encyclical *Laborem exercens,* 25–27), as is also their suffering through which they are called to complete in their bodies what is lacking to the sufferings of Christ (Col. 1:24; apostolic letter *Salvific doloris,* 24).

I urge you, therefore, to insist, with ever greater commitment, on the continuous spiritual, doctrinal, and catechetical formation of your members as your statutes demand (III, 1) — a formation which is firmly rooted in the Word of God, faithful to the teaching of the Church, in accord with conciliar directives (*Apostolicam actuositatem,* 22–32), which communicates not only the knowledge, but also the meaning of the ever living love of Christ the Redeemer for all men and women and the meaning of their apostolic vocation and universal solidarity.

For these spiritual ends, I do not doubt that you will put at the service of the local and particular Churches all the means of social communication that are available to you, in order to transmit to all the experience of an authentic prayer, adapted to different cultures and incarnated in their historical context, in particular, prayer in families, which I myself have recommended so many times (apostolic exhortation *Familiaris consortio,* 59–62).

Thus will be accomplished Pius XII's hope that "the Apostleship of Prayer ... be so united to the other pious associations that it penetrates them like a breath of fresh air through which supernatural life and apostolic activity are ever renewed and strengthened" (Address to the participants of the International Congress of the Apostleship of Prayer, September 17, 1956: *ASS* 48 [1956], 676ff.).

With these wishes I put this worldwide pious association into your hands as a precious treasure from the pope's heart and the Heart of Christ. Put all your talents and all your strength in the accomplishment of this mission that I entrust to you today.

May Mary Most Holy, Mother of the Church, be with you in these days in the Cenacle and may she follow you in your ministry throughout the world and I invoke her maternal intercession on the work of the Congress and impart the apostolic blessing to you here present, to your collaborators, and to all the members of the Apostleship of Prayer.

Letter to Father Peter-Hans Kolvenbach, superior general of the Society of Jesus and director general of the Apostleship of Prayer, on the occasion of the 150th anniversary of the founding of the Apostleship of Prayer, December 3, 1994

On the occasion of the 150th anniversary of the founding of the Apostleship of Prayer, I wish to express to you as its director general and through you to all its members, my deep appreciation of the great good it has accomplished and is still accomplishing in the Church. I also earnestly encourage you and all its members to persevere in this work which has proved so extraordinarily precious in the spiritual lives of the faithful and their communities.

It was on the feast of St. Francis Xavier, December 3, 1844, at the Jesuit house of studies at Vals in France, that Father Francis Xavier Gautrelet providentially invited the students to offer their activities, prayers and sacrifices as a way of collaborating spiritually with the apostolic activities of their colleagues in diverse fields of ministry.

This was the birth of the Apostleship of Prayer. Approved by the bishop of Le Puy, it expanded rapidly and by the end of the century its members numbered over 13 million in various parts of the world.

The Apostleship of Prayer has always been especially close to the Roman Pontiffs. Pius IX approved its first statutes and exhorted its members to make the daily offering of their work and prayers for the intentions of the Church and the pope. Every pope since then has given special attention to this association, emphasizing the efficacious contribution it makes to apostolic activities.

The adaptation of the statutes of the Apostleship of Prayer to the teaching and spirit of the Second Vatican Council was approved by Pope Paul VI on March 27, 1968. In my address of April 13, 1985, to the Congress of National Secretaries of the Apostleship of Prayer, I myself recalled the consoling truth that Christians everywhere collaborate actively in the mystery of the Redemption when they daily offer their lives and their work to the Heart of Christ. Each year I personally give to you, as director general of the Apostleship of Prayer, the monthly prayer intentions I have selected for the following year.

As the dawn of the third millennium approaches a world in which many sectors have become quite pagan, it is obvious how urgent it is for members of the Apostleship of Prayer to be involved in the service of the new evangelization.

For Christ has come to preach the Good News to the poor, and the Apostleship of Prayer has always considered itself a form of popular piety for the masses. As such it has performed an important service during the past 150 years by giving new life to people's awareness of how valuable their lives are to God for the building up of his kingdom.

In the dechristianized society of today, what greater service can the Apostleship of Prayer offer than to rededicate itself with enthusiasm to the new evangelization, by opening the eyes of the little ones to the liberating message of revelation?

Members of the Apostleship of Prayer should feel themselves called to teach others to pray with the word of God, especially those who have lost the habit. Christ is the living Word who personally brings life and truth to every mind and heart. Meditating on the Sacred Scriptures helps the faithful to embrace the will of God with joy and, strengthened by the grace received in the Eucharist, to apply it to their daily lives.

The more one learns to inspire one's own prayer with the word of God, the more intimately that person is permeated with the sentiments of the Heart of Christ. In this way participation in the liturgical life becomes extraordinarily effective. It will be the task of the Apostleship of Prayer to promote this lively participation fully aware of its essential importance for the success of the new evangelization.

The new evangelization will also be effective insofar as it strengthens the bonds of ecclesial communion with the grace that flows from the Heart of Christ. The Apostleship of Prayer during the past century and a half has created a profound communion of prayer among hundreds of millions of believers. Nothing less is expected of it in the future.

It should continue to induce as many people as possible to pray together to the Father in the name of the Son with the grace of the Holy Spirit for the intentions of the Church.

This immense communion of prayer will contribute effectively to building up both the universal Church and the local Churches. So, as I exhort all to persevere in prayers for the urgent needs of the whole Church, I also wish to invite the faithful to pray for local Churches and their own communities.

Beginning with you, Reverend Father, and remembering the national secretaries and diocesan directors, parish priests and their collaborators, catechists and promoters, I express my gratitude to all who nourish the spirituality of the Apostleship of Prayer. I impart to all my affectionate blessing, as a pledge of the graces that spring from the Heart of Christ, so full of love and mercy.

Summary

There are three types of messages included here, all of them centered on the Apostleship of Prayer. There are greetings given to parish groups of members of the Apostleship of Prayer either at the end of general audiences or at parish visits. There are remarks given to groups of priest-directors of the Apostleship of Prayer at the end of general audiences, and there are directives on the nature of the Apostleship of Prayer. The latter are the most important and include the last two documents given here: the address of the Holy Father to the World Congress of National Secretaries of the Apostleship of Prayer in 1985 and the letter of December 3, 1994, to the superior general of the Society of Jesus, who is also the director general of the Apostleship of Prayer, on the occasion of the 150th anniversary of the founding of the Apostleship of Prayer. These two documents, along with the letter the pope gave to the superior general of the Society of Jesus at Paray-le-Monial in 1986 (see above p. 75) are extremely valuable in presenting in summary and practical form devotion to the Sacred Heart.

On pp. 157 and 158 are lists of the principal papal documents on devotion to the Sacred Heart. The documents in this chapter are also important because of their teaching on the value of prayer.

Chapter 17

Angelus Messages

Pope John Paul II has used many of his Angelus messages, that is, the messages he gives before praying the Angelus on Sundays and feast days, to offer reflections on various aspects of the Sacred Heart. The longest series of Angelus messages was given by the Holy Father on the invocations of the Litany of the Sacred Heart, a total of thirty-three talks. This series was given during the summer months of 1985, 1986, and 1989; it was completed with the final two invocations in November 1989. These thirty-three talks are not included in this book: they were published originally in 1992 as a small book and are still in print (see above p. 59).

Earlier, on June 27, 1982, the pope had given a talk on the litany. This talk is referenced here and is included in chapter 6 on the Litany of the Sacred Heart of Jesus.

Included here are eleven other Angelus messages on the Heart of Jesus. On some of his pastoral visits in Italy outside Rome or to other countries, the Holy Father also delivered Angelus messages. These are not included here but are found with the talks he gave on that pastoral visit.

The sacrament of love at the heart of the Church, June 8, 1980

In the first part the Holy Father speaks of the Eucharist on the feast of Corpus Christi; in the second part he speaks of the Heart of Jesus.

"Hail, O real Body, born of the Virgin Mary..."

While today, here in St. Peter's Square, we wish to manifest the special worship of the Eucharist, of the most Sacred Body of Christ, our thoughts go to her from whom God, the Son of God, took this Body: the Virgin whose name is Mary. [The rest of the first part is omitted.]

As I am preparing together with you, dear Brothers and Sisters, for the adoration of the Body of Christ in St. Peter's Square, here in Rome, there appear before my eyes two moments of my recent visit to Paris, which are particularly engraved in my heart.

In the first place, last Saturday afternoon, the visit to Rue du Bac: the special shrine of Mary Immaculate hidden in a modest chapel of the Generalate of the Daughters of Charity of St. Vincent de Paul — for over a hundred years, a place of incessant prayer of men and women of Paris, France, and the world.

The following Sunday, almost at midnight, the visit to the Basilica of the Sacred Heart at Montmartre, in which ceaseless adoration of the Blessed Sacrament has been going on for almost a century, without a break, day and night [see above p. 44]. And without a break there are people who pray, who worship, who, in the spirit of St. Margaret Mary, offer atonement to that Heart, which so dearly loved the world and people in this world, and which is outraged and forgotten so much by it.

These two places, the two shrines of the great city of Paris, unite at this moment in my grateful memory, as we prepare to adore, here in St. Peter's Square, the sacrament of love: "Hail, O real Body, born of the Virgin Mary ... "

The Heart which has loved so much, June 15, 1980

"I have loved you with an everlasting love" (Jer. 31:3). These marvelous words of Holy Scripture come into my mind when the Church gathers near the Heart of Jesus, meditating on his mysteries. This devout reflection embraces the whole month of June, but it reaches its peak in the Solemnity of the Sacred Heart, which we celebrated last Friday. Today, in our joint prayer of the Angelus, let there ring out again the fervent echo of that feast, which has a centuries-old tradition and an ever living topicality in the Church. Let each of us reflect on what attracts us to that Heart which loved us so much.

Listening to certain biblical affirmations about the Lord's eternal love, which was revealed in the Heart of the Man-God, drawing everyone to it, before my eyes there appear in the first place the smiling children, boys and girls, who came in large numbers last Sunday to the meeting with Jesus in the Eucharist, here in this square. A few days ago, they approached Holy Communion for the first time, and they continue to enjoy the solemn atmosphere of that day, which is manifested even in their dress. The Lord Jesus has drawn them so strongly to himself and has attracted them to his Heart. May they never move away from him. May they always keep the living memory of their first Communion and the cordial friendship with their Divine Friend. May they find in that Heart, which never disappoints, a strong and loving support, throughout their lives.

Today, again, the words of eternal love, with which God loved us, drawing us to the Heart of his only-begotten Son, will find a highly significant expression in another important event, for which the venerated Basilica of St. Peter is preparing: forty-five deacons will receive priestly ordination, through my ministry. Thinking of each of them, and reflecting on the sacrament of the priesthood, which will be conferred on them, I raise my prayer to the Eternal Priest of our souls, in order that each of these young priests may find and deepen perfectly that bond with which they have been united for some time to the Heart of Christ.

The priest's vocation is nothing, in fact, but the discovery of that eternal love which attracts and calls, which can fill with full joy the heart of the elect, opening it at the same time toward all those brothers and sisters whom Providence will place on the way of his pastoral ministry. Let each one to be ordained discover even more fully this very sweet bond and gain vigorous new strength from it. May the number ever increase of those to whom eternal love is revealed in their own hearts as the greatest, those who feel the call to the priestly service and follow it without looking back.

Reciting the Angelus, let us invoke today the Mother of the Eternal Priest for this great ecclesial intention.

The Litany of the Sacred Heart of Jesus reflects the deepest experiences of human hearts, June 27, 1982

See above p. 57.

Mother, teach us to open our hearts to the love of your Son's Sacred Heart, July 1, 1984

During the whole month of June the Church placed before us the mysteries of the Heart of Jesus, the God-Man. These mysteries are expressed in a penetrating way in the Litany of the Most Sacred Heart, which can be sung and can be recited, but above all, must be meditated upon.

In the last days of the month of June, these mysteries have been proposed in their sum total in the liturgy of the Solemnity of the Most Sacred Heart.

Here are the words of St. John the Apostle: "Not that we have loved God but that he has loved us and has sent his Son as an offering for our sins" (1 John 4:10) ... "that we might have life through him" (1 John 4:9).

Here we have the synthesis of all the mysteries hidden in the Heart of God's Son: prevenient love — satisfactory love — life-giving love.

This Heart beats with the human blood that was poured out on the cross. This Heart beats with all the inexhaustible love that is eternally in God. With this love, it is always open to us through the wound that the centurion's lance opened in it on the cross.

"If God has loved us so, we must have the same love for one another" (1 John 4:11): love gives birth to love, it releases love and is fulfilled through love. Every particle of true love in the human heart has in itself something of what fills the Heart of the God-Man limitlessly.

Therefore he asks us in the liturgy of the Solemnity of the Sacred Heart: "Come to me, all you who are weary and find life burdensome, and I will refresh you. Take my yoke upon your shoulders and learn from me" (Matt. 11:28–29).

You, O Mother of Christ, were the first to heed this call. In the Angelus prayer, while meditating on the mystery of the Annunciation, we pray to you: teach us to open our hearts to the love that is in the Heart of Jesus, as you opened your heart to it right from your first "fiat," and as you have always opened it. Teach us, Mother, to be in intimacy, in truth, and in love with the Divine Heart of your Son.

The Holy Spirit strengthens "the inner man," June 8, 1986

"I bow my knees before the Father . . . that according to the riches of his glory he may grant you to be strengthened with might through his Spirit in the inner man" (Eph. 3:14–16). Thus the Apostle of Christ prays in the words of the Letter to the Ephesians.

I want to introduce these words of the Apostle into our prayer, as we gather to recite the Sunday Angelus, while we are with Mary, Mother of Christ.

Last Friday the Church celebrated the Solemnity of the Sacred Heart of Jesus. The entire month of June is dedicated to the mystery of his Divine Heart.

Yet, who can be nearer to the Heart of the Son than the mother? Together with her we bow our knees before the Father. Together with her we pray that devotion to the Heart of the Redeemer of the world may realize for all of us, through the Holy Spirit, the strengthening with might in the inner man.

Yes, through the Holy Spirit.

The meaning of that "strengthening with might in the inner man," the work of the Holy Spirit who acts in our hearts, is explained in the next part of the Letter to the Ephesians where we read: "May Christ dwell in our hearts through faith: that you, being rooted and grounded in love, may have power to comprehend . . . and to know the love of Christ which surpasses knowledge, that you may be filled with all the fullness of God" (Eph. 3:17–19).

Only the Holy Spirit can accomplish this in our human spirit. Only the Holy Spirit can open to us this fullness of the "inner man," which is found in the Heart of Christ.

Only he can ensure that from this fullness strength can gradually be drawn, even by our human hearts, our "inner man," which must not be absorbed only by passing things, but "rooted and grounded" in that "love" which does not pass away.

May the humble handmaid of the Lord preside over our prayer, that our human hearts may be "rooted and grounded" in God, who alone is the love which does not pass away.

This love is revealed in the human Heart of her Son.

The gift of piety is the root of the "civilization of love," May 28, 1989

Our reflection on the gifts of the Holy Spirit leads us today to speak of another important gift, piety. With it, the Spirit heals our hearts of every form of hardness, and opens them to tenderness toward God and our brothers and sisters.

Tenderness, as a truly filial attitude toward God, is expressed in prayer. The experience of one's own existential poverty, of the void which earthly things leave in the soul, gives rise to the need to have recourse to God in order to obtain grace, help, and pardon. The gift of piety directs and nourishes such a need, enriching it with sentiments of profound confidence in God, trusted as a good and generous Father. In this sense, St. Paul wrote: "God sent his Son ... that we might receive adoption. As proof that you are children, God sent the Spirit of his Son into your hearts, crying out: 'Abba, Father!' So you are no longer a slave but a son ... " (Gal. 4:4–7; see Rom. 8:15).

Tenderness, an authentically fraternal openness toward one's neighbor, is manifested in meekness. With the gift of piety the Spirit infuses into the believer a new capacity for love of the brethren, making his heart participate in some manner in the very meekness of the Heart of Christ. The "pious" Christian always sees others as children of the same Father, called to be part of the family of God which is the Church. He feels urged to treat them with the kindness and friendliness which are proper to a frank and fraternal relationship.

The gift of piety further extinguishes in the heart those fires of tension and division which are bitterness, anger, and impatience, and nourishes feelings of understanding, tolerance, and pardon. Such a gift is, therefore, at the root of that new human community which is based on the civilization of love.

Let us ask the Holy Spirit for a renewed outpouring of this gift, entrusting our prayer to the intercession of Mary, sublime model of fervent prayer and maternal tenderness. May she, whom the Church salutes in the Litany of Loreto as the "Singular vessel of devotion," teach us to adore God "in spirit and truth" (John 4:23) and to open ourselves with meek and receptive hearts to all who are her children and therefore our brothers and sisters. Let us ask her in the words of the Salve Regina: "O clement, O loving, O sweet Virgin Mary!"

The Sacred Heart: Living witness to God's desire to redeem us, June 16, 1991

During the month of June, popular Christian devotion directs our hearts, following a beautiful tradition, toward the mystery of the Heart of Jesus; we celebrated the liturgical solemnity of this Friday a week ago [June 7].

Today, I would like to pause to reflect on this topic with you, taking our starting point from the Collect of today's Mass in which the Church addresses God, the "strength" of those who hope in him, because they are aware of their own "weakness" and of the fact that "without his help they can do nothing." The Church addresses God, comforted by Christ's solemn promise that prayer expressed in his name has a guaranteed value and will be heard (John 14:13f).

In this moment of recollection we, too, confident in the love of the Lord Jesus and the charity of his Heart, turn to God the Father and say to him: "Help us with your grace."

The Heart of Jesus is offered to us as a living witness of God's desire to save us and to do everything possible so that, according to his holy will, we can be pleasing to him "in our intentions and acts."

If in every person there is the tragic experience of moral evil, of guilt which separates him or her from the Lord, of disobedience to his will, it is from this very situation that we know that only the love of Christ's Heart can free us.

Rich in mercy toward all those who are oppressed by sin, the Sacred Heart is the origin and foundation of peace and true hope. Jesus restores every person to communion with the Father, through the cross drawing to himself the gaze of all who seek salvation (John 19:37). May we always be mindful that his pierced Heart is the endless source of the divine charity which pardons, regenerates, and restores life.

May Mary lead us to this Heart, propitiation for the sins of the world. May she lead to him every person who suffers from the sadness of evil and perhaps despairs of regaining friendship with God.

Immaculate Heart of Mary, draw us near to the Sacred Heart of your Son, Jesus!

The Sacred Heart encourages us in redemptive suffering, June 30, 1991

During the month of June, which ends today, we have had the opportunity to reflect on the mystery of the love of God, manifest to the world in the Heart of Christ; and on that feast day, we celebrated "the great things" which this Heart has done for us. We know and we believe that the Lord Jesus has loved us and loves us with an eternal, merciful love, and therefore fills us with every gift of grace.

Today, in praying the Angelus, we want to pause and consider the vocation of the Christian as a response to this love. This response is expressed above all through prayer and redemptive suffering.

The mystery of the redemption, which is brought about through the cross, always remains alive in the Church, who is conscious that each of her children must bear his share of suffering in order, together with Christ, to make reparation for the sins of the world. She, therefore, announces to humanity the riches of the Heart of Christ and invites all to draw near with full confidence to the throne of grace in order to find timely help there (Heb. 4:16); she asks Christians also to share the infinite charity of the Redeemer and to participate in this work for the salvation of the world.

How many Christians, touched by this invitation, have offered and continue to offer themselves, in union with Christ, as victims for the salvation of their brothers and sisters and in their own flesh make up that which is lacking in his sufferings on behalf of his body which is the Church (Col. 1:24)! Their example, as shown throughout the entire history of the Church, is still valid and encouraging.

May this brief reference to the primacy of the Heart of Jesus in the economy of salvation lead us to a better understanding of the obligation of reparation for the offenses committed against God. Contemplation of the Heart of Jesus, patient and rich in mercy, impels us, toward the greater degree of love that is expressed in sharing the suffering and in commitment to expiation.

The Virgin Mary, present at the foot of the cross, is for all of us the supreme model because of her direct participation in the passion of Christ, from whose pierced Heart saving grace is poured out upon the world.

Reflections on the Sacred Heart:
Christ teaches us to create conditions for true peace,
September 22, 1991

The human person sees in peace a fundamental imperative for his own life. It is in peace that he finds the essential conditions for his complete self-fulfillment. It should not be surprising, then, if in the presence of the grave threats to which peace is exposed today, cries of alarm are raised with increasing insistence in various national and international circles, inviting persons of good will to commit themselves urgently to protecting it.

If there is a place in which this invitation should find a favorable echo and a generous response it is certainly the heart of every religious person. The longing for peace, in fact, must be recognized as an expectation and a hope by anyone who sincerely aims for the Absolute. The attempt to enter into relationship with the transcendent Mystery of God presupposes an interior attitude of detachment, openness, and attention which constitutes the premises of a true and lasting peace.

This is valid in a special way for the Christian: he has been taught by his faith to experience God as the one who "scatters the peoples who delight in war" (Ps 67[68]:31), because he "loves all things that are and loathes nothing that he has made" (Wisd. 11:24). Furthermore, the Christian is continually faced with the programmatic words of the Sermon on the Mount: "Blessed are the meek, for they will inherit the land.... Blessed are the peacemakers, for they will be called children of God" (Matt. 5:5, 9).

He also knows where to find the inexhaustible source from which he can draw the necessary energy to be an authentic "peacemaker." It flows from the Heart of him who came into the world so that men "may have life and have it more abundantly" (John 10:10). From the Heart of Christ peace is waiting to well up into a stream of new life in the hearts of all persons of good will.

Supported by faith, the Christian is taught to create new conditions for a true peace. These conditions were already pointed out in that elegant phrase of the prophet Isaiah, which my predecessor Pius XII chose as the motto of his pontificate: "Justice will bring about peace" (Isa. 32:17).

Without justice there is no peace!

Priests according to the Heart of Christ, June 14, 1992

In one of the Angelus messages of his spiritual pilgrimage of Latin American Marian sanctuaries, the pope turned his thoughts to the Virgin venerated in the cathedral of Lima, Peru, under the title of "Our Lady of Evangelization" and prayed that there would never be lacking on the Latin American continent "priests according to the Heart of Christ."

Christ's Heart spurs us to full unity, June 28, 1998

We have reached the last Sunday of June, the month dedicated to the Sacred Heart of Jesus, while in July the Church expresses with special intensity her devotion to his Most Precious Blood. Through these spiritual emphases, tradition invites us to fix our gaze of faith on the mystery of God's love, revealed in the Incarnation of the Son. Christ offers his human and Divine Heart, source of reconciliation and principle of new life in the Holy Spirit, to today's men and women who are immersed in a secularized world and risk losing the center of gravity in their lives.

On the threshold of the third millennium, the Church proclaims to all people with renewed emphasis: Christ is the Heart of the world; the paschal mystery of his death and resurrection is the center of history which, thanks to him, is the history of salvation; his love draws every creature to himself and makes those who believe in him one heart and one mind, spurring Christians of every age to search for full unity.

Christ's Blood: pledge of reconciliation, July 2, 2000

Last Friday we celebrated the Solemnity of the Sacred Heart of Jesus, that Heart which began to beat two thousand years ago in the womb of Mary most holy and brought the fire of God's love into the world.

The Heart of Jesus contains a message for everyone; it also speaks to today's world. In a society where technology and informatics are developing at a growing rate, where people are caught up in thousands of often conflicting interests, they risk losing their center, the center of their very selves. By showing us his Heart, Jesus reminds us first of all that it is there, deep within oneself, that each person's destiny is decided, his death or life in the definitive sense.

He gives us life in abundance, which allows our hearts, sometimes hardened by indifference and selfishness, to be opened to a higher form of life.

The Heart of the crucified and risen Christ is the inexhaustible source of grace from which every individual can always draw love, truth, and mercy, especially during this special year of the Great Jubilee.

The Blood of Christ has redeemed us. This is the truth which we proclaimed just yesterday, at the beginning of July, the month traditionally dedicated to the Precious Blood of Christ.

How much blood has been unjustly shed in the world! How much violence, how much contempt for human life!

This humanity, often wounded by hatred and violence, more than ever needs to experience the efficacy of Christ's redeeming Blood. That Blood, which was not shed in vain, contains all the power of God's love and is the pledge of hope, redemption, and reconciliation. But in order to draw from this source, we must turn to the cross of Christ and fix our gaze on the Son of God, on his pierced Heart, on that Blood poured out.

Mary stood beneath the cross, sharing in the passion of her Son. She offers her Mother's Heart as a refuge to everyone in search of forgiveness, hope, and peace, as we have been reminded by the feast of her Immaculate Heart. Mary washed the blood from her crucified Son. We entrust to her the blood of the victims of violence, so that it may be redeemed by the Blood which Jesus shed for the world's salvation.

Summary

This chapter gives us eleven Angelus messages and a reference to another quoted elsewhere. In addition to the thirty-three Angelus messages on the Litany of the Sacred Heart, this totals forty-five talks the Holy Father gave on the Sacred Heart. They develop different aspects of the devotion to the Sacred Heart, including its relation to the Eucharist and to the Immaculate Heart of Mary. Most of them relate in some way to the month of June, the month traditionally devoted to the Heart of Jesus.

Chapter 18

General Audiences

Usually the Holy Father did not devote an entire discourse of his Wednesday catecheses to the Sacred Heart. The exception would be the occasions after one of his times in the hospital when in place of a Wednesday general audience he delivered a message from his window in the way he did for his Sunday Angelus messages. At other times he occasionally said something briefly about the Sacred Heart in a catechetical instruction on another topic.

General audience of July 29, 1987

In this general audience, the pope spoke about Jesus' prayer of thanksgiving for the revelation given to little ones. Jesus said: "I give praise to you, Father, Lord of heaven and earth, for although you have hidden these things from the wise and the learned you have revealed them to the children" (Matt. 11:25). In this discourse there is a reference to the Sacred Heart toward the end.

The hymn of thanksgiving of the Church which accompanies the celebration of the Eucharist arises from the depth of the heart of the Church and also from the Heart itself of the Son who lived that thanksgiving.

General audience of December 9, 1987

The catechesis of this general audience treated the miracles of Jesus as a manifestation of his saving love (Matt. 8:16–17).

"Signs" of divine omnipotence and the salvific power of the Son of God, the miracles narrated in the Gospels, are also the revelation of God toward men and women, especially for those who suffer, who are in need, who beg for healing and forgiveness. They are "signs" of the merciful love proclaimed in the Old and the New Testaments. Especially the reading of the Gospel makes us understand and "feel" that the miracles of Jesus have their source in the loving and merciful Heart of God, which lives and vibrates in his own human Heart.

General audience of June 8, 1988

Jesus, the faithful witness. The pope quotes the words of Jesus, "Learn from me" and twice later refers to the meekness and humility of the Heart of Jesus.

General audience of August 10, 1988

Christ frees humankind for a "new life." The pope begins by noting that it is worth repeating what he has said in recent catecheses when considering the salvific mission of Christ as liberation and Jesus as Liberator. This is liberation from sin and for the truth and new life. He quotes from the parable of the Good Shepherd: "I have come that they [the sheep] may have life and have it to the full" (John 10:10). That is also what Jesus says in figurative but very evocative language in his conversation with the Samaritan woman at the well in Sychar in the imagery of "living water."

Jesus also repeated this truth in very similar words to the crowd, when he was teaching them during the feast of Tents. "Whoever is thirsty let him come to me and let whoever believes in me come and drink. As Scripture says, from his breast shall flow a river of living water" (John 7:37–38). Rivers of living water are an image of the new life in which they share by virtue of the death of Christ on the cross. The tradition of the Fathers and the liturgy understand in the same sense the text of John where it is related that from the side (the Heart) of Christ, after his death on the cross there came forth "blood and water" when a Roman soldier "struck his side" (John 19:34).

According to an interpretation dear to many of the oriental Fathers and now accepted by different exegetes, rivers of living water shall also flow "from the breast" of the one who drinks the "water" of truth and grace of Christ. "From the breast" means: from the heart. In fact, "a new heart" is created within the human person as the prophets, and in particular Jeremiah and Ezekiel, announced very clearly.

In Jeremiah we read: "This will be the covenant that I will make with the house of Israel when those days arrive, says the Lord. I will plant my law, I will write it in their hearts. Then I will be their God and they shall be my people" (Jer. 31:33). In Ezekiel it is stated even more explicitly: "I shall give you a new heart and put a new spirit in you; I shall remove the heart of stone from you and give you a heart of flesh instead. I shall put my spirit in you and make you live according to my precepts and make you observe and keep my laws" (Ezek. 36:26–27).

It is a question therefore of a profound spiritual transformation which God himself works within the human person by means of "the breath of his Spirit" (Ezek. 36:26). The rivers of living water of which Jesus speaks mean the source of a new life which is life in the spirit and in truth, a life worthy of "true adorers of the Father" (John 4:23–24).

The rest of the catechesis develops the idea of this new life of the believer who becomes a new creation in Christ and says nothing more about the Heart of Jesus.

General audience of November 16, 1988

Catechesis on Christ's last words on the cross: "Father, forgive them..."
There is a brief mention of the Heart of Jesus when the pope speaks of
the "ignorance" of those who crucified Jesus.

Perhaps no sinner completely escapes that "ignorance" and is therefore beyond the range of that intercession for forgiveness which
issues from the most tender Heart of Christ dying on the cross.

General audience of December 14, 1988

First signs of the fruitfulness of Christ's redemptive death. The pope
begins by speaking of the centurion who witnessed Jesus breathe his last
and came to believe in him, as he said: "Truly this man was the Son of
God" (Mark 14:39). This was the first sign of Redemption accomplished.
The rest of the discourse is devoted to the piercing of the Heart of Jesus.

Another sign is recorded by John when he writes that "one of the
soldiers pierced his side with a spear, and at once there came out
blood and water" (John 19:34).

Be it noted that Jesus is already dead. He died before the two
criminals who had been crucified with him. This is a proof of the
intensity of his sufferings.

The thrust of the spear, therefore, is not a new suffering inflicted
on Jesus. It serves rather as a sign of the total gift which he had
made of himself, a sign marked in his very flesh by the piercing
of his side, and it may be said, with the opening of his Heart, a
symbolic representation of that love through which Jesus has given
everything and will continue to give everything to humankind.

From that opening of his Heart there flow blood and water. It is a
fact that can be explained physiologically. However, the evangelist
mentions it for its symbolic value: it is a sign and announcement

of the fruitfulness of the sacrifice. So great is the importance attributed to it by the evangelist that, immediately after narrating the episode, he adds: "He who saw it has borne witness, and his testimony is true: he knows that he is speaking the truth, so that you also may believe" (John 19:35). He appeals to direct observation, made by himself, to emphasize that it is a fact full of great significance concerning the motives and effects of Christ's sacrifice.

Indeed the evangelist perceives in the event the fulfillment of two prophecies. The first concerns the paschal lamb of the Jews, of which "not a bone shall be broken" (Exod. 12:46; Num. 9:12; see Ps. 34:21). For the evangelist, Christ crucified is therefore the paschal lamb and the "lamb bled dry," as St. Catherine of Siena says, the lamb of the New Covenant, prefigured in the pasch of the old law and "effective sign" of the new liberation not only of Israel but of all humankind from the slavery of sin.

John's other biblical citation is an obscure text attributed to the prophet Zechariah who says: "They shall look on him whom they have pierced" (Zech. 12:10). The prophecy concerns the liberation of Jerusalem and Judah by a king, for whose coming the nation acknowledges its guilt and mourns over him whom it has pierced as one mourns the loss of an only son. The evangelist applies this text to Jesus pierced and crucified, now contemplated with love. The hostile glances of his enemies were followed by the loving gaze of those converted. This possible interpretation helps us to understand the theological-prophetical perspective in which the evangelist considers the history that he sees developing from the open Heart of Jesus.

The symbolic meaning of the blood and water have been given various interpretations.

In John's Gospel it is possible to note a relationship between the water that flows from the pierced side and Jesus' invitation on the feast of Tabernacles: "If any one thirst, let him come to me and drink. He who believes in me, as the scripture has said, 'Out of his heart shall flow rivers of living water'" (John 7:37–38; see

4:10–14; Rev. 22:1). The evangelist then makes clear that Jesus was speaking of the Spirit which those who believed in him were to receive (John 7:39).

Some have interpreted the blood as the symbol of the forgiveness of sins through the sacrifice of expiation, and the water as the symbol of purification.

Others relate the blood and water to the Eucharist and baptism.

The evangelist has not provided sufficient grounds for precise interpretations. However, we seem to have an indication from the text on the pierced side from which flow blood and water, namely, the outpouring of grace flowing from the sacrifice, as John himself, from the very beginning of his Gospel, says of the Word Incarnate: "From his fullness have we all received grace upon grace" (John 1:16).

We wish to conclude by observing that the testimony of the beloved disciple acquires its full meaning if we recall that this disciple had rested his head on Jesus' breast during the Last Supper. Now he beheld this breast torn open. Hence he felt the need to emphasize the symbol of infinite charity which he had discovered in that Heart, and he invited the readers of his Gospel and all Christians to contemplate that Heart "that has so loved men and women" as to give himself in sacrifice for them.

General audience of June 1, 1994

Grace flows from the Sacred Heart: Devotion to Christ's Heart cannot be separated from the Eucharist. In place of the regular General audience on Wednesday, June 1, the Holy Father came to the window of his study and greeted the pilgrims in St. Peter's Square.

My cordial welcome to you all who have gathered in St. Peter's Square for this somewhat unusual Audience, as I return to my weekly meetings with pilgrims.

Today begins the month of June, dedicated to the Sacred Heart of Jesus, that Divine Heart pierced by a lance on the cross so that the treasures of grace would flow from it for all men and women. It is an everlasting source from which every believer and the whole Church draw the ever new vigor of faith, hope, and charity.

Devotion to Christ's Heart cannot be separated from the Eucharist, the sacrament of the Lord's Body and Blood, whose solemn feast occurs precisely tomorrow. Here in Rome it will be celebrated with the traditional moving procession from St. John Lateran to St. Mary Major.

In the rest of Italy the celebration is postponed till next Sunday. The Italian faithful are spending a week marked by the Eucharist. During these days the National Eucharistic Congress is being held in Siena and will conclude next Sunday. I invite all Christians, especially families, to be of one heart and soul, and to offer thanks to the Father for the priceless gift of the Lord's Body and Blood, which has found truly marvelous expression in art and culture, and particularly in the lives of the saints of this beloved country, this Italy.

As I hope that you will all welcome the life-giving strength of God's love, as did Mary most holy, I cordially impart to you my apostolic blessing, which I extend to your loved ones and children, to the sick and the suffering.

General audience of June 8, 1994

Jesus' Heart still speaks to us. From the window of his study the pope again addressed pilgrims and visitors gathered in St. Peter's Square at the customary time of the General audience.

The day after tomorrow is the Solemnity of the Sacred Heart of Jesus. It is a liturgical feast that sets a particular spiritual tone for the whole month of June. It is important for the faithful to have a deep sensitivity to the message it gives: in Christ's Heart the love of God has reached out to all humanity.

In our day this message has an extraordinary timeliness. Contemporary men and women, in fact, are often confused, divided, as if lacking an inner principle to create unity and harmony in their being and acting. Unfortunately rather widespread behavioral patterns intensify their rational and technological dimension, or on the contrary, the instinctual aspect, even though the core of the person is neither pure reason nor pure instinct. A person's center is what the Bible calls the "heart."

At the end of the twentieth century, the long-dominant unbelief of the Enlightenment school now seems obsolete. People feel an intense nostalgia for God, but they have lost the way to the inner sanctuary where his presence dwells: that sanctuary is precisely the heart, where freedom and intellect encounter the love of the Father who is in heaven.

The Heart of Christ is the universal seat of communion with God the Father; it is the seat of the Holy Spirit. To know God, one must know Jesus and live in harmony with his Heart by loving God and neighbor as he does.

Devotion to the Sacred Heart, as it developed in the Europe of two centuries ago under the impetus of the mystical experiences of St. Margaret Mary Alacoque, has been the response to Jansenistic rigorism, which ended up misunderstanding God's infinite mercy. Today, devotion to Jesus' Heart offers an authentic and harmonious fullness, in the perspective of a hope that does not disappoint, to a one-dimensional humanity or to one even tempted to give in to forms of a certainly practical, if not theoretical, nihilism.

About a century ago a well-known thinker announced the "death of God." Well, an unending spring of life, giving hope to every person, has streamed precisely from the Heart of God's Son, who died on the cross. From the Heart of Christ crucified is born the new humanity redeemed from sin. The man of the year 2000 needs

Christ's Heart to know God and to know himself; he needs it to build the civilization of love.

Therefore, dear brothers and sisters, I invite you to look with confidence to the Sacred Heart of Jesus and to repeat often, especially during this month of June: Most Sacred Heart of Jesus, I trust in you!

General audience of June 7, 1995

The scope of the recent brief visit of the Holy Father to Belgium was to beatify Father Damien de Veuster, missionary of the Congregation of the Sacred Hearts of Jesus and Mary, who gave his life serving the lepers on the island of Molokai in the archipelago of Hawaii. The pope devoted his talk to a review of his visit to Belgium and the beatification of Blessed Damien. One section of his talk was on the Sacred Heart.

June is the month dedicated to the Sacred Heart of Jesus. This was significantly underlined by the fact that the beatification of Father Damien took place in Brussels against the background of the Basilica of the Sacred Heart at Koekelberg. There, in spite of the rain, the beatification was followed with attentive recollection and saw pressing around the altar faithful coming from various cities and nations. One delegation came from the island of Molokai to receive the relic of their missionary and to take it back to their homeland. The Church in Belgium constructed the Basilica of the Sacred Heart after the end of the First World War, which had seen many victims.

Summary

This chapter contains nine excerpts from the catechesis of the general audiences, most of them on other topics. We note that there are certain ideas or themes that keep recurring. The pope repeatedly speaks of the piercing of Christ's side and Heart on Calvary. Rivers of living water, an image of the new life, flow from the pierced Heart of Christ. He also speaks of the varied symbolism of the blood and water that flowed from the pierced Heart of Christ. Devotion to Christ's Heart cannot be separated from devotion to the Eucharist. We are to learn from Jesus, who is meek and humble of Heart.

Chapter 19

Greetings to
Various Groups of People
Young People, the Sick, Newlyweds

After the general audience, usually held on Wednesdays, and after his Angelus message on Sundays and special feast days, the Holy Father frequently greeted various groups of pilgrims from various parts of the world who were present for the occasion. At the general audiences, this almost always included special greetings to young people, the sick, and newlyweds. He gave his greetings in various languages.

In some of these remarks the pope spoke of the Sacred Heart because the group had some particular connection with devotion to the Sacred Heart or because it was June, the month dedicated in a special way to the Heart of Jesus. These greetings were naturally very brief and even when the Holy Father spoke in a number of languages about the same topic, such as just before the Solemnity of the Sacred Heart, he tried to find different things to say about the topic so as not just to repeat the same thing in different languages.

Most of the greetings that referred to the Sacred Heart were given during June, the month of the Sacred Heart, but there are some from other times of the year when a group connected with the Sacred Heart was present.

This chapter on the pope's greetings to various groups of people will not attempt to give all the greetings that he gave, but will offer a sampling of these greetings.

At the general audience of June 15, 1983:
To the sick

And now my particularly affectionate greeting to the sick who, over-coming hardships and difficulties, have wished to be present at this audience and to unite themselves to all the other pilgrims to wit-ness their sincere love for the Church. In expressing my satisfaction for your act of faith and reverence, I urge you to turn your glance — especially in this month of June — to that Heart which has so loved and loves men and women: the Heart of Christ, salvation of those who trust in him. From this Heart it is possible to obtain comfort and relief from your own pain, strength and support for your own Calvary of sorrow, value and merit for your own suffering with se-cure spiritual benefit for yourselves and for the entire Church. To you and to those who lovingly assist you, I impart from the heart my Blessing.

At the general audience of November 16, 1983:
To Italian students

In a special way I wish to remember the great German mystic St. Gertrude (1256–1301) whose liturgical memorial occurs today and who is justly called "the theologian of the Sacred Heart." As a matter of fact it is important to know the personality and the spirituality of our saints in order to be able to imitate them in the life of grace and of witness and to be able to call upon them in moments of confusion and temptation. As St. Gertrude often rec-ommended, I exhort you also to always have a complete trusting confidence in Jesus as Redeemer and Friend, to be able to be tal-ented students and worthy of esteem, bringing joy to yourselves and to those you love.

At the general audience of June 20, 1990:
To young people, to the sick, and to newlyweds

The day after tomorrow is the Solemnity of the Sacred Heart of Jesus: a feast dear to the Christian people. I invite you young people to discover the riches that are hidden in the Heart of Jesus. Let your hearts open themselves to the school of the love of Christ and in this way learn to love in a way that is noble and ennobling.

And you too, dear sick people, who suffer in body and in spirit, turn your gaze to the Heart of Jesus and you will find peace, comfort, and hope. Suffering in fact is a school of love.

The Sacred Heart of Jesus also teaches you, newlyweds, to love and to support each other mutually all along the course of your family life, which was inaugurated with the sacrament of matrimony.

At the general audience of June 2, 1993:
To a group of Japanese Sisters, members of
the Definitorio of the Institute "Miyazaki Charitas"

The month dedicated to the Sacred Heart of Jesus has begun. It reminds us of his unbounded love for us. Because you bear the name itself of "charity," consider yourselves especially spurred on to pour out the love of Jesus among people, under the guidance of the Mother of Jesus.

At the general audience of June 2, 1993:
To a group of Czech pilgrims

The piety of Catholics dedicates the month of June to a special devotion to the Sacred Heart of Jesus. The love of the Father is manifested to us in the Heart of his Son Jesus. Let us entrust ourselves to him: Jesus, meek and humble of Heart, Jesus good and great in love, transform our hearts and teach us to love God and our neighbor with generosity.

At the general audience of June 9, 1993:
To a group of Japanese pilgrims of the "Don Bosco Group"

The month dedicated to the Sacred Heart of Jesus makes us recall the unbounded love of him who sacrificed himself for the good of men and women, and whose love consequently was completely "altruistic," as was the love of the Madonna for all of us. May this pilgrimage of yours be spiritually fruitful for you as St. John Bosco desired.

At the general audience of June 1, 1994:
To groups of the faithful

It is my pleasure to greet French-speaking people at the beginning of the month dedicated to the Sacred Heart. Call upon Christ to pour out his love on humanity and he will grant the gifts of reconciliation and of peace. May God bless you.

Dear English-speaking visitors and pilgrims: during the month of June, the Church turns with confidence to the Sacred Heart of Jesus, symbol of forgiveness and grace. It is time therefore for us all to pray with greater intensity for the needs of the Church and of the whole human family. May God's love be with you all.

At the beginning of a new month, dedicated in a special way to worship of the Sacred Heart of Jesus, I cordially greet you, dear brothers and sisters, German-speaking pilgrims. May the Lord by his presence strengthen you in faith. For this I impart to you from my heart the apostolic blessing.

I greet all people, families, and groups coming from different countries of Latin America and Spain. At the beginning of the month of June, dedicated to the Heart of Jesus, I impart to you with great affection my apostolic blessing.

I also cordially greet the groups from Poland on the first day of the month of June, dedicated in a special way to the Most Sacred Heart of Jesus. This month is very close to us just as is the month of May, the Marian month. May the Lord bless all present here, all diocesan, parochial, and tourist groups.

At the general audience of June 8, 1994:
To groups of the faithful

To the faithful coming from Poland: Next Friday we celebrate the Solemnity of the Most Sacred Heart of Jesus. The entire month of June is dedicated to this Heart in a special way. In Poland we have the tradition of celebrating "the devotion of June" [chanting the Litany of the Sacred Heart]. In the month of May we celebrate the devotion in honor of our Lady, whereas in June it is in honor of the Heart of Jesus. I cordially unite myself to you in this month by means of devotion to the Most Sacred Heart of Jesus, which in Poland has a long history. May Jesus Christ be praised.

Dear French-speaking pilgrims, just two days from the feast of the Sacred Heart, which is due in a special way to St. Margaret Mary Alacoque, I invite you to invoke fervently the merciful Christ, whose Heart is the eternal source of life, the foundation of our hope. May God bless you with his redemptive love.

Dear English-speaking brothers and sisters: on Friday, the Church will celebrate the Solemnity of the Sacred Heart of Jesus, to remind us that the love of God for us has been made present in the world through Jesus Christ. Modern men and women need to rediscover the depths of Christ's love, so clearly manifested on the cross, if they are to be healed in their need for interior integrity and harmony. Heart of Jesus, fill us with hope and love!

My cordial greetings of welcome also to you, dear sisters and brothers of German-speaking countries. Next Friday the Church celebrates the Solemnity of the Sacred Heart of Jesus. Whoever desires to know God must know Jesus and live in harmony with his Heart, and love God and neighbor just as he has done. With this desire, I impart my apostolic blessing to all.

Sacred Heart of Jesus, I trust in you. Dear brothers and sisters: with this fervent ejaculation in this month dedicated to the Heart of Jesus, I desire to greet all persons, families, and groups coming from different countries of Latin America and Spain, present at this meeting. I impart to you with great affection my apostolic blessing.

Dear Portuguese-speaking pilgrims: the man of the year 2000 needs the Heart of Jesus in order to know God and to know himself. People today have a great hunger for God, but they do not find the door to enter the inner sanctuary where God makes his dwelling place, which is precisely the human heart. The door by which to enter is the Heart of Christ opened by the soldier's lance. Dear sisters and brothers, may you find your own happiness and that of others in consecration ever renewed to the Divine Heart who loves and blesses you!

At the general audience of September 7, 1994

To many participants of the National Congress of the "Apostleship of Prayer" and to members of the "Youth Eucharistic Movement" who have come to Rome to celebrate respectively the 150th and the 50th anniversaries of their foundations: I learn with pleasure that these associations, competently animated by the Society of

Jesus, continue to grow and to labor, providing a fruitful spiritual service in all the dioceses of Italy. I wish to express to you my sincere appreciation for the effective and concrete contribution you offer to the diffusion on all levels of the great and consoling truth that every Christian by prayer and the offering of one's own activity can efficaciously collaborate in the redemptive work of Christ.

At the general audience of June 12, 1996

To a group of Czechs, pilgrims from Moravia: Christ will be the only King of my heart. Therefore I will shun the spirit of this world and live in the spirit of Jesus. I wish to labor with him, where — and as — it is possible for me. All this I desire to do moved by love.

This is the purpose of the consecration to the Heart of Jesus which we will renew on this feast which is very close. I ask for you the grace to carry it out fully.

I bless you from the heart together with all your dear ones in your homeland. May Jesus Christ be praised!

To a large pilgrimage from the Republic of Slovakia: With affection I welcome the Slovak pilgrims from Kosice and Bratislava, from Konska and Dolny Kubin.

Dear brothers and sisters, the day after tomorrow is the feast of the Sacred Heart of Jesus and the World Day for the sanctification of priests. The Lord Jesus, High Priest, for love has undergone death to give life to the world. And this life he continuously communicates to individuals in his Church by means of priests. Pray for your priests and for all priests of the world so that they may be truly "men of God," who with love pray and sacrifice themselves for the salvation of men and women. Carry this my charge with you from Rome to Slovakia.

To young people, to the sick, and to newlyweds: My cordial greeting goes now to young people, to the sick, and to newlyweds.

Dearly beloved, the feast of the Sacred Heart of Jesus and the memorial of the Immaculate Heart of Mary, which the Church prepares to celebrate in the next few days, reminds us of the need to respond to the redemptive love of Christ and invites us to entrust ourselves with confidence to the intercession of the Mother of the Lord.

You, dear young people, continue to devote yourselves with the enthusiasm that is proper to you to the construction of a civilization whose foundations are truth and love, peace and solidarity.

You, dear sick people, unite your sufferings to the infinite love of the Heart of Christ for the salvation of humanity.

You, dear newlyweds, know how to progress ever more on the way of love and mutual respect. To all of you my blessing.

At the general audience of June 23, 1999

To pilgrims from Poland: In Poland faith was nourished and greatly supported by devotion to the Sacred Heart and to the Blessed Virgin Mary. Veneration of the Divine Heart of Jesus had special prominence in this [1999] pilgrimage [to Poland]: in the background was the consecration of the human race to the Sacred Heart which my revered predecessor Leo XIII performed for the first time exactly one hundred years ago. Humanity needs to enter the new millennium with trust in God's merciful love. However, this will be possible only if we turn to Christ the Savior, the inexhaustible fountain of life and holiness.

To pilgrims from Slovakia: Pray for newly ordained priests and for all priests that they may be priests according to the Heart of Jesus.

Summary

This chapter gives samples of the greetings of the pope to various groups on ten different occasions. Each occasion may include several different language groups. Naturally the greetings are very brief. When speaking to several groups on the same occasion the pope tries to say something different to each group. The greetings selected here all refer in some way to the Sacred Heart. The Holy Father recommends joining the offering of prayers and sacrifices for the needs of the Church and the world as a particularly effective form of devotion to the Sacred Heart of Jesus.

Chapter 20

Civilization of Love

The expression "civilization of love" was coined by Pope Paul VI. He used it in his New Year's message to the cardinals in 1976. Pope John Paul II has made the expression his own and has used it on many occasions, some of them related to the Sacred Heart, but not all. One of the clearest explanations was given by the pope in a homily to the People of Nuoro, Sardinia, on October 19, 1985, when he said:

The civilization of love is born of God, because God is love, and in Christ this love, which is God, "appeared among us." God is a love that has revealed its infinite dimension in the unreserved gift of the Crucified, of the Son of God who sacrificed himself for us. Thus it is from the pierced Heart of Christ crucified that the civilization of love flows. In the sanctuary of that Heart, God bent down to men and women and gave them the gifts of his mercy, in turn making them capable of opening themselves in mercy and pardon to his own brothers and sisters.

For this reason, he who does not accept love, he who does not believe in love, does not believe in God. But at the same time, he who does not know God, he who does not believe in him, can neither believe in love nor know or desire the civilization of love.

In the letter the pope gave to the superior general of the Society of Jesus on October 5, 1986, he said:

This is the true meaning of the reparation demanded by the Heart of the Savior — on the ruins accumulated through hatred and violence can be built the civilization of love so greatly desired, the kingdom of the Heart of Christ.

Earlier, on June 1, 1980, in the pope's originally prepared message for the young people of Paris, the Holy Father had said:

Young people of France, it is more than ever the time to work hand-in-hand at the civilization of love, according to the expression dear to my great predecessor Paul VI. What a gigantic workyard! What a stirring task!

In the homily at a Mass celebrated in New Orleans on September 12, 1987, Pope John Paul II said:

May we not hope for what Pope Paul VI described as the "civilization of love" instead of "an eye for an eye and a tooth for a tooth," the attitude which ravages the face of the earth and scars the family of humankind? As I have said, this love, based on the forgiveness which Jesus described to Peter, does not mean that the objective demands of justice, which people legitimately seek, are thereby cancelled out. Sometimes those demands, however, are very complex.

Later in the same homily, the Holy Father quotes the United States bishops in their pastoral message on the American economy.

We write ... as heirs of the biblical prophets who summon us "to do justice, to love kindness, and to walk humbly with our God" (Mic. 6:8).... We speak as moral teachers, not economic technicians. We seek ... to lift up the human and ethical dimensions of economic life ... (4, 7). To do justice, yes — but also to love. This is at the heart of Christ's message. It is the only way to reach that "civilization of love" that ensures peace for ourselves and for the world.

In a series of reflections on the gifts of the Holy Spirit, the pope on May 28, 1989, spoke of the gift of piety.

Such a gift is at the root of that new human community which is based on the civilization of love.

To the Priests of the Sacred Heart in a talk to their twentieth ordinary General Chapter on May 30, 1997, the pope said:

Father Dehon's charism is a fruitful gift for building the civilization of love, since the soul of the new evangelization is the witness of divine charity: "God so loved the world that he gave his only Son" (John 3:16).

Finally, speaking to more than seven thousand members of the Italian National Confederation of Mercy and of the "Fratres" Blood Donor Groups on June 14, 1986, the pope said of the civilization of love but again with no mention of the Sacred Heart:

Be promoters and builders of the civilization of love, be tireless witnesses to the culture of charity, whose power lifts, aids, and transfigures men and women, bringing them to participate in the fullness of Redemption.

There has been no attempt in this chapter to cite all the instances where Pope John Paul II has spoken of a civilization of love, not even when he referred it to the Sacred Heart, but merely to call attention to this important concept of the civilization of love.

Summary

The concept of a civilization of love is a fruitful topic for reflection in itself and in its relation to the Sacred Heart. One might also be aware of this concept while reading other parts of this book and what the pope has said on other occasions, for frequently the concept of a civilization of love is mentioned almost in passing.

Part Four

Saints and Blesseds of the Sacred Heart

Chapter 21

St. John Eudes

**Letter to Father Pierre Drouin, superior general of
the Congregation of Jesus and Mary, February 27, 1993**

This letter was written for the 350th anniversary of the founding of the
Congregation of Jesus and Mary, popularly known as Eudists after their
founder, St. John Eudes.

In 1643, St. John Eudes, together with a group of priests, founded
the Congregation of Jesus and Mary in Caen, to establish seminaries. According to his own words, it was the "day on which the Son
of God was made man and the Holy Virgin was made the Mother
of God" (*Complete Works*, XII, 112). On the occasion of the congregation's celebration of the 350th anniversary of its foundation, I
am happy to join in the thanksgiving and prayer of hope of all the
Eudists and their associates.

Priests, candidates to the priesthood, and lay associates of your
society of apostolic life, you gratefully recall the holy figure of him
who was an untiring missionary, perpetually at pains to train good
evangelizers. St. John Eudes had a leading role in the religious life
of France in the eighteenth century; he personally contributed to
the deep, spiritual movement which was later called the French
school, courageously responding to the needs and appeals of his
contemporaries through his preaching, his writing, and his many
initiatives in the fields of education and charity.

Your founder left you a spiritual inheritance of great value which
continues to inspire your congregation today. One example is the

Constitutions, based on the *Regula Domini Jesu* of John Eudes, which describe the "foundations" of the Eudists' life as divine grace, to be communicated to others, the divine will, to be served, the cross of Jesus, so that they may walk in the footsteps of the Lord, and a deep love for Jesus and Mary, to whom the congregation belongs and who are their family (no. 3).

You do well today to study once again the essential ideas of your founder. He unceasingly contemplated Christ, the only-begotten Son of God, sacrificed for the salvation of the world. He was so immersed in the message of the word of God that he formulated the Rule which he proposed to his brothers using the very words of Sacred Scripture. He harmoniously combined the depth of theological reflection, taken from St. Paul and St. John, with the spiritual ardor of a life of prayer, rich in love. Was he not perhaps drawing a self-portrait when he wrote: "We must be inspired by the spirit of Jesus, live his life, walk in his path, be clothed with his sentiments and ways, and carry out our every action according to the directions and intentions with which he carried out his" (*Royaume de Jesus,* II, 2)? He understood and was able to show the fruitfulness of devotion to the Sacred Heart of Jesus, which he himself helped to spread.

He never separated his contemplation of Jesus from that of his Mother: "Oh, Jesus, only-begotten Son of God, only-begotten Son of Mary, I contemplate you and I adore you, living and reigning in your Blessed Mother, and he who is all and does all in her" (*Royaume de Jesus,* V, 9). Furthermore, at the time of his glorification, he was recognized as "Father, Doctor, and Apostle of devotion to the Sacred Hearts," so great was his love for the Hearts of Jesus and Mary.

This anniversary, celebrated three and a half centuries after the often tormented history of your congregation, is an invitation to all Eudists to turn to their founder and his message as the living sources of their present vocation. Reviving the inspiration which gives life to the institute, and the constantly renewed experience of successive generations of its members, are additional graces which, if received, can enlighten the mission to work together enthusiastically in response to the new requirements of our time.

"The Eudists, laborers for evangelization, work for the renewal of the faith in the People of God" (*Constitutions,* 2). This mission assumes different forms depending on the time and place; however, for his sons the total commitment of St. John Eudes remains an example and guide for those who consecrate themselves to preaching the Good News of salvation in order to show their brothers and sisters the light of the love of Jesus and Mary. They especially cooperate "in training lay people for various apostolic tasks" (*Constitutions,* 33).

In a very special way I would like to encourage the Eudists to continue today the work which inspired their foundation: the formation of candidates to the priesthood and the ongoing formation of priests. Conditions have changed, but the basic idea remains the same. St. John Eudes had a very noble concept of the priesthood. Thus he wrote to his brothers: "The Son of God joins you to him in the most noble perfection and in the most divine actions, making you share in his function as mediator between God and men..." (*Memorial de la vie ecclesiastique,* I). It is necessary to work so that this ministry of mediation may continue with enlightened generosity. I have been given the occasion to address this letter to you a year after the publication of the exhortation *Pastores dabo vobis,* which followed on the Synod of Bishops on the formation of priests in recent circumstances. I know that the Church can count on the sons of St. John Eudes to be among the first to put these essential guidelines into practice. May they continue to be enthusiastic and exacting, both with themselves and those to whose formation they contribute, so that the Lord may give Christian communities the workers for the harvests that they themselves asked for in prayer.

St. John Eudes was also the founder or the inspiration of a whole family of institutes faithful to his spirituality, to his apostolic dynamism, and to the impulse he gave to charitable activity. It is right that the men and women who share a common heritage should unite in the joy and hope of their Eudist brothers.

Addressing the members of the Congregation of Jesus and Mary, I conclude this message by recalling an exhortation of St. John Eudes himself: "Give yourselves to Jesus in order to enter into the immensity of his great Heart, which contains the Heart of his holy Mother and of all the saints, thus to love ourselves in this abyss of love, charity, mercy, humility, purity, patience, submission, and holiness" (*Coeur admirable*, III, 2).

My wish for the superiors, priests and lay associates of the congregation, is that they may experience the happiness of an authentic interior renewal on the occasion of the celebrations of this year's anniversary. To them I express the Church's confidence and gratitude for the service they render through evangelization, especially in the formation of priests in three continents: Europe, America, and Africa. While invoking with them St. John Eudes, and imploring the Mother of the Lord and her admirable Heart, I entrust them and their ministry to Christ the High Priest. With great affection I impart my apostolic blessing to them.

Summary

Pope John Paul II writes a short letter recalling the most important facts of the life and words of St. John Eudes, as "Father, Doctor, and Apostle of devotion to the Sacred Hearts" of Jesus and Mary. The pope concludes his letter by quoting the words of St. John Eudes: "Give yourselves to Jesus in order to enter into the immensity of his great Heart, which contains the Heart of his holy Mother and of all the saints."

Chapter 22

St. Margaret Mary Alacoque

Letter to Bishop Raymond Seguy, Bishop of Autun, Chalon, and Macon, June 22, 1990

This letter on the Sacred Heart was written on the occasion of the third centenary of the death of St. Margaret Mary.

The third centenary of the death of St. Margaret Mary, canonized by my predecessor Benedict XV in 1920, recalls the memory of one who, from 1673 to 1675, was favored with appearances of the Lord Jesus and was entrusted with a message whose widespread influence in the Church has been tremendous. It was during the Octave of Corpus Christi in 1675, in the Grand Century when so many writers and artists penetrated the riches of the human soul, that the young Visitandine of Paray-le-Monial heard these bewildering words: "Behold this Heart which has so loved human beings and which has spared itself nothing even to exhausting and spending itself to give witness to this love; and in recompense for the most part I have received only ingratitude."

When I was on pilgrimage in 1986 to the tomb of Margaret Mary, I asked, in the spirit of what has been handed down in the Church, that veneration of the Sacred Heart be faithfully restored. For it is in the Heart of Christ that the human heart learns to know the true and unique meaning of its life and destiny; it is in the Heart of Christ that the human heart receives its capacity to love.

St. Margaret Mary learned the grace of loving by means of the cross. In it she delivers to us a message that is ever relevant. It is necessary, she says, "to make ourselves living copies of our crucified Spouse, by expressing him in ourselves in all our actions" (letter of January 5, 1689). She invites us to contemplate the Heart of Christ, that is, to recognize in the humanity of the Word incarnate the infinite riches of his love for the Father and for all human beings. It is the love of Christ which makes a person worthy of being loved. Created in the image and likeness of God, the human person has received a heart eager for love and capable of loving. The love of the Redeemer, which heals it from the wound of sin, elevates it to its filial condition. With St. Margaret Mary, united to the Savior also in his suffering offered for love, we shall ask for the grace of knowing the infinite value of every person.

To give to veneration of the Sacred Heart the place due to it in the Church, it is necessary to take up again the exhortation of St. Paul: "Have within you the sentiments which were in Christ Jesus" (Phil. 2:5). All the Gospel accounts should be reread from this perspective: each verse, meditated with love, will reveal an aspect of the mystery hidden for centuries and now revealed to our eyes (Col. 1:26). The only Son of God, in becoming incarnate, takes a human heart. Through the years he passed in the midst of men, "gentle and humble of heart" (Matt. 11:29), he revealed the riches of his interior life by each of his gestures, his looks, his words, his silences. In Christ Jesus is fulfilled the fullness of the commandment of the Old Testament: "You shall love the Lord with all your heart" (Deut. 6:4). In fact, only the Heart of Christ has loved the Father with an undivided love.

And behold we are called to share in this love and to receive through the Holy Spirit this extraordinary capacity to love. After their encounter with the Risen One on the road to Emmaus, the disciples were filled with amazement: "Were not our hearts burning inside us as he talked to us on the road and explained the Scriptures to us?" (Luke 24:32). Yes, the human heart is inflamed by contact with the Heart of Christ, for it discovers in this love for the Father that the risen Lord has accomplished "all that the prophets have announced" (Luke 24:25).

The humanity of the Lord Jesus dead and risen reveals itself to us through contemplation of his Heart. Nourished by meditation on the Word of God, prayer of adoration places us in the closest, most intimate relationship with this "Heart that has so loved human beings." Understood in this way, devotion to the Sacred Heart fosters active participation of the faithful at times of grace in the Eucharist and the sacrament of penance; intimately bound to the humanity of Christ given for the salvation of the world, the faithful thus derive the desire to be united to all who suffer and the courage to be witnesses of the Good News.

I encourage pastors, religious communities, and all animators of pilgrimages to Paray-le-Monial to contribute to the diffusion of the message received by St. Margaret Mary. And to you, pastor of the Church of Autun, and to all who will allow themselves to be moved by this teaching, I hope you will discover in the Heart of Christ the force of love, the sources of grace, the real presence of the Lord in his Church by the gift daily renewed of his Body and Blood. To each of you, I willingly grant my apostolic blessing.

Summary

On the feast of the Sacred Heart in 1990, the pope sent a letter to the bishop of the diocese in which Paray-le-Monial is located to commemorate the third centenary of the death of St. Margaret Mary. As he had done during his visit to Paray-le-Monial in 1986, the pope once again encourages devotion to the Sacred Heart in the spirit of St. Margaret Mary Alacoque. The Holy Father has often referred to her in his other talks, for example, when speaking of her spiritual director, St. Claude La Colombière.

Chapter 23

Canonization of
St. Claude La Colombière

Homily at the Mass of the canonization of
Blessed Claude La Colombière, May 31, 1992

Claude La Colombière was a seventeenth-century French Jesuit priest who is especially known for being the spiritual director of St. Margaret Mary Alacoque and for spreading devotion to the Sacred Heart of Jesus. The homily was given in Italian and French.

"So that your love for me may live in them" (John 17:26).

Christ prays in the Upper Room. He prays on the evening in which he instituted the Eucharist. He prays for the Apostles and for all those who will believe through their word (John 17:20) down the generations and centuries. He is asking the Father that all "may be one," as the Father is in the Son and the Son is in the Father: "That they may be one in us" (John 17:21).

To be one: the unity of divinity and the unity of communication of the persons — the unity of the Father in the Son and of the Son with the Father in the Holy Spirit. Unity through love.

Christ prays for love: "So that your love for me may live in them" (John 17:26). Christ reveals the secret of his Heart. Precisely this human Heart of God's Son is an ineffable sanctuary which contains all the treasures of love: it is a Heart "overflowing with goodness and love" (Litany of the Sacred Heart).

The prayer offered by Christ in the Upper Room continues in the Church: from century to century, from generation to generation, it is a perennial "fountain of life and holiness" (Litany of the Sacred Heart). But there are particular moments in history, specially chosen places and persons who discover and reveal anew this perennial and undying truth about love.

The man whom the church today proclaims a saint — Blessed Claude La Colombière — is certainly one of these persons.

In France the seventeenth century has been called "the great century of souls." It was a time of high human culture, of the development of the institutions of that prestigious European nation. But it was also a time of cruel conflict and human poverty. The clergy and religious orders were often decadent; as a result the people remained far from the light of faith, from the benefits of the spiritual life and of ecclesial communion. However, after the Council of Trent, after founders such as Francis de Sales, Berulle, and Vincent de Paul, an intense spiritual movement enlivened the Church in France. A great work of reform took place: the priestly ministry was renewed, notably through the establishment of seminaries; religious returned to the authenticity of their vocation, new foundations came into being; evangelization of the countryside took on new vitality through parish missions; a flowering of mysticism was joined to theological reflection.

In the middle of this century lived Claude La Colombière, who entered the Society of Jesus at a young age. He exercised his mission in Paris and in several provinces; he had a notable influence because of his intellectual effort, and even more, because of the dynamism of the Christian life which he knew how to communicate. A true companion of St. Ignatius, Claude learned to master his strong sensitivity. He humbly maintained a sense of "his wretchedness" so as to rely only on his hope in God and his trust in grace. He resolutely took the way of holiness. He adhered with all his being to the Constitutions and Rules of the Society, rejecting all tepidness. Fidelity and obedience were expressed, before God, by the "desire ... for trust, love, resignation, and perfect sacrifice" (Retraite, no. 28).

Father Claude forged his spirituality in the school of the Exercises. We still have his impressive journal. He dedicated himself first of all to "meditating a great deal on the life of Jesus Christ, who is a model for our own life" (ibid., no. 33). Contemplating Christ allowed him to live in familiarity with him so as to belong to him totally: "I see that I absolutely must belong to him" (ibid., no. 71). And if Claude dared to aim for this total fidelity, it was in virtue of his acute awareness of the power of grace which transformed him. He attained the perfect freedom of one who gives himself unreservedly to the will of God: "I have a free heart," he said (ibid., no. 12). Trials or sacrifices he accepted, "thinking that God only expects these things of us out of friendship" (ibid., no. 38). His whole taste for friendship led him to respond to God's friendship with a loving zeal renewed each day.

Father La Colombière was active in the apostolate with the conviction that he was the instrument of God's work: "To do much for God, one must belong entirely to him" (ibid., no. 37). Prayer, he also said, is "the only way ... to have God united to us so that we may do something for his glory" (ibid. no. 52). In the apostolate fruits and success come less from personal abilities than from fidelity to the divine will and openness to his action.

This pure-hearted and free religious was prepared to understand and to preach the message that the Heart of Jesus was entrusting to Sr. Margaret Mary Alacoque at the same time. Paray-le-Monial, in our eyes, would be the most fruitful stage in Claude La Colombière's short journey. He came to this town, long rich for its tradition of religious life, to have a providential meeting with the humble Visitandine engaged in constant dialogue with her "divine Master," who promised her "the delights of [his] pure love." He found her to be a religious who ardently desired the "all-pure cross" (Memoire, no. 49) and who offered her penance and sorrows without hesitation.

Father La Colombière, with highly reliable discernment, straight-away authenticated the mystical experience of this "beloved dis-ciple [of the] Sacred Heart" (ibid., no. 4), with whom he had a beautiful spiritual kinship. He received from her the message which would have great repercussions: "Behold the Heart which has so loved men that it spared nothing to exhaust and consume itself in testimony of its love" (Retraite, no. 135). The Lord asked that a feast be established to honor his Heart and that a "reparation of honor" be made to him in Eucharistic communion. Margaret Mary passed on to "the faithful servant and perfect friend," whom she recog-nized in Father La Colombière, the mission of "establishing this devotion and of giving this pleasure to my Divine Heart" (ibid.). Claude, in the years left to him, interiorized these "infinite riches." His spiritual life then developed in the perspective of the "repara-tion" and "infinite mercy" so underscored at Paray. He gave himself completely to the Sacred Heart "ever burning with love." Even in trials he practiced forgetfulness of self in order to attain purity of love and to raise the world to God. Sensing his own weakness, he gave himself over to the power of grace: "Accomplish your will in me, Lord.... It belongs to you to do everything, Divine Heart of Jesus Christ" (ibid., Offrande, no. 152).

The past three centuries allow us to evaluate the importance of the message which was entrusted to Claude La Colombière. In a period of contrasts between the fervor of some and the indifference or impiety of many, here is a devotion centered on the humanity of Christ, on his presence, on his love of mercy, and on forgiveness. The call to "reparation," characteristic of Paray-le-Monial, can be variously understood, but essentially it is a matter of sinners, which all human beings are, returning to the Lord, touched by his love, and offering a more intense fidelity in the future, a life aflame with charity. If there is solidarity in sin, there is also solidarity in salvation. The offering of each is made for the good of all. Following the example of Claude La Colombière, the faithful understand that such a spiritual attitude can only be the action of Christ in them, shown through Eucharistic communion: to receive in their hearts the Heart of Christ and to be united to the sacrifice which he alone can offer worthily to the Father.

Devotion to the Heart of Christ would be a source of balance and spiritual strengthening for Christian communities so often faced with increasing unbelief over the coming centuries: an impersonal conception of God will spread; individuals, moving away from a personal encounter with Christ and the sources of grace, will want to be the sole masters of their history and to become a law unto themselves, to the point of being ruthless in pursuing their own ambitions. The message of Paray, accessible to the humble as well as to the great of this world, answers such aberrations by clarifying the relationship of the human person with God and with the world in the light which comes from the Heart of God: in conformity with the Church's Tradition, it turns his gaze toward the cross of the world's Redeemer, toward "him whom they have pierced" (John 19:37).

We give thanks, again today, for the message entrusted to the saints of Paray, which has never ceased to extend its radiance. At the beginning of our century Pope Leo XIII hailed "in the Sacred Heart of Jesus a symbol and clear image of Jesus Christ's infinite love, a love which impels us to love one another" (encyclical *Annum Sacrum,* 1900). Pius XI and Pius XII encouraged this devotion and saw in it a spiritual answer to the difficulties which the faith and the Church were facing.

Certainly, forms of expression and sensitivities develop, but the essential element remains. When one has discovered in Eucharistic adoration and meditation the Heart of Jesus "ever burning with love for human beings" (Retraite, no. 150), how could one let oneself be seduced by forms of meditation which turn in on the self without welcoming the presence of the Lord? How could one be attracted by the proliferation of conceptions of the sacred which only mask a tragic spiritual emptiness?

For evangelization today the Heart of Christ must be recognized as the heart of the Church: it is he who calls us to conversion, to reconciliation. It is he who leads pure hearts and those hungering for justice along the way of the Beatitudes. It is he who achieves the warm communion of the members of the one Body. It is he who enables us to adhere to the Good News and to accept the promise of eternal life. It is he who sends us out on mission. The heart-to-heart with Jesus broadens the human heart on a global scale.

May the canonization of Claude La Colombière be for the whole church an appeal to live the consecration to the Heart of Christ, a consecration which is a self-giving that allows the charity of Christ to inspire us, pardon us and lead us in his ardent desire to open the ways of truth and life to all our brothers and sisters!

"Righteous Father, the world also does not know you, but I know you, and they know that you sent me" (John 17:25). They: the saints — the Church in ever new periods of her history. They: Claude La Colombière — Margaret Mary Alacoque. The Church.

During the Easter season the Church relives the theophanies of her Redeemer and Lord — the Good Shepherd who "lays down his life for the sheep" (John 10:15).

And the Church looks to heaven together with Stephen the deacon, the first martyr stoned to death in Jerusalem. The Church looks to heaven as Stephen did at the moment of his death as a martyr. "Behold, I see the heavens opened and the Son of Man standing at the right hand of God.... Lord Jesus, receive my spirit" (Acts 7:56–59). Amen.

Talk, given in French, to a special audience after the canonization, for pilgrims who came to Rome from the Diocese of Autun, Chalon, and Macon, May 31, 1992

After the canonization of Claude La Colombière, I am pleased to meet with you for a moment, pilgrims from the Diocese of Autun, Chalon, and Macon, led by Bishop Raymond Seguy. You have come to share the joy of the whole Church in seeing enrolled in the list of the saints this son of your land, this great witness of the spiritual history of your country.

In welcoming you, the precious memories of my pilgrimage to Paray-le-Monial come to life again. I am pleased to greet you as representatives of this city of long monastic and religious tradition, ever vibrant and constantly renewed, and in particular honored by the saintly Visitandine Margaret Mary and the saintly Jesuit Claude.

In the seventeenth century, the choice of the Lord, in a way, caused a new source to arise in your city, a source of merciful and infinitely generous love from which generations of pilgrims have come. The fecundity of grace which is attached to the worship of the Sacred Heart is manifested particularly by the developments which for several years pilgrimages to Paray have recognized. Along with the diocese, various communities have contributed to sharing with many the riches of the message confided to the saints of your city.

I rejoice to know that Paray nourishes the spirituality of many priests and religious and inspires the early formation of a number of candidates for the priesthood. The meetings which gather notably the young and families are a true motive for hope for the vitality of the Church in your country, without overlooking the participation of pilgrims from other nations. In this way you have the care to give a large part to sacred art, which it is good to foster, so that we at the present time can better express the praise of God and celebrate the treasures of his love.

To all those who work in the daily pastoral life and in arranging for the pilgrimages and meetings, I offer my encouragement: I think especially of the monastic communities, of the priests of the diocese, of the Jesuit Fathers, of the Community of Emmanuel, of the faithful of the city and of Saone-et-Loire, as well as all who are united to them with a like fervor. May St. Claude La Colombière and St. Margaret Mary sustain you with their intercession and obtain from the Lord to render ever more radiant the spiritual fire that he has desired to make of Paray-le-Monial.

In the joy of this feast I readily call down upon you the blessing of God.

Talk to a special audience for those who came to Rome from various countries for the canonization of Claude La Colombière, June 1, 1992

Among those present were Father Peter-Hans Kolvenbach, superior general of the Society of Jesus, and Father Giuseppe Pittau, rector of the Gregorian University. The talk was given in Italian, French, Spanish, and English.

[Italian] I am happy to welcome you to this special audience after yesterday's solemn celebration in which I had the joy of enrolling Blessed Claude La Colombière in the list of saints. I address my affectionate greeting to all of you present, with a particular thought for the bishops accompanying you and for the priests of the Society of Jesus who have seen one of their fellow religious raised to the glory of the altars.

The decisive event which marked the life and spirituality of St. Claude La Colombière was certainly the meeting with Sister Margaret Mary Alacoque, which took place in the Visitation Monastery in Paray-le-Monial in February 1675. On the occasion of a meditation which he gave the community, an interior voice suggested to the religious to turn to him in confidence: "This is the one I am sending you." In fact, from her first confession, Father Claude was aware of the authenticity of the mystical experience of the young Visitandine Sister and Margaret Mary knew she was seeing the fulfillment of the vision of the flaming Heart of Jesus with two other hearts which became lost in the Divine Heart: hers and that of the spiritual director opportunely who had been sent to her.

In her autobiography the great mystic then fully described the vision she had on June 15, 1675, in which Jesus, showing her his Heart, said to her: "Behold the Heart which has so loved men and women that it spared nothing to exhaust and consume itself in testimony of its love, and in place of gratitude receives ingratitude from the majority of them. . . . " For this reason Jesus himself asked that the first Friday after the octave of Corpus Christi be dedicated especially to honoring his Heart with participation in the Eucharist and with special prayers of reparation for the offenses committed against the sacrament of love.

Not knowing how to do everything that was expected of her, Sister Margaret Mary hesitatingly asked Jesus for some direction; this is what she wrote in her autobiography: "He told me to turn to his servant whom he had sent me to fulfill this plan." Father Claude accepted the mission and thus became a fervent apostle of devotion to the Sacred Heart and of commitment to reparation.

As you know, Father Claude's stay in Paray-le-Monial was brief; however, he had perfectly understood that against the coldness of Jansenism and the religious indifference of many Christians, and even of consecrated persons, it was necessary to preach and help people feel deeply the true motive behind creation and redemption: Love. Consequently he continued to be the tireless herald of that message for the rest of his life.

Today too St. Claude La Colombière, that master of enlightened spirituality, teaches us that Jesus Christ alone leads us to the true God, that love alone — which the Bible symbolizes as the Heart, the expression of Jesus' whole Person and mission — enables us to penetrate the mysteries of God, our Creator, Redeemer, and Rewarder.

In fact, in the Heart of Jesus God shows that he wants to be understood in his absolute desire to love, forgive, and save; in the Heart of Jesus, God teaches that the Church, in its ministry and teaching, must always be loving and sensitive, never aggressive or oppressive, although it must always condemn evil and correct error; in the Heart of Jesus God has us understand that it is necessary to share in his work of salvation through the "apostolate of prayer" and "commitment to reparation."

Justly, therefore, the movement of the "Apostleship of Prayer" has these three ideals and goals: the proclamation of and witness to the infinite treasures of the Heart of Jesus, who wants only to love his creatures and be loved; the constant sense of Jesus' true presence in the Eucharist, maintaining a deep, lively Eucharistic devotion through Mass, Communion, and adoration of the Blessed Sacrament; the commitment to reparation — including sacrifice and suffering, which Jesus himself expressed a desire for in his message to Margaret Mary. Thus St. Claude La Colombière once wrote to a person he was directing: "I do not recognize devotion unless there is mortification" (*Letters,* no. 74).

Conversion, salvation, and the sanctification of souls is the true content of the devotion to the Heart of Jesus and of the undying message of St. Claude La Colombière.

[French] With pleasure I greet all the French-speaking pilgrims present; I would especially like to address the superiors and fathers of the Society of Jesus. With you I give thanks for the canonization of your companion, Claude La Colombière. You recognize in him a faithful son of St. Ignatius, a model and an intercessor for the Jesuits of today. His writings, which eloquently testify to his spiritual life, reveal his profound experience of the Exercises. He achieved an unlimited assent to the kingdom of God; he gave his consent to the person of Christ. The sorrow caused him due to sin was equal to nothing but his unshakeable trust in the merciful forgiveness. In the image of the Son, he conformed his will to that of the Father, which he unceasingly translated into prayer and preaching: "Just as I cannot live without you, make me never live but for you" (Sermon 56). May the intercession of St. Claude sustain you in your very diverse ministries on all continents, such as spiritual direction, preaching, education, research, theological research and instruction, the many forms of apostolate entrusted to you, and the mission *ad gentes!*

Naturally, the canonization of Claude La Colombière leads me to emphasize the "most delightful task" [*munus suavissimum*] which he himself received from the Lord, to spread and preach the mystery of his Sacred Heart. It is the whole Society which continues to have this charge, as I myself had the joy of confirming for you at Paray-le-Monial near the tomb of St. Claude. There is a genuine kinship between Ignatian spirituality and that of the Sacred Heart. Do not cease to show your brothers and sisters that "near the Heart of Christ the human heart learns to recognize the genuine, unique meaning of its life and destiny,... and to have a filial love for God and love of neighbor" (letter to Father Kolvenbach, October 5, 1986).

[Spanish] I am pleased now to greet the Spanish-speaking pilgrims, present for the solemn canonization of Blessed Claude La Colombière, priest of the Society of Jesus. The Church wants to present him as an apostle of devotion to the Sacred Heart of Jesus. This devotion was spread beginning with Father La Colombière's meeting with St. Margaret Mary Alacoque in Paray-le-Monial. In the Sacred Heart is represented the infinite, merciful love which God poured out on the world through his divine Son. May the new saint help all of us to be apostles of this devotion and to witness the love of Christ for the human family.

Commending you to his intercession, I impart to you and to your families my apostolic blessing.

[English] To the English-speaking pilgrims who have come for the canonization of Claude La Colombière I extend a cordial welcome: I invite you to learn from the life and teaching of the new saint the value of personal and intense fellowship with our Lord Jesus Christ, the supreme object and revelation of the Father's eternal love. In the Heart of Jesus is revealed, in fact, all the richness of God's plan to lead humankind to full maturity and full happiness in the vision of his glory and in communion with the Blessed Trinity. Holiness, piety, and apostolic commitment in the Church are all essentially related to the strength of our faith in the Redeemer and our imitation of his "compassion on the multitudes" (Matt. 9:36). Entrusting you and your families to the intercession of St. Claude La Colombière, I invoke upon you the gifts of peace and joy in the Holy Spirit.

[Italian] I now affectionally impart my apostolic blessing to everyone.

Summary

The key figure in God's providence for promoting the popular devotion to the Sacred Heart we have known today was certainly St. Margaret Mary Alacoque. But next to her was her spiritual director, St. Claude La Colombière, who is now recognized for the unique role he played both in the life of St. Margaret Mary and in promoting devotion to the Heart of Christ.

Chapter 24

Sister Faustina Kowalska and Divine Mercy

Helen Kowalska was born on August 25, 1905, in Glogwiec, Poland, and entered the Congregation of the Sisters of Our Lady of Mercy in 1925, taking the name of Sister Maria Faustina. She lived for thirteen years in various houses of the congregation, especially in Krakow and Plock (Poland) and Vilnius (Lithuania), and died in Krakow on October 5, 1938.

Sister Faustina received unusual graces from God (visions, apparitions, hidden stigmata, and other gifts). She is best known for promoting devotion to Divine Mercy expressed particularly through veneration of the image of the Merciful Jesus, painted at her direction and bearing the inscription, "Jesus, I trust you."

Devotion to Divine Mercy is sometimes contrasted to devotion to the Sacred Heart, but for Sister Faustina there was no conflict or contrast. She had great devotion to the Sacred Heart, as seen in her autobiographical Diary. Pope John Paul II expressed the relationship between Divine Mercy and the Sacred Heart when he wrote in his encyclical *Dives in misericordia* (1980): "The Church seems in a particular way to profess the mercy of God and to venerate it when she directs herself to the Heart of Christ. In fact, it is precisely this drawing close to Christ in the mystery of his Heart which enables us to dwell on this point... of the revelation of the merciful love of the Father" (no. 13).

On November 22, 1981, early in his pontificate, Pope John Paul II had visited the Sanctuary of Merciful Love at Collevalenza, but in his talks there he did not speak of the Sacred Heart but only of Merciful Love.

In a message before the Regina Coeli on April 26, 1992, the pope spoke of Divine Mercy but did not mention the Sacred Heart, whereas two years later on April 10, 1994, he also mentioned the Sacred Heart. Both of these messages were delivered on the second Sunday of Easter. On April 10, 1994, the pope said: "The peace brought by the Risen One is the triumph of Divine Mercy." He concluded with a short prayer to the Blessed Virgin before praying the Regina Coeli: "O Mary, Mother of Mercy! You know the Heart of your divine Son better than anyone. Instill in us the filial trust in Jesus practiced by the saints, the trust that animated Blessed Faustina Kowalska, the great apostle of Divine Mercy in our time."

Pope John Paul II had introduced the cause of the beatification and canonization of Sister Faustina when he was still cardinal archbishop of Krakow. She was beatified by him on April 18, 1993, and canonized on April 30, 2000, both days being the second Sunday of Easter and Divine Mercy Sunday.

On April 27, 1995, also Divine Mercy Sunday, the Holy Father visited the Church of the Holy Spirit "in Sassia" to bless the image of the Merciful Jesus, a copy of the one which had been painted according to the directions of Sister Faustina, and to dedicate the Center of Spirituality of Divine Mercy in the Church of the Holy Spirit. The pope spoke of Divine Mercy and Blessed Faustina but did not mention the Sacred Heart.

Some saw this visit of the Holy Father to the Church of the Holy Spirit as referred to by Sister Faustina in her Diary when she described a vision she had on May 23, 1937: "The solemn celebration of the feast of Mercy took place in Rome in a beautiful church a few steps from St. Peter's when the Holy Father celebrated this festival with all the clergy." The Church of the Holy Spirit is on Borgo Santo Spirito very close to St. Peter's.

By a decree of the Congregation of Divine Worship and the Discipline of the Sacraments, dated January 23, 1995, Poland was granted permission to add "of Divine Mercy" to the designation of the second Sunday of Easter. On May 5, 2000, this was extended to the entire Church. The decree read: The Supreme Pontiff John Paul II has graciously determined that in the Roman Missal, after the title "Second Sunday of Easter," there shall henceforth be added the appellation "(or Divine Mercy Sunday)," and has prescribed that the texts assigned for that day in the same Missal and the Liturgy of the Hours of the Roman Rite are always to be used for the liturgical celebration of this Sunday.

During his sixth visit to Poland in 1997, the Holy Father on Saturday evening, June 7, visited the Shrine of Divine Mercy, located in the former convent chapel of the Sisters of the Blessed Virgin Mary at Krakow, and he prayed at the tomb of Blessed Faustina. In his address he spoke of Divine Mercy and Blessed Faustina and also referred to the Sacred Heart of Jesus: Anyone can come here, he said, look at this picture of the merciful Jesus, his Heart radiating grace, and hear in the depths of his own soul what Blessed Faustina heard: "Fear nothing. I am with you always" (Diary, q. II). And if this person responds with a sincere heart: "Jesus, I trust in you," he will find comfort in all his anxieties and fears.

There were four other persons beatified with Sister Faustina on April 18, 1993, and in the homily there was no mention of the Sacred Heart. But in the homily during the Mass of the Canonization of Blessed Faustina on April 30, 2000, the pope did speak of the Sacred Heart and explained the symbolism of the image of Divine Mercy.

Homily on the canonization of Sister Maria Faustina Kowalska, April 30, 2000

"Give thanks to the Lord for he is good; his steadfast love endures for ever" (Ps. 118:1).

So the Church sings on the octave of Easter, as if receiving from Christ's lips these words of the psalm; from the lips of the risen Christ, who bears the great message of Divine Mercy and entrusts its ministry to the apostles in the Upper Room: "Peace be with you. As the Father has sent me, even so I send you.... Receive the Holy

Spirit. If you forgive the sins of any, they are forgiven; if you retain the sins of any, they are retained" (John 20:21–23).

Before speaking these words, Jesus shows his hands and his side. He points, that is, to the wounds of his passion, especially the wound in his Heart, the source from which flows the great wave of mercy poured out on humanity. From that Heart Sister Faustina Kowalska, the Blessed whom from now on we will call a saint, will see two rays of light shining from that Heart and illuminating the world: "The two rays," Jesus himself explained to her one day, "represent blood and water" (Diary, p. 132).

Blood and water! We immediately think of the testimony given by the Evangelist John, who, when a soldier on Calvary pierced Christ's side with his spear, sees blood and water flowing from it (John 19:34). Moreover, if the blood recalls the sacrifice of the cross and the gift of the Eucharist, the water, in Johannine symbolism, represents not only baptism but also the gift of the Holy Spirit (John 3:5; 4:14; 7:37–39).

Divine Mercy reaches human beings through the Heart of Christ crucified: "My daughter, say that I am love and mercy personified," Jesus will ask Sister Faustina (Diary, p. 374). Christ pours out this mercy on humanity through the sending of the Spirit who, in the Trinity, is the Person-Love. And is not mercy love's "second name" (*Dives in misericordia,* 7), understood in its deepest and most tender aspect, in its ability to take upon itself the burden of any need and, especially, in its immense capacity for forgiveness? . . .

It is important that we accept the whole message that comes to us from the Word of God on this second Sunday of Easter, which from now on throughout the Church will be called "Divine Mercy Sunday. . . ."

It is not easy to love with a deep love, which lies in the authentic gift of self. This love can only be learned by penetrating the mystery of God's love. Looking at him, being one with his fatherly

Heart, we are able to look with new eyes at our brothers and sisters, with an attitude of unselfishness and solidarity, of generosity and forgiveness. All this is mercy!...

This consoling message is addressed above all to those who, afflicted by a particularly harsh trial or crushed by the weight of the sins they committed, have lost all confidence in life and are tempted to give in to despair. To them the gentle face of Christ is offered; those rays from his Heart touch them and shine upon them, warm them, show them the way and fill them with hope. How many souls have been consoled by the prayer "Jesus, I trust in you," which Providence intimated through Sister Faustina! This simple act of abandonment to Jesus dispels the thickest clouds and lets a ray of light penetrate every life. Christ Jesus, I trust in you! Jezu, ufam tobie!

On that same day of the canonization of St. Faustina Kowalska, during the message before praying the Regina Coeli, the Holy Father spoke of Divine Mercy but did not mention the Sacred Heart. In the evening, at the close of the prayer service that is held each evening of the Jubilee Year, the pope again spoke to the crowds gathered in St. Peter's Square, but did not mention the Sacred Heart. He urged the faithful to make Sister Faustina's prayer their own: "Jesus, I trust in you."

Homily at Mass on Divine Mercy Sunday in St. Peter's Square, a year after the canonization of St. Faustina, April 22, 2001

The Heart of Christ! His "Sacred Heart" has given us everything: redemption, salvation, sanctification. St. Faustina Kowalska saw coming from this Heart that was overflowing with generous love, two rays of light which illuminated the world. "The two rays," according to what Jesus himself told her, "represent the blood and the water" (Diary, p. 132). The blood recalls the sacrifice of Golgotha and the mystery of the Eucharist; the water, according to the rich symbolism of the Evangelist John, makes us think of baptism and the gift of the Holy Spirit (John 3:5; 4:14).

Through the mystery of this wounded Heart, the restorative tide of God's merciful love continues to spread over the men and women of our time. Here alone can those who long for true and lasting happiness find its secret.

"Jesus, I trust in you." This prayer, dear to so many of the devout, clearly expresses the attitude with which we too would like to abandon ourselves trustfully in your hands, O Lord, our only Savior.

You are burning with the desire to be loved and those in tune with the sentiments of your Heart learn how to build the new civilization of love. A simple act of abandonment is enough to overcome the barriers of darkness and sorrow, of doubt and desperation. The rays of your Divine Mercy restore hope, in a special way, to those who feel overwhelmed by the burden of sin.

Mary, Mother of Mercy, help us always to have this trust in our Son, our Redeemer. Help us too, St. Faustina, whom we remember today with special affection. Fixing our weak gaze on the divine Savior's face, we would like to repeat with you: "Jesus, I trust in you." Now and for ever. Amen.

Summary

St. Faustina herself gives the meaning of the two rays of light she saw coming from the Heart of Jesus, a meaning given by Our Lord himself. St. Faustina was very devoted to the Heart of Christ and saw no contrast or conflict in speaking of Divine Mercy and devotion to the Sacred Heart. See above p. 105 for the full text of the address of the pope at the Shrine of Divine Mercy in Krakow during his sixth visit to Poland on June 7, 1997.

Chapter 25

Canonizations of Saints Devoted to the Sacred Heart of Jesus

St. Paula Frassinetti (1809–82), foundress of the Sisters of St. Dorothy in Genoa, Italy, canonized March 11, 1984

The interior force which led her to live out so integrally the folly of the cross was her tender devotion to the Heart of Jesus Christ. With her authentically apostolic sensibility, St. Paula was aware that no one could carry out a true apostolate if he or she did not have impressed on one's own heart the stigmata of Christ, if there is not operative interiorly that ineffable blending of love and sorrow which is found in the Sacred Heart of Jesus. Therefore she desired that in her institute devotion to the Heart of Jesus would be practiced according to the rule: by rule they were to fast on the vigil of the feast of the Sacred Heart; Sisters and pupils on every First Friday of the month would take their turn of adoration before the Blessed Sacrament.

In 1782 the entire institute was consecrated to the Sacred Heart of Jesus.

St. Eustochia Emerald Calafato (1434–68), Franciscan foundress of Messina, canonized June 11, 1988

Today St. Eustochia teaches us the value of total consecration to Christ, of living with a spousal love that is devout and complete.

230

When a person adheres to him, he is loved by that same Heart, which has an infinite capacity for love.

Another distinctive note of the spirituality of St. Eustochia is adoration of the Eucharistic Jesus and the celebration of the Liturgy of the Hours.

I ask you before the sacrament of the Body and Blood of Christ, in imitation of St. Eustochia, that you be capable of perceiving the throbbing of the Heart of Jesus, who invites you to an every closer union with him, with your bishop and the auxiliary bishops, as well as with your collaborators.

St. Rose Philippine Duchesne (1769–1852), a member of the Society of the Sacred Heart, canonized July 3, 1988

St. Rose Philippine led a group of four companions to the United States and was known to the Potowatami Indians as "the woman who prays always."

St. Rose Philippine was a woman of lively faith and constant prayer, a woman full of zeal for the missionary needs of the Church. Her love, which knew no limits, was always eager to reach out to those in need in countries and cultures different from her own. By the time she got to her long-awaited mission among the American Indians, she could write to St. Madeleine Sophie Barat that "to go to teach the Indian children is a grace — a gift of God, not just a service." And her enthusiasm never wavered.

How does one account for such untiring zeal, such constant dedication to the Church's missionary efforts? Surely, it could only be the result of a heart on fire with love of God, a heart that was always in loving harmony with the Sacred Heart of Jesus the Lord.

St. Gaspar Bertoni (1777–1835), apostolic missionary, founder of the Stigmatines, the Congregation of the Sacred Stigmata of our Lord Jesus Christ, canonized November 1, 1989

St. Gaspar drew up a project of Christian life which foresaw for all people, regardless of their state of life, the call to holiness....His friends, the "Apostolic Missionaries," in communion of pastoral life with the bishops, were called to preach this message: the universal call to holiness with the conviction that hope flows for all from the sacrifice of Christ, from his merciful Heart, from his wounds.

St. Richard Pampuri (1897–1930), a member of the Order of the Hospitaller Brothers of St. John of God, canonized November 1, 1989

In a community that made mercy the principal motto of its own ministry, St. Richard felt that he had to respond with a new sign and a new availability to Christ "with a correspondence that was always more ready and generous, with an abandonment that was always more total, always more perfect, toward the most Sacred Heart of Jesus" (letter to his sister, October 1923).

St. Mary of St. Ignatius (Claudine) Thevenet (1774–1837), foundress of the Congregation of the Religious of Jesus and Mary, canonized March 21, 1993

In order to accomplish her mission, Claudine Thevenet inspired a group of young girls who, filled with a zeal like hers, drew their energy from the fountain of the Heart of Christ and of his Mother. With a strong link of unity between constant attention to God, love of Jesus and Mary, as well as faithful obedience to the Church,

Mother Mary of St. Ignatius founded the Religious of Jesus and Mary, which allowed her work to spread.

St. Claude La Colombière (1641–82), canonized May 31, 1992

See chapter 23.

St. Benedict Menni (1841–1914), beatified by Pope John Paul on June 23, 1985, canonized November 21, 1999

At the beatification, the pope said of St. Benedict:

His extraordinary activity was constantly sustained and animated by an intimate and profound devotion to the Sacred Heart of Jesus and by a particular veneration for the Mother of God, especially under the title of Our Lady of the Sacred Heart of Jesus.

At his canonization, the pope said:

His spirituality was born of his own experience of God's love for him. In his great devotion to the Heart of Jesus, King of heaven and earth, and to the Virgin Mary, he found the strength for his charitable service to others, especially the suffering: the elderly, children with scrofula and poliomyelitis, and the mentally ill. He carried out his service to the order and to society with a humility based on hospitality and blameless integrity, which made him a model for many. He organized various initiatives, guiding some young women who formed the first nucleus of a new religious institute, and founding the Hospitaller Sisters of the Sacred Heart of Jesus in Ciempozuelos (Madrid). His spirit of prayer led him to contemplate deeply Christ's paschal mystery, the source for understanding human suffering and the path to resurrection. On this day of Christ the King, the example of St. Benedict Menni's life sheds light on those who want to follow in the footsteps of the Master along the paths of welcoming hospitality.

St. Faustina Kowalska (1905–38), canonized April 18, 1993

See chapter 24.

St. Teresa Eustochio Verzeri (1801–52), foundress of the Daughters of the Sacred Heart of Jesus for the education and assistance of poor girls, canonized June 11, 2001

In her spiritual path she was particularly attracted by the Sacred Heart of Jesus, which she offered to the devotion of her sisters exhorting them to an obedient, generous, and gentle religious life. The soul who wants to follow Jesus, she loved to repeat, should imitate him in everything, especially participating in his redemptive passion, after the example of Mary.

To learn from the Heart of Jesus, to let oneself be directed by the feelings of that Heart and to pour them out in the service of our brothers and sisters: that is the message Teresa transmits to us, at the dawn of the third millennium, inviting each of us to cooperate actively in the evangelizing action of the Church.

Summary

Each of these ten saints canonized by Pope John Paul II had a special devotion to the Sacred Heart of Jesus, and that devotion influenced his or her life. To be recommended is a book published by Our Sunday Visitor in 1999, entitled *John Paul II's Book of Saints*, which gives a short biography of each of the persons canonized or beatified by Pope John Paul II. Anyone interested in more details of the life of a particular saint would do well to read a more complete biography. Usually within a short time after the canonization of a new saint, biographies are available; some of them appear after the beatification.

Chapter 26

Beatifications of Those Devoted to the Sacred Heart

**Blessed Ursula Ledochowska (1865–1939),
foundress of the Ursuline Sisters of the Sacred Heart
of Jesus in Agony (the Grey Ursulines),
beatified in Poland June 20, 1983**

The Holy Father gave an audience and an address to the members of the congregation on the first celebration of the feast of Blessed Ursula, May 29, 1984.

The specific mission of the Congregation of the Ursulines of the Sacred Heart of Jesus in Agony is to announce the love of his Heart by means of all the activities which have as their scope to spread and deepen the faith, especially through teaching and educating children and young people and the service of the most needy and oppressed.

The spirit of your foundress is the availability for sacrifice which the Heart of the Redeemer in Agony inspires in you.

The inexhaustible source of every spiritual energy is the Heart of Christ.

Blessed Louis-Zephirin Moreau (1824–1901), fourth bishop of St. Hyacinth, near Montreal, Canada, beatified May 10, 1987

Despite his physical frailty, he lived a demanding austerity. He was not able to confront his enormous responsibilities except by the power which he put on prayer. He described this himself when he wrote: "We do not do well the great things with which we are charged except by an intimate union with Our Lord." He could be called the "Bishop of the Sacred Heart": from day to day the pastor gave his life for his sheep, because he loved them with the ardent love of Christ.

Blessed Joseph Gerard (1831–1914), Missionary Oblate of Mary Immaculate, beatified September 15, 1988

On the day after the feast of the Triumph of the Cross of Christ the liturgy of the Church directs our attention toward her who is found at the foot of the cross, to the Mother of Christ, Mary.

It is with great joy that I join you in prayer today, my brothers and sisters of the Church in Lesotho (Africa). I know that many of you have had to make many sacrifices to be here, and I assure you of my happiness and gratitude that you have come. Your presence at this liturgy is a sign of your love for the Church and an expression of your willingness to bear witness to the Kingdom of Christ.

I am also aware that many people would have liked to be with us, but have been unable to do so: the sick and suffering, those who live too far away, those who are too young or too old. To all of them I say with deep affection: the pope embraces you and loves you in the Sacred Heart of Jesus Christ our Redeemer.

Blessed Joseph Gerard, pray for us; lead us to Jesus through the Immaculate Heart of Mary, our Mother in faith. Amen.

Blessed Mary Margaret Caiani (1861–1921), foundress of the Minim Sisters of the Sacred Heart, beatified April 23, 1989

In the beatification homily for the five who were beatified, the pope said something about each. The power of the message of charity was understood by Mary Margaret Caiani through contemplation of Christ and his pierced Heart. In the light of the divine love revealed in the divine Savior, Margaret learned to serve her brothers and sisters among the humble people of her native Tuscany and wanted to dedicate herself to the neediest and the lowliest: the marginalized children, the children of rural areas, the elderly, soldiers who were wounded in war and those recovering in military hospitals. She taught her spiritual daughters, the Minim Sisters of the Sacred Heart, to serve their neighbor with the intention of making reparation for the offences committed against Christ's love and always to be inspired by this love in the exercise of their charity.

The horizon of charity required by "the new commandment" is, indeed, limitless, since it is a precept that calls every believer to participate in Christ's infinite love. It is the charity of Jesus which, as the rule and norm, raises the soul to share in his work and involves our feeble efforts so that they become a sign and sacrament of the very charity of God. The space, the breadth of Christian charity, is measured by the fullness of divine love. In meditating on the suffering and the mystery of the pierced Heart of Christ, Mary Margaret Caiani was able to understand that it was necessary to "make reparation," that is, to compensate by her deeper awareness of the precept of charity for humanity's lack of understanding of God's infinite and merciful love. Among the basic counsels she gave her sisters, there is this: "You will console our sweet Jesus and make reparation for the many injuries inflicted upon his most loving Heart."

Blessed Mary Catherine of St. Augustine (1632–68), beatified April 23, 1989

"As I have loved you." This is Christ's rule of love, to let one's self be so carried away with Christ, to love with him, to model all of one's actions on his infinite generosity.

Mary Catherine of St. Augustine was animated by such a love. Very early in life she responded unreservedly to the Lord's call, humbly faithful to all the spiritual, community, apostolic, and charitable demands that marked the life of the Augustinians of Mercy. She knew how to "belong to God and desire nothing but to serve him."

In the secret of her soul she received the gift of being ceaselessly present to God, to Christ the Redeemer. She lived in union with the Sacred Heart of Jesus and placed all her confidence in the Heart of Mary. The painful torments of temptation were not able to affect her serenity nor lessen her extraordinary mystical experience. However, she accepted her intimate and hidden suffering, "taking upon herself the ills of others." In the face of the sins of people, her response was to sacrifice herself, united to the Savior's cross, to "win hearts for God."

Blessed Lorenzo Maria Salvi, Passionist, beatified October 1, 1989

Lorenzo "competed well for the faith," according to the spirit of his religious congregation, working intensely in preaching parish missions, in the course of retreats, in the ministry of confessions. He tried to instill love for the poor and humble Christ in anyone who drew near to him, through devotion to Jesus' childhood and passion, moments in which the Savior's humility and sweetness were most perfectly revealed. Convinced of the infinite mercy of the Heart of

Christ, he did not tire of exhorting people to confidence, following the example of the baby who entrusts himself in everything to the loving and strong embrace of its father.

Blessed Marie of Jesus Deluil-Martiny (1841–84), foundress of the Daughters of the Sacred Heart of Jesus, beatified October 22, 1989

"Here I am. I come to do your will" (Heb. 10:9). These words from the Letter to the Hebrews attributed to Christ show what Marie Deluil-Martiny was called to accomplish throughout her life. At a very early age she was touched by "Jesus' injured love" and by the all-too-frequent rejection of God in society. At the same time she discovered the greatness of the gift which Jesus made to the Father to save humankind, the wealth of love which radiated from his Heart, the fruitfulness of the blood and water which flowed from his open side. She was convinced that it was necessary to participate in the redemptive suffering of Christ, in a spirit of reparation for the sins of the world. Marie of Jesus offered herself to the Lord, at the price of trial and in a constant purification. She could truly say, "I have a passion for Jesus.... His life in mine; my life in him" (1884).

At a very young age Marie was able to share with her neighbors her ardent desire to live the Savior's oblation through ardent participation in the Sacrifice of the Mass. When she founded the Daughters of the Heart of Jesus, she put Eucharistic adoration at the center of their religious life. Deeply understanding Christ's sacrifice, she wanted people to unite themselves continually to the offering of the Blood of Christ to the Blessed Trinity. With a correct understanding of the Eucharist she included among the directives of the institute both a "continual thanksgiving" to the Heart of Jesus for his benefits and mercy and "pressing supplication to obtain the coming of Jesus' Kingdom into the world." Among her intentions she gave special place to priests, their holiness and fidelity.

Blessed Joseph Baldo (1843–1915), founder of the Congregation of the Little Daughters of St. Joseph, beatified October 31, 1989

"The heart of the priest," he wrote, "must be like the priestly Heart of Jesus: it must spread the light of all that is truly beautiful, lovable, and virtuous. It must spread the brilliance of the doctrine of Jesus Christ."

Blessed José María de Yermo y Parres (1851–1904), founder of the Congregation of the Servants of the Sacred Heart of Jesus and the Poor, beatified May 6, 1990

Father José María — the Apostle of Charity, as his contemporaries called him — combined love of God with love of neighbor, the synthesis of evangelical perfection, with a great devotion to the Heart of Jesus and with special love for the poor. His burning zeal for God's glory led him also to desire that all be truly missionaries.

All missionaries. All apostles of the Heart of Christ. Especially his daughters, the congregation he founded, the Servants of the Sacred Heart of Jesus and the Poor, to whom he left two loves as a charismatic inheritance: Christ and the poor. These two loves were a fire in his heart and were always to be his daughters' purest glory.

Blessed Annibale Maria di Francia (1851–1927), founder of two religious congregations: the Rogationist Fathers of the Heart of Jesus and the Daughters of Divine Zeal, beatified October 7, 1990

He himself deeply loved his priesthood: he lived it with consistency, he exalted its greatness before the People of God. He often repeated that the Church, in order to carry out her mission, needs "many holy" priests, "after the Heart of God." He felt that was an essential problem and insisted that prayer and spiritual formation be primary in priestly preparations.

In a talk given on December 6, 2001, to representatives of the Rogationist Family during the year-long commemoration of the 150th anniversary of their founder's birth, the Holy Father said:

By welcoming you, who represent the Rogationists, the Daughters of Divine Zeal, the Rogationist Missionaries, the graduates and Lay Vocation Promoters who share the same charism, I wish to greet your colleagues and all who form a network of apostolic life in your religious families. On every continent they give themselves humbly, generously, and joyfully for the spreading of "Rogate" (Ask the Master) born from the Heart of Christ.

Blessed Louise Thérèse de Montaignac de Chauvance (1820–85), foundress of the Oblates of the Sacred Heart of Jesus, dedicated to service and reparation, beatified November 4, 1990

A daughter of the Church and a woman of the Church, she knew that "serving the Lord and serving the Church are the same thing." Moved by an ardent apostolic spirit and sustained by great devotion to the Heart of Jesus, she set to work in close contact with her bishop, with the priests of her parish, and with the lay faithful. She founded the Oblates, who were called to be the leaven of unity through their union with Christ and one another.

Together, let us ask Blessed Louise Thérèse de Montaignac de Chauvance to help us "recognize the love of the Heart of Jesus and ceaselessly remind people about it," as she was able to do so well during her entire life.

Blessed Maria Schinina (1844–1910), co-foundress of the Sisters of the Sacred Heart of Jesus, beatified November 4, 1990

The spiritual journey of Blessed Maria Schinina of the Sacred Heart began with a deep penetration by God's love, which is expressed in the symbol of the Heart of Jesus; in order to respond to this love in her spirituality she emphasized contemplation, adoration and reparation.

Blessed Marie-Thérèse of the Sacred Heart of Jesus Haze (1782–1876), foundress of the Daughters of the Cross, beatified April 21, 1991

"See what love the Father has bestowed on us" (1 John 3:1). Mother Marie-Thérèse Haze knew how to accept that love; she knew how to respond to it each day. She experienced trials but, at the side of Our Lady of Sorrows, she ceaselessly contemplated the Heart of Christ pierced on the cross for the world's salvation. Showing her sisters the way, she was able to say "that a crushed heart becomes the throne of grace." For her the Redeemer's presence in the Blessed Sacrament was a constant source of serene submission to God's will, of wisdom for guiding her actions, of courage for undertaking many foundations.

Blessed Josef Sebastian Pelczar (1842–1924), beatified June 2, 1991

Blessed Josef was beatified during Pope John Paul II's fourth visit to Poland. See above p. 85.

Blessed Francis Spinelli (1853–1909), founder of the Sisters of Perpetual Adoration of the Blessed Sacrament, beatified June 21, 1992

Love for the Eucharistic Christ and service to the poor, the image of Christ: here in synthesis is the life and priestly ministry of Blessed Francis Spinelli, whose witness seems particularly timely and eloquent today.

In an age like ours, marked by notable social changes, he continues to remind us that for the people of all eras only the pierced Heart of the Redeemer is the unending source of selfless love which purifies and renews. Father Spinelli entirely understood the truth of the message of the cross and, therefore, he is now held up as an example to imitate and an intercessor to invoke.

The Church offers him as a model of an authentic apostle especially to you, the priests whom Providence calls to be stewards of the mysteries of salvation. In your daily ministry may you draw light and courage from the Eucharist, in order to become faithful disciples of the divine Master.

Blessed Dina Belanger (1897–1929), beatified March 20, 1993

The intimacy of Christ's presence in Dina Belanger, the life of the Blessed Trinity in her, appear particularly in her spirit of offering to the Heart of the Son of God. Jesus is, she writes, "the life of my life," because she always sought to make her heart beat in unison with his. She knows he is with her at every moment, in the eternal present which makes St. Paul say: "Behold, now is a very acceptable time; behold, now is the day of salvation" (2 Cor. 6:2). Entirely caught up in the desire to respond to the divine will, she lives in the freedom which God grants his children, in the spirit of her motto: "Jesus and Mary, the rule of my love, and my love the rule of my life." From this fidelity to the intentions of the Eucharistic Heart of Jesus and the Immaculate Heart of his mother spring the simplest and most beautiful characteristic of charity toward her sisters. As if she had received the grace of St. Thérèse of the Child Jesus, who left this world the very same year in which she was born, Dina Belanger wanted to "consume the whole world in love"; she became an apostle and missionary after the Heart of God.

Blessed Damien Joseph de Veuster (1840–89), missionary to the lepers, beatified in the Brussels cathedral, June 4, 1995

It is in intimacy with Christ, in the faithful appointment with the Liturgy of the Hours and lectio divina, and in contemplation that Damien's activity found meaning and fulfillment. Through lectio divina religious, like the faithful, can "discover the Heart of God in the word of God" (St. Gregory the Great, *Letters*, 4, 31). Strong in this spiritual intimacy, Damien could write to his parents after his ordination to the priesthood: "Do not worry about me, because when one serves God, one is happy everywhere." Contemplation does not distance us from men and it is not time wasted. By meditating on the Heart of Christ, like the beloved disciple, the apostle of the lepers found the necessary energy for his extraordinary activity.

The fact that the congregation to which Father Damien belongs is consecrated to the Heart of Jesus and to the Heart of his Mother is eloquent. Between these two Hearts there is an exchange of gifts in the mystery of the Incarnation and the Redemption. Father Damien drew inspiration from this exchange and he followed it to the end. "How sweet it is to die as a son of the Sacred Heart," he would say on the day of his death, Monday of Holy Week 1889. Today, his gift is returned to the hands of that same Mother, to whom he entrusted himself and gave himself from the very beginning of his vocation: this gift becomes total in the glory of God. Rejoice, heavenly Mother! Be joyful, motherland of Father Damien! Be happy, people of the Hawaiian Islands! In your land Father Damien sowed the Word of God, whose love is demonstrated through the Gospel and the life of his disciples.

Through the intercession of Blessed Damien, today I especially pray to the Lord for the men and women religious of the Congregation of the Sacred Hearts. May they be worthy descendants of the apostle of Molokai, bringing the Gospel untiringly to the places where they are sent! ... The mystery of the Eucharist and the love of the Sacred Hearts must remain the pillars and foundation of the congregation's spirituality.

Blessed Genoveva Torres Morales (1870–1956), foundress of the Sisters of the Sacred Heart of Jesus and the Holy Angels, also called the "Angelicas," beatified June 29, 1995

A woman of humble origin and background, she possessed the knowledge of divine love, acquired through her intense devotion to the Sacred Heart of Jesus Christ. She used to say: "Love conquers all." This love led her to devote her life to caring for retired women, to remedy the loneliness and deprivation in which many of them lived, looking after them materially and spiritually in a true home, beside them like an "Angel of solitude." To this end she founded in Valencia the Institute of the Sisters of the Sacred Heart of Jesus and the Holy Angels.

Blessed Daniel Comboni (1831–81), first bishop of Central Africa, founder of the Comboni Missionaries of the Heart of Jesus and the Comboni Missionary Sisters, beatified March 17, 1996

On the day following the beatification, the pope sent a message which was read by the vicar general of the Comboni Missionaries at a Mass of thanksgiving in St. Peter's Basilica.

From contemplation of the cross and devotion to the Sacred Heart of Jesus, your blessed founder was able to draw support and strength to face every trial. Physical hardship and moral suffering did not dampen his evangelizing zeal but, on the contrary, shed even brighter light on its value and soundness.

Blessed María Encarnación of the Sacred Heart Rosal (1815–86), religious reformer of the Institute of the Bethlemite Sisters, beatified May 4, 1997

Mother María Encarnación Rosal, the first woman from Guatemala to be beatified, was chosen to continue the charism of Blessed Pedro de San José Betancourt, founder of the Order of Bethlemites, the first Latin American order. Today its fruit endures in the Beth-lemite Sisters who, together with all the members of the great family of the Lay Association, strive to put his evangelizing charism into practice in their service to the Church.

Basing herself on the lessons learned in the school of Bethlehem, that is, love, humility, poverty, the generous gift of self, and austerity, she lived a splendid synthesis of contemplation and action, uniting to her educational activities the spirit of penance, adoration, and reparation to the Sacred Heart of Jesus.

In his talk to pilgrims on the following day, the pope said:

Blessed María Encarnación enriched the Church by helping to pre-serve the spirituality of Bethlehem. A tenacious and strong woman with an extraordinary personality and great love for the Sacred Heart, she did not despair in the face of difficulties and thus suc-ceeded in actively and faithfully cooperating with the plan of God, "who desires all men to be saved and to come to the knowledge of the truth" (1 Tim. 2:4).

Blessed Anna Schaffer (1882–1925), beatified March 7, 1999

Precisely in the most intense pain, Anna Schaffer realized that every Christian is responsible for his neighbor's salvation. For this purpose she used the pen. Her sickbed was the cradle of an extensive letter-writing apostolate. She used what was left of her strength to do embroidery work and in this way give joy to others. In her letters and in her handwork her favorite motif was the Heart of Jesus as the symbol of God's love. She did not depict the flames of Jesus' Heart as tongues of fire, but as ears of wheat. The reference to the Eucharist, which Anna Schaffer received from her parish priest every day, is unmistakable. The Heart of Jesus, as she portrayed it, will thus be the symbol of this new Blessed.

What this new Blessed did from her sickbed on earth, she now accomplishes even more effectively in heaven. She ceaselessly speaks to God on our behalf. Thanks be to God for giving us such a powerful intercessor.

Blessed Maria Bernardina Jablonska (1878–1940), beatified June 6, 1997

Blessed Maria Bernardina Jablonska was beatified during John Paul II's sixth visit to Poland (see above p. 98).

Blessed Maria Karlowska (1865–1935), beatified June 6, 1997

Blessed Maria Karlowska was also beatified during John Paul II's sixth visit to Poland (see above p. 98).

Blessed Stefan Wincenty Frelichowski (1913–45), beatified June 7, 1999

Blessed Stefan was beatified during John Paul II's seventh visit to Poland (see above p. 110).

Blessed Catherine Volpicelli (1839–94), foundress of the Servants of the Sacred Heart, beatified April 29, 2001

"Worthy is the Lamb who was slain, to receive power and wealth and wisdom and might and honor and glory and blessing!" (Rev. 5:12). These words taken from the book of Revelation and proclaimed in the second reading can also be fittingly applied to the

mystical experience of Blessed Catherine Volpicelli. Three significant aspects stand out in her life, which was totally consecrated to
the Heart of the Lamb slain for our salvation: a deep Eucharistic
spirituality, an indomitable fidelity to the Church, and a surprising
apostolic generosity.

The Eucharist, which she adored for long hours and made the
center of her life, to the point of taking a vow as a victim of reparation, was a school of docile and loving obedience to God for her.
At the same time it was a source of tender and merciful love for
her neighbor; in the poorest and most marginalized she loved her
Lord, contemplated at length in the Blessed Sacrament.

She was always able to find in the Eucharist the missionary fervor
which impelled her to express her vocation in the Church with
docility to her pastors and with prophetic intentions of promoting
the laity and new forms of consecrated life. Without determining
places for action or founding specific institutions, she wanted, as she
herself said, to seek solitude in work and fruitful work in solitude.
She was the first "messenger" of the Apostleship of Prayer in Italy,
and left as a legacy, especially to the Servants of the Sacred Heart,
a unique apostolic mission which must continue to be ceaselessly
nourished at the source of the Eucharistic mystery.

On the following day, speaking to pilgrims who had come for the
beatifications, the pope said:

Catherine Volpicelli lived in Naples in the middle of the nineteenth
century. She received a sound human and religious formation from
her family and had the opportunity to meet several men of God
such as Blessed Ludovico da Casoria, the Barnabite Leonardo Mat-
era, and Blessed Bartolo Longo, who deeply marked her spiritual
development. Her heart expanded more and more, in proportion
to the size of the Heart of Christ, whose fervent disciple and

apostle she became. cultivating an intense Eucharistic life and the Apostleship of Prayer.

It was precisely with the first messengers of the Apostleship of Prayer that Catherine founded the Institute of the Servants of the Sacred Heart, which, after being approved by the archbishop of Naples, received the decree of praise from my predecessor, Leo XIII. With such a rich interior life, Catherine and her sisters made themselves "Good Samaritans" in various situations of poverty, not only carrying out a philanthropic and charitable work, but witnessing to genuine Gospel charity with simplicity and discretion, solidarity and respect for the simple and humble people. Her apostolic heritage is a very precious gift for the Church, for which we would like to thank the Lord. May this religious heritage be preserved and increased by his spiritual daughters.

Summary

What was said in chapter 25 for the ten saints canonized by Pope John Paul II can also be applied to these twenty-five new Blesseds. Each followed the Lord Jesus in his or her own way and similarly was influenced by devotion to the Heart of Jesus in a distinct way. Each of us should be able to let the spirituality of the Sacred Heart influence our life and our following of the Lord Jesus in our own personal way.

Part Five

Prayers to
the Sacred Heart

Chapter 27

Centenary of the Consecration of the Human Race to the Sacred Heart of Jesus

Message for the Centenary of the Consecration of the Human Race to the Sacred Heart of Jesus, June 11, 1999

The hundredth anniversary of the Consecration of the Human Race to the Divine Heart of Jesus, prescribed for the whole church by my predecessor Leo XIII in the encyclical letter *Annum sacrum* (May 25, 1899; *Leonis XIII P.M. Acta XIX* [1899], pp. 71–80) and carried out on June 11, 1899, prompts us first of all to give thanks to "him who loves us and has freed us from our sins by his blood and made us a kingdom, priests to his God and Father" (Rev. 1:5–6).

This happy occasion seems a particularly appropriate one for reflecting on the meaning and value of that important ecclesial act. With the encyclical *Annum sacrum,* Pope Leo XIII confirmed all that had been done by his predecessors carefully to preserve and highlight the devotion and spirituality of the Sacred Heart. With that consecration he wished to obtain "extraordinary benefits first for Christianity, but also for the whole human race" (*Annum sacrum,* p. 71). Asking that not only believers but all people should be consecrated, he gave a new direction and sense to the consecration which had already been practiced for two centuries by individuals, groups, dioceses, and nations.

The consecration of the human race to the Heart of Jesus was thus presented by Leo XIII as "the summit and crowning of all

253

the honors which have been customarily paid to the Most Sacred Heart" (*Annum sacrum,* p. 72). Such a consecration, the encyclical explains, is owed to Christ, Redeemer of the human race, for what he is in himself and for what he has done for human beings. Since in the Sacred Heart the believer encounters the symbol and the living image of the infinite love of Christ, which in itself spurs us to love one another, he cannot fail to recognize the need to participate personally in the work of salvation. For this reason every member of the Church is invited to see consecration as the giving and binding of oneself to Jesus Christ, the King "of prodigal sons," the King of all who are waiting to be led "into the light of God and of his kingdom" (Formula of Consecration). Consecration thus understood is to be joined to the missionary activity of the Church herself, because it answers the desire of Jesus' Heart to propagate in the world, through the members of his Body, his total dedication to the kingdom, and to unite the Church ever more closely to his offering to the Father and his being for others.

The value of what took place on June 11, 1899 was authoritatively confirmed in the writings of my predecessors, who offered doctrinal reflections on the devotion to the Sacred Heart and mandated the periodic renewal of the act of consecration. Among these I am pleased to recall the holy successor of Leo XIII, Pope Pius X, who directed in 1906 that the consecration be renewed every year; Pope Pius XI of revered memory, who recalled it in his encyclicals *Quas primas,* in the context of the Holy Year of 1925, and in *Miserentissimus Redemptor;* his successor, the Servant of God Pius XII, who treated it in his encyclicals *Summi Pontificatus* and *Haurietis aquas.* The Servant of God Paul VI, then, in the light of the Second Vatican Council, wished to make reference to it in his apostolic epistle *Investigabiles divitias* and in his letter *Diserti interpretes facti,* addressed on May 25, 1965, to major superiors of institutes named after the Heart of Jesus.

I too have not failed on several occasions to invite my brothers in the episcopate, priests, religious and the faithful to cultivate in their lives the most genuine forms of devotion to the Heart of Christ. In this year dedicated to God the Father, I recall what I wrote in the encyclical *Dives in misericordia:* "The Church seems in a particular way to profess the mercy of God and to venerate it when she directs herself to the Heart of Christ. In fact, it is precisely this drawing close to Christ in the mystery of his Heart which enables us to dwell on this point — a point in a sense central and also most accessible on the human level — of the revelation of the merciful love of the Father, a revelation which constituted the central content of the messianic mission of the Son of God" (no. 13). On the occasion of the Solemnity of the Sacred Heart and the month of June, I have often urged the faithful to persevere in the practice of this devotion, which "contains a message which in our day has an extraordinary timeliness," because "an unending spring of life, giving hope to every person, has streamed precisely from the Heart of God's Son, who died on the cross. From the Heart of Christ crucified is born the new humanity redeemed from sin. The man of the year 2000 needs Christ's Heart to know God and to know himself; he needs it to build the civilization of love" (June 8, 1994).

The consecration of the human race in 1899 represents an extraordinarily important step on the Church's journey and it is still good to renew it every year on the feast of the Sacred Heart. The same should be said of the Act of Reparation which is customarily recited on the feast of Christ the King. The words of Leo XIII still ring true: "We must have recourse to him who is the Way, the Truth, and the Life. We have gone astray and we must return to the right path; darkness has overshadowed our minds, and the gloom must be dispelled by the light of truth; death has seized upon us, and we must lay hold of life" (*Annum sacrum,* p. 78). Is this not the program of the Second Vatican Council and of my own pontificate?

As we prepare to celebrate the Great Jubilee of the Year 2000, this centenary helps us to reflect with hope on our humanity and to see the third millennium illumined by the light of the mystery of Christ, "the Way, the Truth, and the Life" (John 14:6).

In stating that "the imbalances under which the modern world labors are linked with that more basic imbalance rooted in the human heart" (Pastoral Constitution *Gaudium et spes,* 10), faith happily discovers that "it is only in the mystery of the Word made flesh that the mystery of man truly becomes clear" (ibid., 22), since "by his Incarnation the Son of God has united himself in some fashion with every man. He worked with human hands, he thought with a human mind, acted with a human will, and loved with a human heart" (ibid.). God has so willed that the baptized Christian, "associated with the paschal mystery and configured to the death of Christ," should hasten "forward to the resurrection strengthened by hope," but this holds true "also for all people of good will in whose hearts grace works in an unseen way" (ibid.). "All human beings," as the Second Vatican Council reminds us, "are called to this union with Christ, who is the light of the world, from whom we come, through whom we live and toward whom we are led" (Dogmatic Constitution *Lumen gentium,* 3).

The Dogmatic Constitution on the Church authoritatively states that

> by regeneration and the anointing of the Holy Spirit, the baptized are consecrated to be a spiritual house and a holy priesthood, that through all the works of Christians they may offer spiritual sacrifices and proclaim the marvelous works of him who called them out of darkness into his wonderful light (1 Pet. 2:4–10). Therefore all the disciples of Christ, persevering in prayer and praising God (Acts 2:42–47), should offer themselves as a sacrifice, living, holy and pleasing to God (Rom. 12:1). They should everywhere on earth bear witness

to Christ and give an answer to those who seek an account of that hope of eternal life which is in them. (Ibid., 10)

In facing the challenge of the new evangelization, the Christian who looks upon the Heart of Christ and consecrates himself as well as his brothers and sisters to him, the Lord of time and history, rediscovers that he is the bearer of his light. Motivated by this spirit of service, he cooperates in opening to all human beings the prospect of being raised to their own personal and communal fullness. "From the Heart of Christ, man's heart learns to know the genuine and unique meaning of his life and of his destiny, to understand the value of an authentically Christian life, to keep himself from certain perversions of the human heart, and to unite the filial love of God with love of neighbor" (*Message to the Society of Jesus,* October 5, 1986).

I wish to express my approval and encouragement to all who in any way continue to foster, study, and promote devotion to the Heart of Christ in the church with language and forms adapted to our times, so that it may be transmitted to future generations in the spirit which has always animated it. The faithful still need to be guided to contemplate adoringly the mystery of Christ, the God-Man, in order to become men and women of interior life, people who feel and live the call to new life, to holiness, to reparation which is apostolic cooperation in the salvation of the world, people who prepare themselves for the new evangelization, recognizing the Heart of Christ as the heart of the Church; it is urgent for the world to understand that Christianity is the religion of love.

The Savior's Heart invites us to return to the Father's love, which is the source of every authentic love: "In this is love, not that we loved God but that he loved us and sent his Son to be the expiation for our sins" (1 John 4:10). Jesus ceaselessly receives from the Father, rich in mercy and compassion, the love which he lavishes upon human beings (Eph. 2:4; James 5:11). His Heart particularly reveals the generosity of God toward sinners. God's reaction to sin is not to lessen his love, but to expand it into a flow of mercy which becomes the initiative of the Redemption.

Contemplation of the Heart of Jesus in the Eucharist will spur the faithful to seek in that Heart the inexhaustible mystery of the priesthood of Christ and of the Church. It will enable them to taste, in communion with their brothers and sisters, the spiritual sweetness of charity at its very source. By helping all to rediscover their own baptism, it will make them more aware of having to live their apostolic dimension by spreading love and participating in the mission of evangelization. Each person needs to be more committed to praying the Lord of the harvest (Matt. 9:38) to grant the Church "shepherds after his own Heart" (Jer. 3:15) who, in love with Christ the Good Shepherd, will pattern their own hearts on his and be ready to go out into the highways of the world to proclaim to all that he is the Way, the Truth, and the Life (postsynodal apostolic exhortation *Pastores dabo vobis,* 82). To this we must add effective action so that many of today's young people, docile to the voice of the Holy Spirit, may be taught to let the great expectations of the Church and of humanity resonate in the depths of their hearts and to respond to Christ's invitation to consecrate themselves enthusiastically and joyously with him "for the life of the world" (John 6:51).

The coincidence of this centenary with the last year of preparation for the Great Jubilee of the Year 2000, which is "aimed at broadening the horizons of believers, so that they will see things in the perspective of Christ; in the perspective of the 'Father who is in heaven' (Matt. 5:45)" (apostolic letter *Tertio millennio adveniente,* 49) offers a fitting opportunity to present the Heart of Jesus "the burning furnace of love, . . . the symbol and the expressive image of the eternal love with which 'God so loved the world, that he gave his only begotten Son' (John 3:16)" (Paul VI, apostolic epistle *Investigabiles divitias*). The Father "is love" (1 John 4:8, 16), and the only-begotten Son, Christ, manifests this mystery while fully revealing man to man.

Devotion to the Heart of Jesus has given form to the prophetic words recalled by St. John: "They shall look on him whom they have pierced" (John 19:37; see also Zech. 12:10). It is a contemplative gaze, which strives to enter deeply into the sentiments of Christ, true God and true man. In this devotion the believer confirms and deepens the acceptance of the mystery of the Incarnation, which has made the Word one with human beings and thus given witness to the Father's search for them. This seeking is born in the intimate depths of God, who "loves" man "eternally in the Word, and wishes to raise him in Christ to the dignity of an adoptive son" (*Tertio millennio adveniente,* 7). At the same time devotion to the Heart of Jesus searches the mystery of the Redemption in order to discover the measure of love which prompted his sacrifice for our salvation.

The Heart of Christ is alive with the action of the Holy Spirit, to whom Jesus attributed the inspiration of his mission (Luke 4:18; see also Isa. 61:1) and whose sending he had promised at the Last Supper. It is the Spirit who enables us to grasp the richness of the sign of Christ's pierced side, from which the Church has sprung (Constitution *Sacrosanctum concilium,* 5). "The Church, in fact," as Paul VI wrote, "was born from the pierced Heart of the Redeemer and from that Heart receives her nourishment, for Christ 'gave himself up for her, that he might sanctify her, having cleansed her by the washing of water with the word' (Eph. 5:25–26)" (letter *Diserti interpretes facti*). Through the Holy Spirit, then, the love which permeates the Heart of Jesus is poured out in the hearts of men (Rom. 5:5), and moves them to adoration of his "unsearchable riches" (Eph. 3:8) and to filial and trusting petition to the Father (Rom. 8:15–16) through the Risen One, who "always lives to make intercession for us" (Heb. 7:25).

Devotion to the Heart of Christ, "the universal seat of communion with God the Father, ... seat of the Holy Spirit" (June 8, 1994), aims at strengthening our bond with the Holy Trinity. Thus, the celebration of the centenary of the consecration of the human race to the Sacred Heart prepares the faithful for the Great Jubilee because it concerns its objective of "giving glory to the Trinity, from whom everything in the world and in history comes and to whom everything returns" (*Tertio millennio adveniente,* 53) and because of its orientation to the Eucharist (ibid.), in which the life that Christ came to bring in abundance (John 10:10) is communicated to those who feed on him in order to have life because of him (John 6:57). The entire devotion to the Heart of Jesus in its every manifestation is profoundly Eucharistic: it is expressed in religious practices which stir the faithful to live in harmony with Christ, "meek and humble of Heart" (Matt. 11:29), and it is intensified in adoration. It is rooted and finds its summit in participation in Holy Mass, especially Sunday Mass, where the hearts of the faithful, fraternally assembled in joy, listen to the word of God and learn to offer with Christ themselves and the whole of their lives (*Sacrosanctum concilium,* 48). There they are nourished at the paschal banquet of the Redeemer's Body and Blood and, sharing fully the love which beats in his Heart, they strive to be ever more effective evangelizers and witnesses of solidarity and hope.

We give thanks to God, our Father, who has revealed his love in the Heart of Christ and has consecrated us by the anointing of the Holy Spirit (Dogmatic Constitution *Lumen gentium,*10) so that, in union with Christ, we may adore him in every place and by our holy actions consecrate to him the world itself (ibid., 34) and the new millennium.

Conscious of the great challenge that lies before us, we call upon the help of the Blessed Virgin, Mother of Christ and Mother of the Church. May she guide the People of God across the threshold of the millennium soon to begin. May she enlighten them on the ways of faith, hope, and love! In particular, may she help every Christian to live with generous consistency the consecration to Christ which has its basis in the sacrament of baptism and is fittingly confirmed in personal consecration to the Most Sacred Heart of Jesus, in whom alone humanity can find forgiveness and salvation.

Message for the feast of the Sacred Heart and the hundredth anniversary of Pope Leo XIII's Consecration of the Human Race to the Sacred Heart of Jesus, June 4, 1999

To the Most Reverend Louis-Marie Bille, archbishop of Lyons, president of the Bishops' Conference of France:

As numerous pilgrims prepare solemnly to celebrate the feast of the Sacred Heart at Paray-le-Monial and to commemorate the centenary of Pope Leo XIII's consecration of the human race to the Sacred Heart of Jesus, I am pleased to extend my cordial greetings to them through you, and in prayer to join their spiritual journey and that of everyone who is making an act of offering to the Sacred Heart on this day.

Following St. John Eudes, who taught us to contemplate Jesus, the Heart of hearts, in the Heart of Mary and to make them both loved, devotion to the Sacred Heart became widespread, particularly because of St. Margaret Mary, a Visitation nun at Paray-le-Monial. On June 11, 1899, inviting all the bishops to join him, Leo XIII asked the Lord to be the King of all the faithful, as well as of those who had turned away from him or did not know him, imploring him to lead them to the Truth and to the One who is the Life. In the encyclical *Annum sacrum* he expressed his compassion for people who are far from God and his desire to entrust them to Christ the Redeemer.

The Church ceaselessly contemplates God's love, expressed sublimely and especially on Calvary, the moment of Christ's Passion, a sacrifice that becomes sacramentally present in every Eucharist. "All the sacraments come from the loving Heart of Christ, but especially the greatest of all, the sacrament of love through which Jesus wished to become our life's companion, the nourishment of our souls, a sacrifice of infinite value" (St. Alphonsus Liguori, *Second Meditation on the Loving Heart of Jesus during the Novena of Preparation for the Feast of the Sacred Heart*). Christ is a burning furnace of love who calls with the soothing words: "Come to me...for I am gentle and lowly in heart" (Matt. 11:28–29).

The Heart of the Incarnate Word is the sign of love par excellence; I have therefore personally stressed how important it is for the faithful to penetrate the mystery of this Heart overflowing with love for human beings and containing a message of extraordinary timeliness (see the encyclical *Redemptor hominis,* 8). As St. Claude La Colombière wrote: "This is the Heart which so loved men that it spared nothing, to the point of emptying itself and being consumed, of giving its love to the end" (*Spiritual Writings,* no. 9).

As we near the third millennium, "the love of Christ impels us" (2 Cor. 5:14) to make known and loved the Savior who shed his blood for humankind. "For their sake I consecrate myself, that they also may be consecrated in truth" (John 17:19). Therefore I warmly encourage the faithful to adore Christ, present in the Blessed Sacrament of the altar, letting him heal our consciences and purify us, enlighten us, and unite us. In their encounter with him, Christians will find strength for their spiritual life and their mission in the world. In fact, in communing heart to heart with the divine Teacher, they will discover the Father's infinite love and will be true worshippers in spirit and in truth. Their faith in him will be revitalized; they will enter into God's mystery and be profoundly transformed by Christ. In their trials and joys, they will conform their life to the mystery of our Savior's cross and resurrection (*Gaudium et spes,* 10). Every day they will become more and more sons and daughters in the Son. Then, love will be spread through them in human hearts, in order to build up the Body of Christ which is the Church and to establish a society of justice, peace, and brotherhood. They will be intercessors for all humanity, because every soul which is lifted up to God also lifts up the world and mysteriously contributes to the salvation freely offered by our Father in heaven.

I therefore invite all the faithful fervently to continue their devotion to the Sacred Heart of Jesus, adapting it to our time, so that they may never cease to draw on its unfathomable riches and to respond joyfully by loving God and their brethren, thereby finding peace, pursuing the way of reconciliation and strengthening their hope of one day living fully with God in the company of all the saints (see the Litany of the Sacred Heart). They should also transmit to future generations the desire to meet the Lord, to fix their gaze on him, to answer the call to holiness and to discover their specific mission in the Church and in the world, thus fulfilling their baptismal vocation (*Lumen gentium,* 10). In fact, "divine mercy, the most precious gift of the Heart of Christ and of his Spirit" is communicated to human beings so that they in turn may be witnesses of God's love (Pius XII, encyclical *Haurietis aquas,* 83).

In invoking the intercession of the Virgin Mary, Mother of Christ and of the Church, to whom I consecrated human beings and nations on May 13, 1982, I willingly grant my apostolic blessing to you and to all the faithful who will come on pilgrimage to Paray-le-Monial for the feast of the Sacred Heart or who devoutly participate in a liturgical celebration or another moment of prayer to the Sacred Heart.

Summary

Pope Leo XIII's consecration of the human race to the Sacred Heart of Jesus is a significant date in the history of devotion to the Sacred Heart. It can be called the beginning of the Century of the Sacred Heart as testified by this collection of all that Pope John Paul II has said and written on the Sacred Heart. It is also the century of the significant encyclicals of Pius XI and Pius XII. This message as well as the letter itself of Pope

Leo XIII, *Annum sacrum,* bears repeated reading. This message also serves not only as a fitting conclusion to the century but an introduction to the new millennium. Pope John Paul II's letter of June 11, 1999, contains an excellent summary of the devotion and spirituality of the Sacred Heart of Jesus.

Chapter 28

Prayers to the Sacred Heart of Jesus

Inauguration of perpetual exposition of the Blessed Sacrament in the Basilica of St. Peter, December 2, 1981

A prayer directed to Christ our Lord, which begins with the words, "Stay with us, Lord." There is one reference to the Sacred Heart in the first part of the prayer:

May those who visit this basilica find in it the very fountain "of life and holiness which springs from your Eucharistic Heart."

Prayer to Our Lady of Jasna Gora, June 8, 1983

In the first part of his message at the general audience, our Holy Father quotes the Act of Consecration the Polish bishops made to the Heart of Jesus on October 28, 1951. The second part is a prayer to Our Lady of Jasna Gora and speaks of the Heart of Jesus.

Next Friday is dedicated by the Church to the Solemnity of the Sacred Heart of Jesus. In this perspective I wish to recall the act of consecration to the Divine Heart made by the Polish episcopate on the Solemnity of Christ the King on October 28, 1951, shortly after the end of the Second World War.

These are the words of this act of consecration:

"We give you thanks for all the benefits you have bestowed on our nation, and particularly for having called us to the holy Catholic faith and for your protection over us in difficult historical times...

"We entrust ourselves and consecrate ourselves totally to your Divine Heart in order to be always your people.

"At the same time, we solemnly promise to persevere faithfully in the holy Catholic faith, to defend your holy Church, and to base our personal, family and national life on your gospel!"

Lady of Jasna Gora! You have always been for us the way to your Son's Heart. This Heart, "pierced by a lance" on the cross, has become the "fountain of life and holiness" for everyone.

Bring close to the Divine Heart individuals, families, environments, since this Heart, "made obedient unto death," is the "propitiation for our sins."

May it be also the "source of all consolation" for all the oppressed, injured, and suffering.

O Mother, through your intercession, may the Heart of the Redeemer not cease to be on Polish soil the "King and center of all hearts"... that everyone may be "enriched with his wealth," especially in this Holy Year of the Redemption.

Prayer at the end of the homily at Vancouver Airport (Canada), September 20, 1984

Toward the end of the homily, the pope quotes three invocations from the Litany of the Sacred Heart of Jesus and then concludes with a brief prayer and three more invocations from the litany.

> Heart of Jesus, abode of justice and love!
> Heart of Jesus, patient and most merciful!
> Heart of Jesus, fountain of life and holiness!

Lord Jesus Christ, Eternal Son of the Eternal Father, born of the Virgin Mary, we ask you to continue to reveal to us the mystery of God: so that we may recognize in you "the image of the invisible

God"; that we may find him in you, in your divine Person, in the warmth of your humanity, in the love of your Heart.

Heart of Jesus, in whom dwells the fullness of divinity!
Heart of Jesus, of whose fullness we have all received!
Heart of Jesus, King and center of all hearts,
for ever and ever. Amen.

Consecration of Ecuador to the Sacred Heart of Jesus, January 30, 1985

In the homily, the pope referred to Ecuador as "a consecrated nation." For more than a century, its people had been consecrated to the Sacred Heart of Jesus. At the end of the Mass, the pope renewed this consecration in these words:

This is your people, Lord.
It will always recognize you as its God, O Jesus.
It will not turn its eyes to a star other than
the one of love and of mercy
which shines in the midst of your breast.
Be therefore our God, be therefore your Heart
the luminous beacon of our faith,
the secure ardor of our hope,
the symbol of our banner
the impenetrable shield of our weakness,
the bright dawn of an imperturbable peace,
the tight bond of a holy agreement,
the cloud that makes our field fertile,
the sun that enlightens our horizon,
the rich vein, finally,
of prosperity and abundance of which we stand in need.
And moreover we consecrate and entrust ourselves

without reserve to your Divine Heart.
Multiply endlessly the years of our peace,
eradicate from the boundaries of our land
unbelief and corruption, calamity and misery.
Your gospel gave us our laws,
your justice governs our tribunals,
your clemency and your power
sustain and direct our governors.
Your wisdom, holiness, and zeal
perfects our priests.
May your grace convert all the sons and daughters of Ecuador
and your glory crown them for eternity
so that all peoples and nations of the earth,
contemplating the true joy and happiness of our heart,
may take refuge for their part in your loving Heart
and enjoy the peace it offers to the world
this pure fountain and perfect symbol
of love and charity. Amen.

Prayer of young people for peace, March 30, 1985

The prayer is addressed to the Lord Jesus. There are two references to the heart, first to our heart:

Give us therefore the purity of a pure heart to understand the truth and reject deceitful illusions.

and then to the pierced Heart of Christ:

Lord Jesus Christ, give us your peace, the peace that springs from your pierced Heart, peace in truth, in justice, and in love.

Prayer for the City of Venice, June 16, 1985

The Holy Father prayed for the City of Venice with a prayer to Christ before imparting the Eucharistic Benediction. This is not a prayer directed to the Sacred Heart although there are two phrases that can be applied to the Sacred Heart:

You, Love: love that is not loved,

and:

Give them the grace of reconciliation which flows from your wounded side.

Visit to the cathedral of Lomé (Togo), August 9, 1985

Toward the end of his homily, the Holy Father said:

This cathedral is dedicated to the Sacred Heart of Jesus. It is a precious indication, it is completely a program! Instead of prolonging this discourse I invite you to pray with me to the Sacred Heart.

Sacred Heart of Jesus, perfect image in our human nature
of God the Father, full of mercy,
be blessed for all the graces
of faith, of perseverance, of vocations,
which you have given to this people of Togo.
Conserve it in peace, in joy, in thanksgiving.
And now strengthen the faith, hope, and charity
of those you have called to know in truth
the love of God.
Continue to pour out on them the love
which gives them a filial attitude toward the heavenly Father,
which encourages them to pray as sons and daughters of God.

Give to all the desire constantly to purify their hearts,
to render them transparent to the gospel,
the courage to "break," if need be, with sin,
the ardent desire which develops the life of God
which you have given to them in baptism.
Jesus, meek and humble of Heart,
comfort those who are weary,
give them the repose you have promised.
Make each one of them aware of their original vocation,
of their proper role as baptized, confirmed,
consecrated person, deacon, priest.
Strengthen their unity.
Constantly broaden their charity
to the dimensions of that benevolent love,
inexhaustible, without limits,
that your Divine Heart has never ceased to manifest
among men and women.
May the fire you have brought to earth burn in them,
the passion for your kingdom!
May they participate ever more
in the work of the redemption,
that you have accomplished for them on the cross,
at the cost of your blood!
May they continue their way
toward the fullness of life
to which you draw us all
in the face-to-face meeting in heaven. Amen.

Consecration of the Archdiocese of Delhi (India) to the Sacred Heart of Jesus in the cathedral of Delhi, February 1, 1986

In the solemn joy of this moment, as I begin my pastoral visit to India and as I consecrate the Archdiocese of Delhi to the Sacred Heart of Jesus, let our first action be to praise and bless our God. Let us glorify him for his love for the world which is shown to us in the Heart of his Son. In the human Heart of the Son of Mary the eternal love of God came to abide; and through Christ's human life, and especially through his death on the cross, the tender mercy of God was revealed.

"For God so loved the world that he gave his only Son, that whoever believes in him should not perish but have eternal life" (John 3:16). This is the Good News of our redemption. This is the saving message of the Sacred Heart of Jesus. This is the gospel which I have come here today to proclaim to you. During these days I wish also with you to show my respect and esteem — beyond the limits of the Church — to every person in India. In this too we are impelled by the love of Christ.

O Sacred Heart of Jesus, Burning Fire of Love, have mercy on us and make our hearts like your own.

CONSECRATION TO THE SACRED HEART OF JESUS

Lord Jesus Christ, Redeemer of the human race, to your most Sacred Heart we turn with humility and trust, with reverence and hope, with a deep desire to give to you glory and honor and praise.

Lord Jesus Christ, Savior of the world, we thank you for all that you are and all that you do for the little flock and all the twelve million people living in this Archdiocese of Delhi, which includes those entrusted with the stewardship of this nation.

Lord Jesus Christ, Son of the Living God, we praise you for the love that you have revealed through your Sacred Heart, which was pierced for us and which has become the fountain of our joy, the source of our eternal life.

Gathered together in your Name, which is above all other names, we consecrate ourselves to your most Sacred Heart, in which dwells the fullness of truth and charity.

In consecrating themselves to you, the faithful of the Archdiocese of Delhi renew their desire to respond in love to the rich outpouring of your merciful love.

Lord Jesus Christ, King of love and Prince of peace, reign in our hearts and in our homes. Conquer all the powers of evil and bring us to share in the victory of your Sacred Heart. May all we say and do give glory and praise to you and to the Father and the Holy Spirit, one God living and reigning for ever and ever. Amen.

Prayer for vocations at the end of the message for the twenty-third annual Day of Prayer for Vocations, April 27, 1986

O Jesus, Good Shepherd, raise up in all parish communities priests and deacons, men and women religious, consecrated laity and missionaries, according to the needs of the whole world, which you love and wish to save.

We entrust to you especially our own community; create in us the spiritual climate of the first Christians, so that we may be a cenacle of prayer in loving welcome of the Holy Spirit and of his gifts.

Assist our pastors and all consecrated persons. Guide the steps of those who have generously accepted your call and are preparing themselves for sacred orders or for the profession of the evangelical counsels.

Turn your glance of love toward so many well-disposed young people and call them to follow you. Help them to understand that only in you can they fully realize themselves.

In entrusting these grand desires of your Heart to the powerful intercession of Mary, mother and model of every vocation, we entreat you to sustain our faith in the certainty that the Father will hear what you yourself have commanded us to ask. Amen.

Prayer in the Basilica of the Sacred Heart during the pope's visit to Paray-le-Monial, October 5, 1986

In this place our fathers in the faith
have constructed this basilica for the glory of your Name,
Christ, Lord of the universe.
Under the sign of the beauty and the joy of prayer,
the holy abbots of Cluny and the Benedictine community
have labored for the construction of a civilization of love.

In this city, in the monastery of the Visitation,
Margaret Mary received the revelations of your infinite Love,
Christ, Savior of the world.
In the contemplation of your Heart that has loved so much,
she received the power to announce your mercy.
Guided by Claude La Colombière and in the wake of Francis
    de Sales,
she has helped numerous Christians to set themselves to listen
    to you
to become "disciples of your Heart meek and humble."
  Glory to you for ever.
Today, in this land of Borgogna,
heirs of our brothers and sisters in faith, the saints of all times,
we look to you, to you, Lamb with the pierced Heart.

We look to you, as in the hour of the cross,
did Mary, your holy Mother, and John your beloved disciple.
    Reveal to us the riches of your Heart.
In the hour of your death, under the blow of the lance,
water and blood gushed forth, so that all people, drawn to
        your Heart,
might come to attain with joy to the fountain of salvation.
The Church, your spouse, born from your pierced side, calls
        out to you.
Give her in abundance the living water of the Spirit and the
        blood of sacrifice,
so that she can, in the heart of the world,
witness the vivifying and transfiguring power of the Heart of
        your God.

In the time of the resurrection,
incredulous Thomas uncovered the love of his Savior,
placing his hand in the wound of the side up to the Heart of
        the Risen One.
He has believed and proclaimed; "My Lord and my God."
Give to your spouse, the Church,
to strengthen her faith turning incessantly to your Heart,
to understand, in one continual contemplation,
that would shape the force of love in the burning "brazier" of
        victorious Lord.
    Glory to you for ever.
In the hour of the sending on mission,
Peter understood the meaning of the fundamental question:
"Do you love me?"
And he should answer first by going to feed your flock.
Today your Church understands the same call
addressed to each of us: "Do you love me?"
A call that comes from your Heart, Lord Jesus,

and that wishes to touch each of us in our hearts.
Give us the courage to respond without fear and without
    reticence,
because you have chosen us, each and every one,
to be, at the dawn of the twenty-first century,
"witnesses and builders of a civilization of love."

Jesus, meek and humble of Heart, make our hearts like unto
    yours,
burn our hearts in the fire of yours. Amen.
    Glory to you for ever.

Act of Consecration to the Sacred Heart of Jesus in the cathedral of Plock during the pope's fourth pastoral visit to Poland, June 7, 1991

Make our hearts like unto yours.

On the day the Church shows us the love revealed in the sign of the pierced side of Our Lord Jesus Christ on the cross, from which flowed blood and water, in the presence of the bishops, priests, deacons, and faithful united here, I, Bishop of Rome, Servant of the Servants of God, consecrate the Diocese of Wloclawek, together with the entire flock entrusted to me, to the most Sacred Heart of Jesus, so that it may ever remain "a chosen race, a royal priesthood, a holy nation, a people he claims for his own" (1 Pet. 2:9).

We thank you, Lord Jesus Christ, because "you have made known to us the name of your Father" (John 17:26) and because "you have been given in sacrifice for us" (John 17:19). We promise you our unlimited fidelity and we ask your grace to be able to continue serving you with the spirit and the fervor of our fathers and mothers.

Through the intercession of the Virgin Mary, of her who stood beneath the cross and in front of the cross on which you, O Jesus Christ, have poured out the treasures of your opened Heart, we ask you from the depths of our being: "Jesus, gentle and humble of Heart, make our hearts like unto yours." Amen.

Prayer to St. Aloysius Gonzaga during the pope's visit to his shrine in Castiglione delle Stiviere, June 22, 1991

In the prayer the Holy Father refers to the Divine Heart:

Humbly and confidently you adored the plans of the Divine Heart.

He also refers to Divine Mercy:

O heroic apostle of charity, obtain for us the gift of Divine Mercy, which moves hearts that are hardened by selfishness, and keep the desire for holiness strong in every person.

Prayer before the Regina Coeli on the second Sunday of Easter (Mercy Sunday), April 10, 1994

The Holy Father reflected on the peace of the Risen Christ, which is the triumph of Divine Mercy. He ends with a short prayer to Mary and refers to the Heart of her Son.

O Mary, Mother of mercy! You know the Heart of your divine Son better than anyone. Instill in us the filial trust in Jesus practiced by the saints, the trust that animated Blessed Faustina Kowalska, the great apostle of Divine Mercy in our time.

Look lovingly upon our misery. O Mother, draw us away from the contrary temptations of self-sufficiency and despair, and obtain for us an abundance of saving mercy.

Summary

These prayers of the Holy Father may serve as subject matter for meditation. But some may also find them helpful to use, with some adaptation, as prayers for their own devotion, along with the Litany of the Sacred Heart, which is reprinted in the following chapter.

Chapter 29

Litany of the Sacred Heart of Jesus

Lord, have mercy on us.
Christ, have mercy on us.
Lord, have mercy on us. Christ, hear us.
Christ, graciously hear us.
God the Father of heaven,
Have mercy on us.
God the Son, Redeemer of the world,
Have mercy on us.
God the Holy Spirit,
Have mercy on us.
Holy Trinity, one God,
Have mercy on us.

1. Heart of Jesus, Son of the eternal Father,
   [After each invocation the response is: *"Have mercy on us."*]

2. Heart of Jesus, formed by the Holy Spirit in the womb of the Virgin Mother,

3. Heart of Jesus, substantially united to the Word of God,

4. Heart of Jesus, of infinite majesty,

5. Heart of Jesus, sacred temple of God,

6. Heart of Jesus, tabernacle of the Most High,

7. Heart of Jesus, house of God and gate of heaven,

8. Heart of Jesus, burning furnace of charity,

9. Heart of Jesus, abode of justice and love,

10. Heart of Jesus, full of goodness and love,

11. Heart of Jesus, abyss of all virtue,

12. Heart of Jesus, most worthy of all praise,

13. Heart of Jesus, king and center of all hearts,

14. Heart of Jesus, in whom are all the treasures of wisdom and knowledge,

15. Heart of Jesus, in whom dwells the fullness of the divinity,

16. Heart of Jesus, in whom the Father was well pleased,

17. Heart of Jesus, of whose fullness we have all received,

18. Heart of Jesus, desire of the everlasting hills,

19. Heart of Jesus, patient and most merciful,

20. Heart of Jesus, enriching all who invoke you,

21. Heart of Jesus, fountain of life and holiness,

22. Heart of Jesus, propitiation for our sins,

23. Heart of Jesus, loaded down with opprobrium,

24. Heart of Jesus, bruised for our offenses,

25. Heart of Jesus, obedient unto death,

26. Heart of Jesus, pierced with a lance,

27. Heart of Jesus, source of all consolation,

28. Heart of Jesus, our life and resurrection,

29. Heart of Jesus, our peace and reconciliation,

30. Heart of Jesus, victim for sin,

31. Heart of Jesus, salvation of those who trust in you,

32. Heart of Jesus, hope of those who die in you,

33. Heart of Jesus, delight of all the saints,

Lamb of God, you take away the sins of the world,

Spare us, Lord.

Lamb of God, you take away the sins of the world,

Graciously hear us, O Lord.

Lamb of God, you take away the sins of the world,

Have mercy on us.

V. Jesus, meek and humble of heart.

R. Make our hearts like unto thine.

Let us pray:

Almighty and eternal God, look upon the Heart of your dearly beloved Son and upon the praise and satisfaction he offers you in the name of sinners, and being appeased, grant pardon to those who seek your mercy, in the name of the same Jesus Christ, your Son, who lives and reigns with you in the unity of the Holy Spirit, world without end. Amen.

Conclusion

"A fountain of life and holiness!" These words are a brief statement of what Pope John Paul II understands by the Heart of Christ and what he has tried to say and write on the Sacred Heart of Jesus. Throughout this book we have been able to read and reflect on the words of the pope himself. We cannot fail to be impressed by his love for and dedication to the person of Christ as seen through the mystery of his Heart.

If we look carefully at what Pope John Paul II has said of the Heart of Christ, we find that he does not take back or modify anything that any of his predecessors had said about the devotion; rather he repeats and emphasizes what they said. In the pope's letter to the superior general of the Society of Jesus he says that "this devotion corresponds more than ever to the expectations of our day" and that its "essential elements belong permanently to the spirituality of the Church throughout its history."

The Holy Father explains what is meant by "heart," by "Sacred Heart," and by "devotion to the Sacred Heart." Frequently he goes into the scriptural meaning of "heart" and then shows the scriptural basis of the devotion. He repeatedly cites and explains the principal scriptural texts: the piercing of the side and Heart of Jesus on the cross, the symbolism of the blood and water that flowed from the Heart of Christ and Matthew's text that speaks of Jesus being meek and humble of heart, a text quoted by Vatican II.

The pope recalls the traditional practices of the devotion: observance of the feast of the Sacred Heart, First Friday practices with confession and Communion of reparation, the holy hour, the Litany of the Sacred Heart of Jesus, imitation of the virtues of the Heart of Jesus, and acts of consecration and reparation. In particular he emphasizes the meaning and importance of reparation to the Sacred Heart.

While the pope often simply mentions reparation, in the letter he gave to the superior general of the Society of Jesus he explained the meaning of reparation when he wrote: "This is the true meaning of the reparation demanded by the Heart of the Savior — on the ruins accumulated through hatred and violence can be built the civilization of love so greatly desired, the kingdom of the Heart of Christ." He quotes these words on other occasions as well.

Despite the fact that so much is said of the pope's devotion, there is something that is not recorded here and yet is extremely important because it leads into what we may call the spirituality of the Heart of Jesus. We might even say it is what is distinctive and even unique to Pope John Paul II's understanding of the Sacred Heart.

What is noteworthy is the way that Pope John Paul II, when speaking of other topics, will mention the Heart of Jesus. It is as if the Sacred Heart is so much a part of his life and thinking that instead of saying "Jesus" or "love" or something similar, he says "Sacred Heart" or "Heart of Jesus." Of course, there are also places where he could have said "Sacred Heart" but did not. The point is that the Heart of Jesus is so much a part of his life and way of thinking that it manifests itself frequently, even when we are not expecting it. This, I think, is a distinctive characteristic of Pope John Paul II and his approach to the Heart of Jesus. He himself said that he learned the devotion as a boy, and he learned it so well and it became so much a part of his life that he instinctively speaks of the Heart of Jesus. This illustrates a "spirituality" of the Heart of Jesus, an approach to the mystery of Christ by way of his Heart, a way of living one's relation to the Heart of Jesus.

Is there anything about the Heart of Jesus that the pope could have mentioned or that we might expect him to have mentioned, but he did not? There is one thing that I can think of, one thing I have looked for, namely, the relation of the Sacred Heart and the Holy Spirit. Theology traditionally speaks of the Holy Spirit as Love. If the Heart of Jesus is the symbol of his divine-human love, there must be a close relationship between love as symbolized by the Heart of Jesus and the Divine Love as being the Person of the Holy Spirit in the heart of the Blessed Trinity. This point is touched on but not really developed, as far as I could find.

Pope John Paul frequently mentions the civilization of love. What Pope Paul VI originated has become part of Pope John Paul II's thinking on the Sacred Heart.

For those who wish to deepen their understanding of devotion to the Sacred Heart or spirituality of the Heart of Jesus, what Pope John Paul II has said and written on the subject is a treasure that lends itself to study and reflection. The Heart of Jesus is truly "a fountain of life and holiness."

Selected Bibliography

Alacoque, St. Margaret Mary. *The Autobiography of St. Margaret Mary.* Rockford, Ill.: Tan Books and Publishers, 1986. Translation of the authentic French text by Sisters of the Visitation, Partridge Green, Horsham, West Sussex, England; first published in 1930 by Sisters of Visitation, Roselands, Walmer, Kent, England; reprinted in 1952.

Bunson, Matthew, and Margaret Stephen. *John Paul II's Book of Saints.* Huntington, Ind.: Our Sunday Visitor, 1999. A collection of brief biographies of the more than three hundred canonizations and more than seven hundred beatifications of the pope to date.

Celeste, Sister Marie, S.C. *The Church and Love: A Treatise on the Love of Christ for the People of God.* Lanham, Md.: University Press of America, 1998. Part II of this small book treats the pope's devotion to the Sacred Heart and quotes from *Angelus Meditations on the Litany of the Sacred Heart of Jesus* and the pope's homily at the canonization of St. Claude.

Collantes, Justo, S.J. *El Corazón de Jesús en la Enseñanza de Juan Pablo II (1978–1988).* Madrid: Instituto Internacional del Corazón de Jesús, 1990. Anthology of everything the pope said or wrote on the Sacred Heart during his first ten years as pope (in Spanish).

Croiset, John, S.J. *The Devotion to the Sacred Heart of Jesus.* Rockford, Ill.: Tan Books and Publishers, 1988. First treatise on devotion to the Sacred Heart, written in French during the lifetime of St. Margaret Mary and published in 1691, the year after her death. English translation by Patrick O'Connell from the final French edition, published in Lyons in 1694: 1st English edition 1948, 2nd ed. 1959; republished by Tan Books and Publishers, 1988.

L'Osservatore Romano, original Italian edition, and *L'Osservatore Romano,* English edition. Best source for the documents of the pope.

Pope John Paul II. *Angelus Meditations on the Litany of the Sacred Heart of Jesus.* Ed. with an Introduction by Carl J. Moell, S.J. Huntington, Ind.: Our Sunday Visitor, 1992. Series of pope's talks on the litany.

————. *Pope John Paul II Prays the Litany of the Sacred Heart of Jesus.* Ed. with an Introduction by Carl J. Moell, S.J. Huntington, Ind.: Our Sunday Visitor, 1992. Reprint of the previous book.

Moell, Carl J., S.J. "Devotion to the Sacred Heart." In *New Catholic Encyclopedia,* 12:818–20. This article written for the *NCE* is the basis for the summary of the devotion in the Introduction.

Nouwen, Henri J. M. *Heart Speaks to Heart: Three Prayers to Jesus.* Notre Dame, Ind.: Ave Maria Press, 1989. Personal prayers responding to the Heart of Jesus as revealed in the Gospels.

O'Donnell, Timothy. *The Heart of the Redeemer: An Apologia for the Contemporary and Perennial Value of the Devotion to the Sacred Heart of Jesus.* San Francisco: Ignatius Press, 1992. The section on Pope John Paul II, pp. 225–55, has many quotations from the documents of the pope with comments.

Wright, Wendy M. *Sacred Heart, Gateway to God.* Maryknoll, N.Y.: Orbis Books, 2001. A book of personal reflections about the Sacred Heart, "about the long Christian devotion to that heart — its history, iconography, prayer, theology, hymnody, and liturgical life — told against the present-day backdrop of story, poetry, visual imagery, and song."

Of Related Interest

Avery Cardinal Dulles, S.J.
THE SPLENDOR OF FAITH
The Theological Vision of Pope John Paul II
Revised and Updated Edition

A philosopher and theologian, as well as priest, bishop, and finally pope, John Paul II has written extensively on a wide variety of subjects. With his considerable theological expertise and acumen, Avery Dulles, the first American theologian to be elevated to cardinal, has undertaken the demanding task of synthesizing the pope's theological insights on a complete range of topics from the Trinity and Christology to the economic and social order. In clear and lucid prose, Dulles enters into the thought of John Paul II and reveals the main outlines of his theological vision — a truly comprehensive vision that deserves to be seen as a whole.

"Indispensable. Everything is here: Christology, the evangelization of culture, world missions, Christian unity, eschatology, and Christian understanding of world religions, the theological basis of human rights and much more.... A splendid achievement, warmly recommended to all who would understand the mind of the premier witness to the gospel of Jesus Christ in our time." — *First Things*

Herder & Herder
0-8245-2121-8, $29.95 paperback

crossroad

Of Related Interest

Bruno Steimer and Michael Parker, eds.
DICTIONARY OF POPES AND THE PAPACY

The inaugural volume of the *Encyclopedia for Theology and Church*
features biographies of every pope and antipope, as well as a detailed
look at the institution of the papacy.

Herder & Herder
0-8245-1918-3, cloth, $50.00

John F. Crosby et al.
THE LEGACY OF POPE JOHN PAUL II
His Contribution to Catholic Thought

Herder & Herder
0-8245-1831-4, paper, $12.95

Please support your local bookstore,
or call 1-800-707-0670 for Customer Service.

For a free catalog, write us at

THE CROSSROAD PUBLISHING COMPANY
16 Penn Plaza, 481 Eighth Avenue
New York, NY 10001

Visit our website at
www.crossroadpublishing.com
All prices subject to change.

crossroad